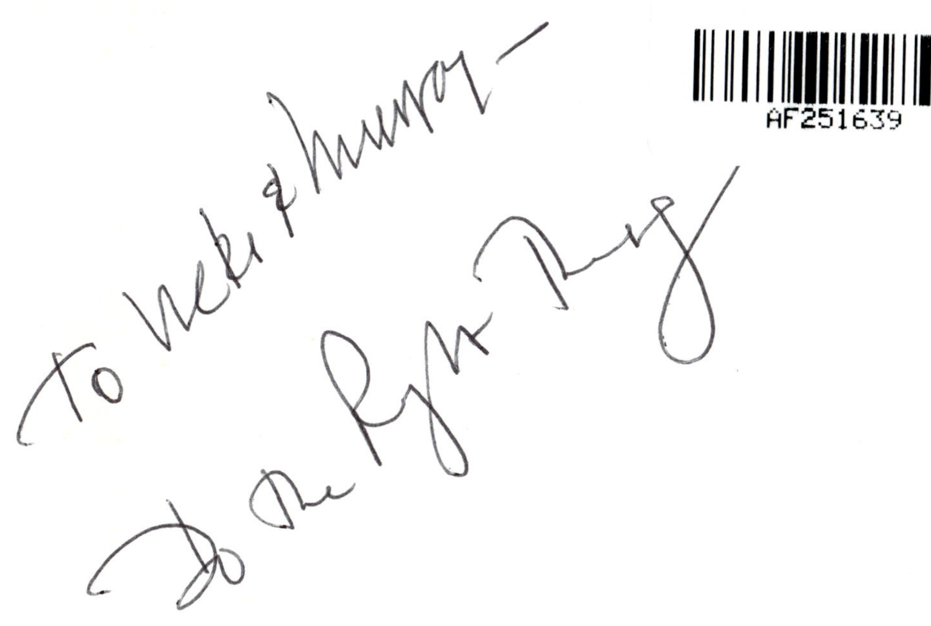

To Vicki & Murray —

Do The Right Thing

THE RIGHT PATH

The Autobiography of a Survivor

THE RIGHT PATH

The Autobiography of a Survivor

by
Edmund Mandel

as told to
Lynn K. Egerman

KTAV Publishing House, Inc.
Hoboken, New Jersey

Library of Congress Cataloging-in-Publication Data

Mandel, Edmund
    The right path : the autobiography of a survivor / Edmund Mandel ;
as told to Lynn K. Egerman.
       p.   cm.
    ISBN 0-88125-498-3 : $29.50
    1. Mandel, Edmund. 2. Jews—Hungary—Biography. 3. Hungarian
Americans—Biography. 4. Holocaust, Jewish (1939-1945)—Hungary—
Personal narrative. I. Egerman, Lynn K. II. Title.
DS135.H9M348   1994
940.53'18'092—dc20   94-6632
                                            CIP

KTAV Publishing House, 900 Jefferson Street, Hoboken NJ, 07030

This book is dedicated

to Pista Virag and the ten thousand young Jewish boys who lost their lives in the copper mines of Bor.

to "Mr. Moto," born Gross Miklós, and for his five-per-three forced-labor battalion.

to Miklós Bloom, the gravedigger's son.

It is dedicated in their memory by someone who took the right path and managed to survive.

CONTENTS

FOREWORD

In recounting his story, Ed Mandel was prone to say that his destiny was based on choosing either the right path or the left. In making what appeared to be a very small choice or having a chance occurrence, one's fate could be irrevocably changed.

Such a small happening as having my son coached by Ed Mandel was an enriching, life-changing event for me.

Ed had an enormous reputation as a coach in our youth soccer region. He was a generation older than the other coaches, without a son or grandson in the league. He had coached for ten years and built a winning legacy. Coach Ed never talked about winning or even about the scores. In his thick Hungarian accent he talked to his raptly listening boys and told them stories about ethics, courage, and heart.

To say he had charisma is to do a disservice to the man. This was no superficial charm. Here was a man capable of responding to deep human chords in others. So the chance occurrence of the random placement of a boy with a coach, this fork in the road of life, was, in all its metaphorical correctness, a life-changing event for all of us involved.

Slowly we became friends, and the more I listened the more I was intrigued about what had created such a person. I wanted to know about the historical events which had molded him and his personal character. I wanted to know the forces and events which had led to the development of such a person who was so full of life and so generous. I wanted to know more about the person who cherished the courage and struggle of others and had such high ethical standards.

So there came about a union of a natural storyteller and a natural listener. This is his story.

I have edited some of the English and grammar, but I hope I have not touched the Old World charm and cadence of Ed's speech.

I chose the title because of its many possibilities: the right path, chosen instead of the left, denotes the promiscuousness of fate. There are many forks in this story where small decisions of choosing when to acquiesce and when to defy meant life or death. There are many choices where listening to one person or another meant well-being or annihilation. The right path connotes also the moral and ethical choices one makes. Ed's story abounds with both.

Lynn K. Egerman

BOOK ONE

- 1-

World War II ended in Kecskemét, Hungary, in December 1944.

The Red Army, as part of the Allied front in its westward advance towards Germany, reached the eastern part of the Danube River in Hungary. The siege of Budapest had begun. Inside the besieged capital city the remnants of Hungarian Jewry who had survived extermination were trapped and struggled to survive until liberated by the Red Army.

In their final assault towards Germany, the Red Army liberated town after town in which thousands of Jews had lived. These towns and villages were now *Judenrein* because of the genocidal policy of the Germans and their Hungarian allies. The same day as the siege of Budapest began, I managed to reach my hometown of Kecskemét, which was fifty-eight miles south of Budapest in the middle of the Great Plain. I had escaped from the Jewish labor battalion and was home.

For the city of Kecskemét the war was over. The city had been liberated. The war was over for the farmers and the orchard workers who lived in the small villages around the city. The Germans had entered Hungary on March 21, 1944. Several weeks later the entire Jewish population was rounded up. What had these farmers thought when in early 1944 the fascist gendarmes had taken away the Jewish families who had lived and worked among them and shared their meager lives for decades? They had been neighbors and friends. In such a small village everyone knew one another.

What did these simple, ordinary people think that early May day in 1944 when a caravan of eight horsedrawn carriages came into the village of Agasegyhaza on the outskirts of Kecskemét? They must have sensed the foreboding aspect of that ominous parade as it stopped in front of the homes of the local Jews of this outlying village. The village was quiet except for this lone caravan of death.

What did these average people think as they watched the Jews, looking bewildered and frightened, taken forcibly from their ancestral homes? Neighbors watched as the Jews were forcibly evicted and carted off, carrying only their bedding, food, pots, and pans. These were the only possessions allowed.

The last Jewish family picked up in this small village was that of the grocer, Aush. Even through the closed doors, the distinct aroma of his village grocery shop emerged. The sweet scent of coffee and the pungent aroma of cheeses, herring, and petrol oil mixed together indicated that there was still merchandize left in the store. Who would get it now?

Aush emerged from the store limping. He had lost his foot in World War I. He had been a much-decorated soldier. Even though he was rushed and pushed by the gendarmes, he had taken time to wear his one holiday jacket with all his war decorations on display. I'll always remember his medals pinned on his jacket, and I'll always wonder what Aush thought as he made this final gesture. He had been so proud to be Hungarian and to serve in the military. He had been one of few Jewish hussars and had regaled all the neighborhood boys with his adventures. He represented pride and heart to me.

The gendarmes tried to shove him into the buggy which held his crying mother, wife, and two sons.

"I will walk," Aush said and looked defiantly in the faces of the cursing, screaming gendarmes.

"I am a war veteran. I lost my foot in the defense of this God-forsaken country of ours."

He walked limping behind the buggy, so proud, so noble, so futile! What did he think of his country now?

What did the driver who drove the Aush family into obscurity think? Did he steel his mind and thoughts away from the future for these human beings? Did he feel sorry for the Aush family and his role in this ignoble ending? Did he have regrets that he had only bought two pounds of sugar on credit from Aush the day before yesterday instead of four pounds? Maybe he thought that he should also have picked up five liters of petrol on credit! Or, perhaps, he felt some guilt. The driver's weatherbeaten, expressionless face didn't register any emotion.

Through their curtained windows, the villagers watched the caravan pass. Their faces registered neutrality, showing neither shame nor guilt, happiness nor sorrow. What did they think about their neighbors being carted away like refuse? Were they relieved that it was others and not them? Had they already began a revisionist history to justify these unjustifiable events? Were they already calculating the booty left behind? Did any of them hide a Jewish child or keep Jewish possessions in trust for the return of their neighbors?

The war ended also for the workers in the city of Kecskemét in December 1944. Among them were the worst and the best of what humankind had to offer. There were those who could hardly wait until their neighbor had been taken away from their home so that they could move in and take whatever they could find. There were also those who demonstrated the kindest, most human traits of courage and generosity.

In 1944 the war also ended for the three whorehouses in the city of Kecskemét. These houses were always very busy. The customers changed from one day to the next during the war years—from Hungarians to Germans to Russians. From this unlikely place, a local Jewish gentleman walked out in December 1944, pale and shaky but alive. His name was Béla Schreiber. Béla came from a well-respected Jewish family. Béla's father was the best-known wagoner in the city. He was very proud of his four beautiful horses. Béla's mother had a prosperous knitting store in the city center. She was a good friend of my mother. Their home at Vak-Bottyan Street became part of the Jewish ghetto in 1944. All the Jews, including my family, were forcibly moved into this ghetto before their train ride to death. I was in the forced-labor camps at that time and was saved. Béla, their oldest son, also survived.

Beginning in 1938 Béla had secretly become a constant visitor of the Pacsirta brothel. He became the steady customer of a Christian prostitute. They left Kecskemét and were married in Budapest, where they attempted to begin a new life. When things started to get difficult for the Jews in Budapest, they returned to Kecskemét. The former prostitute hid her new husband in her former whorehouse. In the whorehouse, that place of dehumanization, two people managed to find love and humanness. They both had managed to save one another. He had saved her from psychic extinction; she saved him from physical death. Somehow they endured and emerged alive. A year later Béla, who had survived humiliation and the Jewish round-up, died from tuberculosis. His wife then committed suicide. They apparently were better suited to save each other than to survive alone.

The war was over also for László Kovacs, an assistant bank manager. He was a frail, skinny, bespectacled man who looked the educated Gentile aesthete he was. In 1942 he was called into the army as an officer. He was assigned to lead a Jewish labor battalion. The Jewish labor battalions were peopled with expendable young men who were prisoners of their own government because of their religion. Their whole purpose was to be disposable labor. László Kovacs brought home all two hundred young Jewish boys assigned to his unit. He saved everybody. In his frail body was a great heart. He had a job to do, but he never ceased being a human being.

The war did not end in December 1944 for Istvan Komlosi. He was a Gentile friend of mine who played soccer with me and the other neighborhood boys. Istvan was a friend in my youth.

For those of us who played side by side, there were bonds. For him, the war didn't end when the Russians besieged the city of Budapest. At that time he and his Arrow Cross gang were in the Budapest ghetto, robbing, murdering, and raping Jews. Istvan Komlosi's war ended six months later in the city fire station's yard at the end of a hangman's noose. Many times I thought I would visit him in prison before his execution. I wanted to know the answers to my burning questions about why he had done those atrocities.

"Do you remember my mother? Did she do anything wrong to you? Do you remember my sister and her baby? What were they guilty of? How could you go from playing side by side with me to murdering and preying on my people and your neighbors? Were you ever my friend? Did I not know you, or did you change?"

I never visited him in prison or asked those questions. I never saw him until the day the hangman put the rope around his neck. I watched him walk up the three steps to the elevated chair. I watched his blank eyes scan the yard as the sentence was read. I watched the blindfold being placed over his eyes, and his chair pushed out. He died without a word. There were no answers to my questions. I wonder if he saw me in the crowd. I will never know. I only know that I felt justice was done. Bitterness, not vengeance, was in my heart that day. All I know is that I left the hanging saddened.

The war also ended for a Jewish girl, Marika Kertesz. She had worked in a barrel-making factory. The owner, Mr. Farago, a married Christian man, hid her and saved her, and she reappeared right after the Germans left. I was amazed at his tolerance and courage, and that of his wife's. Her heart could include a young woman whose presence posed a threat to her family and her own well-being, as well as to the marriage. It had been rumored that Marika and her husband were lovers prior to these horrible times. The wife's heart could surmount her own personal agony for the most human of expressions, that of saving another human being.

A few days after the Germans left Kecskemét, Jewish young men who had survived the labor battalions started to return home. Most of the time, the returnees, all men between the ages of twenty and forty, entered the town in twos and threes. It wasn't safe to travel alone. Among the first returnees were Gyurka and myself.

We had walked home from near Russia. We arrived from the south of the city. The last twenty-eight kilometers we walked from the city of Kiskunfélegyháza. After months of marching and hiding in Eastern Europe, we had attached ourselves to the liberating Soviet army. We were with a unit of typesetters. The printing shop had been loaded on the back of a truck. The truck, with us on it, followed and reported the fighting. When a city was liberated from the Germans, the Soviets moved in with us in tow. At Kiskunfélegyháza we realized that we were close to our home. We decided to depart quietly from our Soviet hosts. We needed to go home.

It was winter. It was snowing. The frozen ground of the highway leading to our home was covered with snow. The roads were filled with Soviet convoys heading towards the front. A motorized artillery unit camouflaged in white passed us at great speed. We walked without really noticing them, immersed in our own private thoughts. Ukrainian units passed us in wagons or on foot. We were almost home. Within hours we would know about Kecskemét and our families.

We knew some of what had happened to the Jews. We had seen abandoned Jewish homes on our long march home. We had seen many cities with no Jewish population. In some cities we had been given Hungarian newspapers, and we had read about Auschwitz. Somehow we still hoped that by some miracle it hadn't happened to our families. We knew that genocide had occurred because we had passed through cities and villages in Ukrainia and didn't find Jews. Foolishly, we clung to hopes that our own city and our own families had been spared. We prayed that this massacre had not happened to Hungary's Jews, for then our families would have been saved. As Gyurka and I walked, we searched for reasons that would separate our families from those who had been killed.

We clung to these distinctions because it was our only hope. Even though these thoughts were ugly in that they in some way minimized the deaths of other Jews, we hoped that these distinctions would mean we could return to an intact life. Perhaps, we hoped, it had happened only in Eastern Europe. Perhaps, we prayed, it had only happened to those Jews who were unassimilated, with their long sidelocks of Jewish Orthodoxy. Perhaps it was only to them that it had happened. Then it might not happen to us, the Jews in the middle of Hungary between the Danube and Tisza Rivers, on the Great Plain. Please God, it could not have happened there. It could not have happened to my family! Please God, let there be a logic or reason behind this that would spare those I knew and loved from annihilation.

When we arrived in the eastern section of Hungary and saw that Jews existed no more, we pretended and wished and hoped that our friends and families had been spared because they were citizens of Hungary, whereas the Jews in these regions were not. Defying all logic, we prayed that it could not have happened to Jews whose fathers and grandfathers had been born in Hungary. So we tried to fool ourselves, to not think about it. Any superstition, any sign of hope, any irrationality which served us, we used to allow sanity and optimism to prevail. Otherwise life as we had known it would have been over. Family, relatives, friends, and all natural order of things would disappear much the way the eight Jewish families from Agasegyhaza had disappeared off the face of the earth. Naturally we talked about the possibility, but we couldn't believe that the horrors would be such personal ones.

That's why we still had the foolish hope that somebody in our family had survived and was waiting for our return. After all, we had survived the labor camps. We were the living proof that survival was possible. We had come home and longed for our homecoming.

My uncle's house was in the southern part of the city, so Gyurka and I turned off from the main road to Zoldfa 7, his address. The house was just a few hundred meters from the main road, but it seemed forever to reach the front yard. A tall fence had once protected the yard and house from the main street. Now a large part of the fence was missing. The front door to the yard was open, attached to the doorjamb with one remaining hinge. The door was leaning sideways, almost touching the frozen ground. It was difficult for us to move it. From the yard we saw that the door to the house was missing. The wind had blown snow into the living quarters. Our hearts were pounding, finally realizing that our hope was futile. No miracle had happened. We did not cry. Our eyes were dry and hardened because now we knew the unknowable: no one had been spared. We realized that no pretending could save us now—genocide had happened, and it had happened to us. All the distinctions we had so clung to in order to imagine our families waiting for us at home evaporated. There was no pretending anymore. We were beyond tears. Tears would come later. We continued our forlorn journey home.

We walked onward. Gyurka's house was locked with a big rusty padlock. We didn't break the lock. Perhaps, in some way, we realized that our lives were permanently and irrevocably changed. Nothing was as it once was. We continued towards my house.

We were just a few hundred meters from my house, behind curving Mikes Street, when someone stopped us. I recognized him immediately. He was a tailor by profession and a great soccer fan. He looked at me. We were malnourished, skinny, sick, and weak.

He asked me, "Are you the soccer-player Mandel boy?"

I said, "Yes."

He said, "I'm glad you made it."

This was the first non-Jewish man who had said any civil words to me in years.

Then he said, "I still remember one of the goals you scored from a corner kick in a soccer game!"

Soccer game! That was centuries ago when I was innocent and believed that life was a given. Somehow that remark made me feel better—maybe life does continue. Maybe I could continue this journey.

We continued our slow walk on Bocskai Street and entered my family's house at Mikes Street 4. The front door was open. Books and pictures were scattered around on the floor. Most of them were already wet from the snow and from people walking all over them. I saw the familiar photographs. I didn't pick them up. I don't know why. Perhaps I was in a daze. Something irrevocable and God-given had ended. Windows were broken; furniture gone or destroyed. Seatcovers from the few remaining chairs and a single mattress lay on the floor, cut to pieces. It looked like someone had been looking for hidden treasures. There was so much irony in that thought. The only treasures in this poor, unassuming home had been dragged into labor camps and death camps.

The chandelier was in the middle of the floor, broken in pieces. A few crystal pieces still sparkled. Browned holes were burnt into the parquet floor, vestiges of campfires made inside our home. In the next room I found straw on the floor. Next to the straw was dried shit and rubber condoms.

"This was the room they brought women to and the room they used as a toilet."

The voice of our former nextdoor neighbor, a blacksmith, broke my angry reverie. He had been watching us from the door.

I stepped out to the garden, and the neighbor followed. I shakily walked a few steps to the well. I looked down our well, which used to be our refrigerator during the summer. I remembered that in carefree days I had lowered watermelons down the well to cool them. I looked around and found bullet holes at chest height on the wall. Someone had been shot here.

I looked at my former neighbor and, with my voice barely hiding my hostility and loathing at his silent complicity, asked him about it.

"Who was doing the shooting here?"

"I don't know," he answered.

"Where were you that day?"

"I wasn't here. I don't remember. Maybe gendarmes executed Hungarian soldiers. Maybe they executed Jews or partisans. Maybe Russian soldiers executed Hungarian gendarmes. Maybe Jews executed Arrow Cross people."

The last sentence hardened my heart further still. I asked him if he had ever seen armed Jews.

"I don't know."

He looked at me and asked in a begging voice, "It doesn't matter now. It's over."

Over! Nothing was over! I hated everyone then—all the morally dead people who looked at me with pleading eyes after the fact. I hated everyone who had not suffered as I had. I knew I would continue to suffer forever! I hated with black, dark anger anyone who could tell me that it didn't matter anymore—that it was over. The only thing that was "over" were generations of Jews—men, women, grandparents, children, and babies. The desire for revenge and justice fueled my hate and tempted me to be violent to this blacksmith. I looked at his pleading eyes. I tried to force myself to believe that he had felt sorry and had compassion when he watched my mother and sisters forced from their home into the ghetto.

I asked him to let me be alone with my friend. We sat in the garden and rested a few minutes, not saying a word. Why had we come home? Could we ever forget what we had seen today? Maybe a new generation would be different. Maybe not everyone had used condoms in the straw in our home. Maybe not everyone had used our quiet garden for human target practice.

We ended up in a former Jewish house where a Gentile woman had moved in. This house had belonged to one of Gyurka's relatives before being sent to the ovens. The woman knew that she had no right to be there. She was afraid that Gyurka would throw her out, but we were too tired physically and emotionally and let her stay. She left us alone. We could not look at one another. We were solemn and quiet. We knew that most of our neighbors were guilty of watching the atrocities happen, even benefiting from them, and that they were now afraid of us. This was no solace.

I started to pace through the living room. There was visibly confiscated furniture in it, different styles and shapes that no one family would collect together. Who had brought in this confiscated furniture? Who else had lived here after the Jews? As I paced I noticed evidence that soldiers had stayed here. Soldiers had enjoyed shooting at pieces of porcelain. Soldiers had enjoyed using family portraits for target practice. Maybe they'd had a shooting contest in this house. I wanted to run from this room and away from my thoughts. But it was dark, and cold, and after curfew.

Nine months later my friend Gyurka married this woman.

From our window, which faced the street that led from the railway station to the town's center, I sometimes saw a familiar face walking slowly in the middle of the street. Young Jewish boys were returning from the labor battalions. They were not used to being free and had forgotten that they could use the sidewalk. They were the remnant of our city's Jewish male youth. Only young ones survived. Whether it was by good fortune or luck or fate, they had managed to make the right moves by not dying in the camps or falling into the hands of the gendarmes or Germans on their long walk home.

By the end of June 1945, young Jewish girls from the death camps started to come home. We tried to find them shelter. Jewish-help organizations had been formed. We were in contact with them in Budapest. A telegram arrived from Budapest that two Jewish girls would be on the next train to our city. That train brought home my two surviving sisters.

Slowly all of us tried to start a new life. We tried to forget what had happened. We didn't want to talk about what had happened to us. We tried to get on with life, telling ourselves that it was over.

The city had two main shopping streets, Rákoczi and Nagykorosi. Once these streets had been dominated by Jewish shopkeepers, bakers, tailors, dressmakers, bookstore owners, watchmakers, and cobblers. Now there was no trace of Jewish life. Non-Jewish children were playing in the temple yard. Children were playing in the street with a homemade soccer ball. There were children, but not the Jewish children who had lived there before. Jewish people used to live here. They had shopped here. Where were they now? Where were my friends? Where was the rest of my family? Only a skeleton of Jews had returned.

Kecskemét had two Jewish temples. In the center of town was the beautiful spacious Neologist temple where most of the Jews had belonged. It was a structural masterpiece in Moorish style with its blue-and-gold dome. This temple served as the centerpiece of many pre–war postcards. I remembered listening to the haunting traditional melodies sung by the cantor and choir. I remembered listening to the organ played by our elementary school teacher, Mr. Szekely.

In 1944, when the city was made *Judenrein*, the Germans had used this temple as a stable. Now in 1945 it looked beyond repair.

The second temple was a much smaller Orthodox synagogue which had been spared by the war. It was the only surviving temple, and it would now be used by the Jews who had survived. It was autumn, the time of the High Holy Days. This small Orthodox synagogue now held all of the surviving Jews from the city's original Jewish population of over twenty-five hundred. Only two hundred survived! Jews from Kecskemét were there. Jews from the neighboring villages came because they no longer had the *minyan* of ten Jewish men the religious laws decreed for services.

The city's young rabbi, Rabbi Schindler, had survived and led the religious service. The cantor, Mr. Popper, had died in

Auschwitz, with his family. Only his son, Shlomo Popper, survived. Shlomo started to chant the first prayers. I looked to where my father had sat. He would sit there no more. I looked to where our friends used to sit. They would never be seen again. I looked at my mother's seat. It would be empty of her forever. It was quiet in the synagogue—deathly, solemnly quiet. The rabbi started to read the names of the families not present at the service. It was a long list of names. Too long! Everybody cried all the tears they had not cried before. This was the last naming of our families, our loved ones. It represented the past, our heritage. This was the day of final recognition and the beginning of the acceptance of the finality of the fate of our loved ones. These were the tears of recognition of the annihilation of neighbors, friends, family, and city. This was the day everyone's innocence was unalterably shattered beyond repair.

The first day of the High Holy Days, everybody was there at the temple, including members of the Communist party and high police officials. At the end of the service, everybody walked home, exhausted and emotionally drained. Ten days later was Yom Kippur. This was the holiest of days. The synagogue was almost empty. The need to put everything behind us was compelling. We could not hear or talk about our losses or experiences, nor could we listen to others telling theirs. It took us years to realize that talking and listening to these experiences could unite us.

Now, fifty years later, I will try to tell my story. I will tell of the way I lived and how I managed to survive. I will be telling my story and the story of many others, some of whom disappeared without a trace. My survival depended for the most part on my having chosen one way or another or having been part of a lucky chance. Others were not so fortunate. All our stories need to be told and retold so that there will never be a reoccurrence. There must never be a genocide of people with neighbors who collude and look the other way. By my very survival I am qualified to tell the story. For who else will tell the story of the ten thousand Jewish young men who were born in 1920 and 1921? They were a few months older than I was. They were taken to Yugoslavia to work the copper mines of Bor. Amongst them was my best friend, Pista Virag. Who will tell his story and the story of the others who disappeared there? Only two hundred returned of the ten thousand who were taken away.

Who else but a survivor will tell the story of "Mr. Moto"? He was the same age as I. He was nicknamed after the Peter Lorre detective because we felt that he resembled this Jewish actor playing a Japanese detective. Both were smart, and both wore glasses. We were called up at the same time for the labor battalions. His fate, though, was different than mine. He was sent to another labor battalion. One from which no one returned.

Who will tell the story of Miklós Bloom? He was the Jewish son of the gravedigger and a very tough kid. He was a good soccer player and an excellent athlete. He disappeared without a trace. One day he was there in the middle of family and friends. The next day he was gone, as well all who were related to him. No one knows when. No one knows why.

Who will remember my teammates who played side by side with me in the Jewish soccer clubs? I am the only survivor of that group.

Who will tell the story of the Tordai brothers? They were such nice quiet boys who liked poems and books. They disappeared with their whole family. No one knows when. No one knows where. No one knows why?

Who else will tell their stories, if not me? How many others disappeared without a trace? Their stories were not different from mine. By fate or luck, I survived. They did not. My story will also be their story. Hopefully I can tell it the right way.

- 2 -

My memory of Kotaj, the village I was born in, was that we were well off. It is the only time in my early life that I remember us as having had enough. We had a farm, and for modest people that was more than enough. My memories of that early time are few.

The village was very small and had a stream running through it. After a heavy summer rain filled the stream, teen-age boys and girls came down to bathe and swim in the cool refreshing water.

The year was 1928, and I was six years old. I went down to the stream with the older village girls, including my sisters and the youngsters they were in charge of. We watched the older boys navigate the bridge and then jump off the bridge into the stream, giving large hoots of joy in the process. They were totally nude. It was totally innocent. Naturally the girls watched the boys furtively and the older boys pretended not to notice.

Everyone was watching the bathing, laughing, jumping nude young men of the village. No one was watching my three-year-old brother, Tibor. On that day Tibor walked away from the group and drowned in the stream.

My father was away on a business trip in Kecskemét at the time of this tragedy. My most vivid memory of the tragedy is of his coming back to our farm after hearing of Tibor's death. I was playing in the yard when he arrived in a topless one-horse buggy. He was both dashing in his top hat and white gloves and crushed with sorrow. As usual he had enormous control of his emotions and bore his pain with quiet, silent dignity.

Another memory of that early time is of visiting my grandparents at their mill. They lived near the city of Tokaj. Memories of these visits are memories of joy. I believe that this was the beginning of hard times for my parents, and their quiet desperation was felt by me, making the visits to my grandparents a joyful respite. My grandmother would sit on my bed and feed me sliced fruits. I think that I was her favorite grandson. My grandfather used to tell me stories about faraway places. While he was talking I remember watching the shadow cast by the oil lamp on the wall of the room. Visiting them was like being in my grandfather's stories.

The happiest time of my childhood was when my grandfather let me visit him in the mill. The small mill was in the front of their house. Being in the mill was being part of his world. I remember sitting on the top of sacks filled with flour, watching him do his work in the relaxed way that he had. He was a good-looking old man. The whole village called him "the good-looking Mishka." With his long white beard made even whiter by the flour particles in the air, he made a striking picture. He talked to me, as he worked, about a united world. He believed in one world, one language, and one money. True to his belief he even tried to teach me a few words of Esperanto. I hardly understood his sophisticated stories, but the tone and nuance of his voice stayed with me. He talked to me as an equal and as someone worthy. It took me years after his death to understand the meaning of his stories and the irony of the world that followed. I was glad he did not live to see the world his grandson inherited.

My father was not a farmer or a businessman. We soon had to leave the village of Kotaj after losing our farm, and with it whatever joy of childhood I can remember. All I recall of the leaving was that our family dog ran after the train for a long time. We moved to the city of Kecskemét. My father went into partnership with a relative in the wine business. The relative embezzled his money. We lost our home again and had to move from a decent house to a much smaller house where my father opened a coal and firewood delivery business. He bought a former army horse, Géza, to carry the coal and firewood. The horse was tall, old, and very skinny. Whenever there was a parade or a band in the city, the horse would trot in cadence. It was funny, and the whole city laughed with us.

Whatever my father touched turned sour, so we were never economically safe or comfortable again. My father was a terrible businessman. One year in springtime apples were going for a very high price, so my father decided that he would invest in apples by buying them and then selling them at a later date at an even higher price. He bought wagonloads of them and stored them in our cellar. Our apples started to rot two or three weeks after we stored them. The family had to go through each box, one by one, turning every single apple and watching for signs of decay. Whenever I eat an apple today, I still smell the scent of rot. They all rotted in our cellar without our having been able to sell a one.

The next year, pumpkin prices were very high. The same thing happened. We ended up renting a truck to come to haul the rotting pumpkins away.

We had to move again to an even less expensive house. This was the house that I remember best. This was the house where, finally, my parents managed to carve out a meager living for the family. Everybody in the family worked. I sold fresh water at the fairs. In one hand I had a dipper filled with a couple of cups. In the other hand I had a bucket of fresh water. I went between the stalls, yelling,

"Fresh water, I have fresh water."

My father was a very proud man. He still considered himself a former landowner. He couldn't acknowledge that I sold water at the fair. When he came across me at the fair, he turned away, pretending that he did not see me and thereby protecting his vulnerable pride.

The last Thursday of every month was fair day. It was always an exciting day. The farm workers arrived in their Sunday best of black pants and black hats. They walked barefoot with their boots neatly tied around their neck in order to save wear and tear on their shoes until they arrived at the fair. Others arrived carrying food and vegetables to sell. The youngsters stood open-mouthed around the candy stalls listening to the sales pitch of the sellers.

"Look here, look here. This is the famous Avar Bomb!"

Avar was a famous center forward on a Budapest soccer team with a very strong shot. His goal were called Avar bombs as they found their way to the net. This candy was named for him.

"Look here, look here, the Turkish honey!"

Market days were always electrifying days. People came from as far as Budapest for the fair. Tents and stalls were put up on Rákoczi Street. This street was the prime area where the richer merchants displayed their wares.

When I was seven I advanced from selling water to selling flypaper at the fair. I bought cases of one hundred and sold them one by one. I bought the flypaper on credit from the wholesale grocery store. One fair day a merchant from Budapest said he would buy the entire case of flypaper from me if each sheet in the case placed end to end was one meter long. Sensing a big sale I ran into the wholesale market.

"Mr. Pataki, how long is the flypaper?"

He answered, "One hundred centimeters long."

I ran back to the merchant and told him it was a deal. I pulled out the flypaper, and the merchant measured it with his yardstick. It was only ninety-nine centimeters long, because the last centimeter was part of the holder, something the gentleman already had known. So I lost the sale, because he bought nothing, and had always intended to trick me. How could he have tried to hurt a child? Why did he try to trick me?

Was he trying to teach me some esoteric lesson in adult logic? Was he just cruelly passing time? My lessons had begun.

Saturdays were bad days for me. My family was religious. I hated everything to do with religion. I hated the Friday evening service and the Saturday noon meals. After school, which ended Saturday around noon, my friends and I went to the country in order not to be home for all the religious observances. I wanted the light, the outdoors, the play of boys, not the dark ardor of devout old men.

There were nine of us: my parents, three sisters, three brothers, and myself. My parents, by the time I was born as next to the youngest, had been beaten by life. My father, who occasionally would laugh and play the violin, became more subdued and submerged by life's burdens. He never seemed to recover from the loss of his farm and the promise it had carried. My mother was dutiful with her family, but never seemed to really enjoy anything that she was doing. I remember undressing for sports in school and being jealous of the neatly darned socks of my classmates. Small white stitches etched stories of devotion and care. I was embarrassed by the way my socks were darned with large stitches of either black or red thread. I was too young to understand that the stitches did not reflect unconcern but, rather, the heavy load of caring for a large family and not having enough. My mother's solace was in her religion. Instead of laughter and conversation there was piety. I did not understand what was happening in the world or in the family. I always felt like a stranger in our home, and I always longed to be elsewhere. By the time I was old enough to truly comprehend her and her devotion to all of us I was in the labor camp. There, in the summer of 1944, somewhere in the Ukraine, in some unexplainable miraculous way, I received a postcard from her. From the date of that brief message I learned later that she had mailed it a day before she was taken to the ghetto. Her letter sustained me as only mother's love can.

My oldest sister, Sara, was a beautiful girl. Young men were constantly around her. Since telephones were a rarity in the city, I became the carrier of her love letters across town. I liked to meet the different people on my journeys, and also enjoyed the fact that I made a few pennies doing this work. The year she turned sixteen, my father was in the business of selling fruit to businessmen from Western Europe who came to our city. They would later ship the fruit to Switzerland. During our famous apricot season, an elegant Swiss gentleman arrived. He purchased wagonloads of beautiful apricots. When he left, my sister Sara left with him. She went only as far as Budapest. As abruptly as she had left, she returned home. This was a grave scandal in our city and a tragic time for the entire family. My sister attempted suicide, and neighbors appeared to stare in our windows. I didn't understand then what had occurred, and the family never talked openly about it. I just knew that my family was mortified and gravely troubled.

In the city was a textile merchant, Karcsi Harsanyi. He was very short, under five feet tall. Karcsi was an important person to me who influenced my entire life. He was a well-educated, smart, good-humored person who was able to make jokes about himself, including his size. He looked at everything positively, including having a relationship with Sara. He loved that sister of mine.

Karcsi managed to remain in my sister's and my life for decades. Although he was madly in love with Sara, she eventually married another. She maintained a twenty-year affair with Karcsi which sustained her through the death camps and another marriage. Sara had the heart of a sensuous rebel in a time and with a family that sanctioned only the traditional. Karcsi remained true to my sister his entire adult life, marrying much later in life a woman who also loved another with unrequited love. While acknowledging that their lifelong loves were others, they also found space in their own lives for each other.

My father was fiercely against Karcsi because this man was hardly a Jew in a religious sense. This "hardly a Jew" taught me how to play chess. This "hardly a Jew" came to my soccer games. To this man I was really somebody. This man taught me about love, loyalty, and integrity. To my father, these attributes were secondary. What was primary to him was Orthodoxy. To me this small man was a giant, a true Jewish giant.

Rozsi was my middle sister. She was a plain, homely girl who stayed in the kitchen helping our mother. She was quiet and shy. She was quite humorless. We were opposites. I was always running around; she always remained at home. She and I had a special antagonism. One of the favorite childhood games was button soccer. To large buttons we would attach labels bearing the names of our favorite offensive and defensive players. A small button was the ball and flicked into play with another button. The trouble was the buttons! I cut them off clothes to equip our game. Rozsi always tattled on me and got me in trouble. Then, when clothes were too old or ragged and eventually discarded, Rozsi would collect the buttons and give them to my brothers, ignoring me.

Of the seven of us, only my youngest sister, Iren, got a formal education. She was serious and focused. A short time after her graduation Iren went to another city near Rumania because one of our aunts got sick. She went down to help the family and stayed for a year, earning money since the family was very rich. The aunt had kids who were a little older than we were. They sent us used clothes to wear. The clothes were too short for me. I remember trying to compensate for the too-short jacket by holding my arms in, hunching my shoulders. My father was furious, as he assumed that this posture was due to my emulating my sister's short boyfriend, Karcsi. I couldn't tell him the truth, which was that he couldn't afford to buy me a perfectly fitted jacket.

Sándor was my oldest brother. He was a deep thinker who always tried to analyze the world around him. He was deeply religious, serious, and considerate to others. Something happened to him when he was eighteen. He came home from the yeshiva, a Jewish religious school, troubled and despondent. During the service on Yom Kippur, which is the most sacred and solemn day in Judaism, he asked me to take a walk with him. Out on the street he suddenly looked very different and distraught. He reached into his pocket and gave me money, ordering me to go and buy him bacon and bread. His request was so shocking that I followed his order without questions. A religious, contemplative Jew disobeying the dietary laws on the holiest of days was beyond belief. He ate with a great urgency, almost in a trance. My immediate and future questions were left unanswered. I did not have the luxury of a long life with him to ask about this episode. By the time I was an adult and could have talked with him about our childhood and our feelings on being a part of this particular family, the family had been annihilated. What kind of feelings burdened his soul and why had I been chosen as a witness remains an unresolved puzzle in my life.

My other brother, József, was the closest to me. We shared secrets. We were friends. Although my brother was two years older and a head taller and stronger, I could intimidate him. I think I could intimidate him because he was so self-assured that he didn't have to prove his prowess. As soon as we stepped out of the house to go to the high school, I would make him carry my books on the long walk. If he refused, I would beat up this mild-mannered brother. I am still amazed. How could have that have happened? The ability to intimidate, although not my proudest trait, did save my life on several occasions. Although mellow and filled with uncomplicated zest for life, József had some mischievousness in him. He worked in a cantina selling wine, and I always wondered about his abundance of money. He told me that he watered down the wine, making one hundred and ten liters with every hundred liters of wine, thereby increasing his profits. József's dream was to emigrate to Palestine.

So my family seemed cleaved into two kinds of people. There were Sara, József, and I, who seemed ready to rush into life and was enthused about the challenge. There were Iren, Rozsi, Sándor, and my parents, who seemed quietened and subdued by the very forces which juiced up the rest of us. Unfortunately I was too young to really understand much of this, and most of the time felt alone and quite alienated.

My life changed when I became twelve. A visiting relative brought me my proudest possession, a soccer ball. It opened the neighborhood and life for me. I spent hours and hours in the parks learning more and more, and practicing new skills on how to handle the soccer ball. A year or so after I received my best possession, I entered high school. The school had only one sport—soccer. I was the first freshman and the first Jewish boy ever selected for the team. It made me proud and my life easier. The other boys looked up to me. That soccer ball had given me an opportunity, a fork in the road. It allowed me to begin to be different and distinct. I had moved beyond the Jewish community, and I had begun to blend into different groups. At the same time I moved and distanced myself further from my family.

I was also a singer in the choir. This was another choice which made me different from most of the Jewish boys in my group. Most of the boys in the choir were chosen from the city orphanage. They were rough kids, and everyone was afraid of them. One day our skinny marching horse passed away, so I made a little note in my book, "Géza died." I put down that day's date. As I was singing, one of the orphans pulled out the notebook from my back pocket and saw the notation. They thought Géza was my father or my brother. This put me at their level of loss, and they began to accept me.

High school in Hungary was mostly Catholic. For one hour twice a week there was religion class. All the boys who had other religions had a "free hour." That free hour was spent in the yard playing soccer and talking about girls.

I had a Gentile friend, Pali Boros. He was physically weak and without any athletic ability. He was the closest non-Jewish friend that I had. Our fates were intermingled in our later years. Pali was a true friend. Pali's family had a tavern and a truckstop at the edge of the city. His family was always decent and caring, and never missed an opportunity for a kind word.

One day we decided to run away and have an adventure. We hid in a woodshed, thinking that in the evening we could jump on the back of a truck and get further away. My older brother, Sándor, came after us. He had found our hiding place, and he took me home. That was the first time my rebellious nature showed itself in planning escapes. It would not be the last.

When I was inducted into the Jewish labor battalion, Pali was inducted into the regular army. I saw him next in 1947 after his release from a Russian prisoner-of-war camp. He had tuberculosis, and was terribly ill. A few months after his return, I found him waiting for me in front of my house. He knew he was always welcome in my house, so his reason for standing outside was that he needed to talk to me privately. Pali told me that the authorities wanted to take away his father's business license. The tavern and the land around it would be lost, but Pali's father hoped to keep his home and the small garden behind the tavern. A local Communist functionary had tried to evict the family from the house, and Pali had come for my help. It was an impossible situation and almost unbearable to listen to. He and his family were true Hungarian patriots. They represented what was best about Hungary. Though drafted, Pali and his family had not complied with the racist fascist policy. He was imprisoned by the liberating Red Army as an enemy and treated brutally. Now the family was being treated bureaucratically and cruelly by the Communist government in power. I went to a former teacher who had become the police chief in Kecskemét. He listened quietly and then advised me to stay away from this problem.

A few weeks later I read a distorted story about how a crazed tavern owner had shot his horse, drained all the wine in the wine cellar, and then committed suicide. I went to Pali's father's funeral to say goodbye to a decent, good man. The secret police watched the funeral from a distance. Pali told me he wanted to escape and wanted my help. I owned a small motor bike at the time, and gave it to him. I never saw him again. Did he escape Hungary? I hope he is alive somewhere and can read of my love for him and for his family.

After my teenage attempt to escape the confines of home, I knew that the next time I would be successful. Three years later I managed it. I had to.

- 3 -

By the mid-1930s, the political situation had worsened. News about Mussolini's Italy and Hitler's Germany became an important part of our everyday lives. Our teachers and the militaristic parents of my classmates were antisemitic jingoists. More and more we heard or read the words *Christian* and *Hungarian* as one word. Somehow, if these two words were joined together, we Jews were set apart. You were either Christian-Hungarian or not Hungarian at all. The Christian-Hungarian gentry felt that they deserved all the rights and privileges. To be Christian-Hungarian meant to be entitled to a good living without effort and without intrinsic capability. This group looked down on everyone not in their class. The Jews were as low as one could get. So the Jews had the impossible position of being despised for being the lowest of the low and at the same time of being blamed for having too much that rightfully belonged to true Hungarians. Basic civil rights only applied to Christian-Hungarians. These men would later become the officers of the Hungarian army. A decade later this was the group that always cried about the good past times when they could confiscate farms and business enterprises they believed should be rightfully theirs. In the mid-thirties these people looked at the example of fascist Mussolini more than at the Nazi enterprise of Adolf Hitler.

Sports were not a major conversational topic among Jews, but when the Jewish American heavyweight champion, Max Baer, defeated the Italian champion, Primo Carnera, the entire Jewish community of Kecskemét celebrated his victory. To us it was a victory against the "master-races" that would make us slaves. Max Baer championed our cause. This was also the time when the Hitler Youth started to vacation in our city as guests of the Hungarian government. We looked at them with mild curiosity when they marched through the city streets.

It was big news when the Italian army entered Ethiopia. Then a few years later the Spanish Civil War became the prelude to World War II. People talked about the possibility of war. What will the English do? Why is there so much silence? Maybe the English feel differently than we do about what will happen next. Are the English angry? Yes! No! We began to think we should emigrate to a safer more hospitable country. We began to dream. It would be so nice to travel, to visit interesting cities, to learn about other people. But they were just dreams.

The 1930s were difficult years for everybody in Hungary. To be thirteen and Jewish made life difficult to comprehend, sometimes painful, and occasionally frightful.

During one of our geography classes, when the subject country was Poland, the teacher added a humorous addendum. In Poland, he said, there were so many Jews that if a Pole threw a stone to chase away a dog, he would probably hit a Jew. Remarks like that made me feel embarrassed, angry, and frustrated at my powerlessness. Outside I reacted as if it were none of my concern and did not bother me at all.

Nationalities was another subject discussed in the classroom. A discussion was underway about the difference between the Germanic and Slavic races when our teacher rather casually remarked that one could easily differentiate Jews by their red noses. I was humiliated by his remarks and unconsciously touched my nose, not realizing that my classmates were watching me. Their reaction was a roar of laughter. I stood up, filled with frustration and anger, and told the teacher that his nose was really red (he was a drunkard) while mine was only sunburned from playing soccer outside. To my amazement he told the class that my nose was not red because I was different from the other Jews. He then picked up his cane and said that my bottom would be red if I didn't sit down. The day ended for me with a blackened eye and bleeding red nose due to the fights I had in the yard with the classmates who had dared laugh at me. I had thought that by being a different type of Jew, I would not be mocked. No! It was not easy to be thirteen and Jewish in Hungary in 1930.

Kecskemét was less than sixty miles from Budapest. At that time this distance was thought to be considerable. At least it was for me, a thirteen-year-old boy. I had not seen the capital city yet. I had not seen a championship soccer game played there. I read in the paper about my favorite team. They would be in Budapest to play for the championship. I tried to get some money for the train ride, but could not. Sunday morning of the day the game was played I got on my bike and pedaled to the big city. It was almost dark by the time I arrived, and the game had almost ended. My team had lost 5 to 0. I left Budapest in a sad mood and arrived back home around midnight.

This was my first adventure and my first dream. I was happy I had made the effort, though sad my team had lost. I gained the knowledge that if I wanted to do something enough, I could.

In our city Jews and Gentiles lived side by side. Gentiles and Jews. Our lives were bound up with one another's during these years, the war years, and after the war. Some of our neighbors were true heroes. Others gave up their humanity for safety or greed. Most of us were just people. These friends, neighbors, and acquaintances had enormous meaning to us because of what happened during the war years and how they and we reacted to these experiences.

Our next-door neighbor was a railroad man. He was gone most of the time. His wife slept around openly with any available man in the neighborhood. We called her affectionately, "the whore Boske." All of us liked her. She was fun-loving and easygoing and dispensed her favors rather generously. We envied her husband for his opportunity to travel and see the world. They were real Christians, without ever claiming it or ever accepting rewards for it. In 1944, when the German Gestapo took my father, along with other Jews, away, her husband followed them secretly to the southern part of Hungary. He reported back to my family that our father and the thirty-five other prominent Jews had been taken to a farm in southern Hungary where they were used instead of farm horses as forced labor. He gave us the last and only information we would ever know about our father. How my father got into that elitist group I never could fathom. He was not wealthy or prominent or famous. By the time the Gestapo took him away he was a fifty-six-year old, beaten man who tried to provide for his family. He tried to maintain some joy of life, playing violin most of the time for himself. The melody of his sad songs and the way he swayed his body to the tune of his fiddle will stay in my memory and heart forever. He was simply our father. How kind these people, our neighbors, were to understand our wish for knowledge of our loved ones!

Our other neighbor was a widowed teacher. The teacher had a son named Zóltan Bibo. He was a young, handsome guy. A female cousin of mine visited us every summer from Budapest. This nice Christian boy fell madly in love with the Jewish girl. Both parents were tolerant of the relationship. In 1942, when I was called up for a labor battalion because I was a Jew, he was drafted into the regular army as a Christian-Hungarian. In a very short time he became an officer. He didn't just wear the army uniform like my friend Pali Boros; he embraced it. By the fall of 1944 he put the green Arrow Cross armband on his uniform. This signified membership in the Hungarian Nazi Party. Long before that he stopped talking to or greeting us. He was one of the first men who visited me when I finally arrived home after the labor camp. Now that the tide had turned and I was on the winning side, he acted as if he were the same love-struck teenager who had been blind to the differences in religion. He tried to show me that the intervening years were of no consequence. To me the fascist uniform was his real character.

Another neighbor was a Gentile art teacher. His name was Imre Gabor. He was quiet, but he was always supportive. Once, in his class, one of the students drew something and at the bottom of his drawing put the slogan, "World proletariat, unite." This teacher and the boy's father had been in jail together for taking part in the short-lived Hungarian Communist revolt in 1919. Almost everybody knew what an inflammatory and dangerous thing this boy had done in the class. Having Communist leanings in this fascist climate was a death sentence for both him and his father. The art teacher turned it into a joke which would not jeopardize himself or the boy. This taciturn man could choose the right words when he needed to. In 1945 he became the city's police chief.

Several houses away from us lived a remote father and a sad mother who was part-gypsy. They had two beautiful daughters. The youngest one was a year younger than I was. Her name was Maria. I was young and in love with her, but had never dared to talk to her. I used to walk in front of her house.

She would come out of her yard singing. I used to pretend she was singing for me. Later she told me she was. Her school was in a different location than mine. I used to tag behind her until she reached her home.

Years later, after we had become friends, she showed me a picture of a soldier, and told me she was in love with him. He had a good-looking, intelligent face. I sincerely wished her good luck and happiness. In 1945, after I returned home, Maria came over to talk to me. She showed me another picture. It was the same man in a different uniform. He wore the gendarme uniform. In the regular army his superiors had refused to let him marry her because she was part-gypsy. They separated, and he became part of the brutal fascist gendarme force. His face under a dark hat now looked brutal. He had been a captain in a gendarme unit that enforced the deportation of Jews from the cities of Szeged, Baja, and Sopron. He was responsible for sending these cities' Jews on their last ride. He had personally cursed, shoved, and pushed people onto the wagons of death.

"Now," she said, "he sits in the jail and sends me a letter asking me to visit him."

She asked me what she should do. She started to cry. I told her that I didn't think she should waste time with a man who had taken part in the murder of thousands and thousands of people, some of them gypsies. Less than a year after our meeting, I met with her at a coffee house where she played the violin so beautifully. She introduced me to her husband, someone she had recently met.

While I began my teenage years attempting to fly on the wings of my independence, the political situation became more foreboding. People would look to the Jewish community elders for their advice. The Jewish leaders said,

"We are Hungarians. We were born here. The hurricane will pass. Hitlers and Mussolinis come and go. We will remain."

So nobody left. Almost nobody.

I had a close friend, Eugene Fischel. One late night he knocked at my window.

He said, "Ed, I'm leaving. I've found a way out of this country. We must leave this country. Come with me."

I hesitated. This was the time when I had met Irenke Gabor. She was my first girlfriend, so I declined to leave with Eugene. Here again, a relatively small choice was shaping my life.

I had fallen in love with Irenke. Neither of us understood what held us together because we were so different from one another. We were not opposites, just different. Each time we met both of us were overwhelmed with tenderness and love. She was my first love. We held hands and kissed in front of other teenagers in courting games. All of our friends knew our secret. Unfortunately, my social status was not good enough for her parents. We were young and in love, but when events forced me to try a new life away from home in my own way, she began to see an older boy. Our relationship ended without any real drama, and perhaps that is why she will remain in my heart forever. I guess that in her short life, I remained the one who held her hand secretly for the first time.

Irenke and I were in love, but had to hide that fact from her parents because I was not welcome in their house. It is interesting to contemplate the social hierarchy which so interfered with our young lives. The Gabors had a small, elegant shoe store which elevated them far above my family's status. In Auschwitz all Jews' status was the same. My sister was in the same group of internees as Irenke. Somehow Irenke had managed to save a picture of us holding hands, and proudly told my sister that we would marry if she came out of the camps. She didn't come back. She died there.

So I chose the path to stay, and Eugene chose his. My path seemed to be one of adolescent naivete and optimism; his was one of adult foreboding. Eugene had a brother in the French Foreign Legion. He wanted to follow his brother, and he wanted me to go with him. After the war, when I was settled in America, my sister sent me a letter from Hungary saying that

Eugene was alive and in Paris. On my next trip there in the late 1970s, I telephoned him. A woman's voice answered the phone in French and relayed the message, "Papa, a Hungarian wants to talk to you."

He came to my hotel. We talked and talked. Our widely divergent paths had both led to survival. Different paths, quite different experiences, but both of us lived through the ordeal.

I was growing and beginning to know myself. I could see myself reflected in the love in Irenke's eyes. I could see myself accepted by peers. I could begin to see the differences that my heritage gave me in the eyes of some of the citizens. But nowhere did I feel more myself than side by side with my teammates on the soccer field. Major-league soccer filled my life and helped me through a lot of difficult times.

When I was fourteen a local Division II team signed up a super-star. He was a nineteen-year-old player, and the papers were full of stories about his soccer prowess. By trade he was a barber. The soccer team gave him five dollars a week so that he could practice twice a week instead of working those days. Something came up with his contract with the soccer association, and he had to wait out a year before the Kecskemét Athletic Club could sign him. The management of the team knew that a player of his caliber could not sit out a year, so they formed a local team around this soccer star, filled with young players and good players past their prime, among them two former Hungarian all-stars. I was selected to play as one of the young players. The official teams had their championship schedules. In order to give us playing time and opposition they organized teams from railroad, city, and factory workers. Because of this legendary player, Béla Koranyi, more people came to watch our unofficial games than the city's championship Division II teams.

I spent almost all of my free time in front of the barber shop watching and idealizing Béla. He was like a god to me, and he liked me in return. In those days soccer was an offensive game. Every team had the same type of line-up. There were two defenders, three midfielders, and five forwards. The player's uniform number coincided with his position. Béla was center forward #9. I was always #8, inside right forward. We played our games on Sundays. Monday was the day for the team to visit the city's steambaths. Massages, patching healing injuries, and brotherly talks were the order of that day.

Coming out of the bathhouse, Béla pulled me aside and said, "Ed, I'm not staying. I've gotten a contract to play in Paris."

I said, "Don't go. Everyone likes you here. They have been loyal to you. You signed a contract. Don't lose face. Don't lose the love and admiration of the city. Stay for your honor."

He didn't go. He finished the season, but our friendship ended after the conversation. Perhaps too much had been said.

In 1945, I had just come back from the war. I could hardly run or walk due to the labor battalion's abuse. A letter came to the Kecskemét soccer club from France. It was from Koranyi. He had become a French all-star thirty-eight times. In his letter he said he would like to return in the fall to play one last game in our city. A game was arranged. In his second letter to the club he inquired about me. Had I survived or not? He asked also about a former Hungarian National all-star, Novometcky. Novo had not survived. He asked that the remnants of the team be assembled for this game. From the forward line, besides himself, only #8 had survived—me.

Finally the game! The stadium was full. Everyone wanted to see him once more. The field was heavy and muddy. I was out of shape. I played way over my exhausted capacity until halftime. I found Béla in the locker room and told him that I couldn't return to the field. I was half-dead. Koranyi looked at me and said, "You have to go onto the field. You promised you would play. The people came to see us play, and they are loyal. Play for your honor."

I finished the game. In 1978 I visited Paris on business. I tried to locate him, but I could find only his French wife. She was a schoolteacher and told me that Koranyi, this great player and my idol, had died in 1976. Rest in peace, Koranyi. We taught each other about honor, didn't we!

- *4* -

Political events took a turn for the worse during these adolescent years. My personal life was progressing at the same time that antisemitism was sweeping Europe. I was sixteen years old in 1938. The theater in the city had begun to advertise a new movie. The film's title was *Jud Suess.* This movie was the most violent antisemitic film made by the Germans. We heard about this movie and the violence and pogroms which followed its showing. Our rabbi advised us to stay out of the area of the theater and to remain indoors at night. A few of us didn't follow his advice. We went out in small groups. We were ready to take a stand and be bloodied for who we were.

The film was shown. Fistfights and arguments ensued. By the second day, the police took us, the few reactive Jewish teenagers, to the city hall for a few hours. They warned us to stay home or else. Us! Not those who cheered on the antisemites. Not those who wallowed in hatred. This was the last straw for me. I'd had enough. I was a tough Jewish boy and needed my own direction. I packed my stuff and took the night train to Budapest.

During the train ride I was fearful about my ability to sustain myself alone in the big city of Budapest. It was dawn when I arrived and saw the bustling crowds heading out towards the main boulevards. In daylight I felt a little more secure. I managed to convince myself about my decision to start a new life without the yoke or support of a traditional religious family life. The first day I found a job in a florist shop as a delivery boy. In addition to my wage I was allowed to sleep in a small storage room of the shop.

In the evenings I went to a nearby park and watched as others kicked the soccer ball. Soon the local youths recognized me as their constant spectator and asked me to play. I joined their team and managed to play a much better game than they did.

A police detective named Virag watched our group. He stopped me afterwards and started to ask personal questions. Personal questions from a Christian policeman usually did not bode well for Jews. Virag, though, was a most unusual human being. I told him who I was. He took me under his wing. He found me a better place to live. He put me up with another boy, a little older than I. My new roommate's name was Vilmos Kiss. Vilmos was a good-looking Gentile boy. He had a good singing voice and was a talented violin player.

I played soccer, and Detective Virag forced me to go to school. I owed him a lot. He was a wonderful person. He took a strange kid under his protection and watched over him. He showed me the right path.

Nineteen thirty-eight was the year of the Anschluss. Germany and Austria became one nation. This union and its expansionist policies gained fanfare and celebration all the way to Vienna. This year was also the end of the failed policies of Chamberlain to appease Hitler. In Budapest, a few weeks after Hitler occupied Czechoslovakia, bank officers, clerks, and teachers started to line up in front of the Arrow Cross and other Nazi-oriented parties to volunteer. This all happened while I played soccer, worked, and went to school under the easy supervision of Mr. Virag. My world had started to crumble at the same time that I was feeling the self-confidence of a young man.

During this time I played under good coaches and got better and better. My dream was that I would be in the papers and named as the best player in Hungary. I played for a left-wing political-oriented team, Torekves S.C. It was a good team. In 1942 the authorities disbanded the team for its political leanings. But at this time, 1938, I was sixteen and felt proud about how I was managing my life. It was not without difficulties and hardships, but it was my life, and I was happy.

There were some days when all I could afford for my daily nourishment was a liter of milk and one kilogram of bread. When I had a little money left after paying my rent, I treated myself to a delicious bowl of bean soup at the Hallo Buffet on the corner of Kiraly Street. I had to eat standing. There were no chairs or tables. It did not matter. I was strong. I was young. Nothing mattered except to get stronger and play better and better.

After our Sunday soccer game the team always had a big meal together in the clubhouse. I was the only Jewish boy on the team. I never heard any remarks about that. I played with my teammates, got drunk with them sometimes, and felt that our bonds were indestructible. The only time I was teased was in the shower. Being circumcised made me different. This teasing stopped after a few weeks. Detective Virag was the club's president. He kept a protective eye on me.

After a rainy Sunday soccer game, as we were leaving the stadium, we heard the news. Germany had occupied Czechoslovakia. People were standing in the rain. On the street corners there were small, mute gatherings. The world around me had stopped. No one seemed to move. This was very frightening. Hungarians are usually talkative and loud. Standing in silence among the crowd along with my teammates, I felt hopelessly lost. The worst part was that the Hungarian army participated in the occupation of defenseless Czechoslovakia. The Hungarians were rewarded by Hitler for their support. The Germans gave part of Czechoslovakia to Hungary.

My Gentile roommate, Vilmos Kiss, volunteered to be a member of the Hungarian *Rongyos Garda*, the "raggedy army." This paramilitary group had been formed to help establish law and order behind the advancing army. This group and Vilmos thought of themselves as Hungarian partisans who were anxious for action and the new world order. Their sole job was to harass the Jewish people. They were the ones who committed the first atrocities against Jews. Vilmos Kiss always considered himself a decent human being and thought of the two of us as friends. For him there was no internal contradiction in this way of thinking, although his stunning lack of conscience and his way of compartmentalizing his acts horrified me. When he returned from his *Garda* activities, he would not answer my questions about his experiences. Once, when he was drunk, he told me that he had seen a rich Jewish merchant murdered in front of his wife and his son.

In 1954, when I was working as a printer in Budapest, this same Vilmos Kiss, now a high-ranking Communist official, came to visit the shop where I was working. He greeted me in a friendly manner. He appeared unfazed by the stunning contradictions in his life. To him there was no disparity between membership in the *Garda* and high rank in the Communist Party. Nothing had changed except the color of his party's affiliation, from fascist tan and black to Communist red.

It was time for me to find another roommate. My new roommate's name was Lajos Berger. He was a simple boy, good-natured and a bit shy. I got to know him at the soccer clubhouse. We rented a room with a separate entrance in an easily accessible location. I packed up my scanty belongings and left Vilmos without explaining the reason. I think he was relieved also. My very presence was a witness to his irrationality. After I left, Vilmos became a member of a right-wing organization, the *Turul.* Once in a while I would see him proudly wearing his uniform. I have to say that he never failed to greet me in a friendly manner, even when he was with his fascist cronies. Somehow what he did in private had no relationship with what he did as a member of a group.

The political situation became more radicalized, and a wave of atrocities followed. Quite a few Jews managed to escape from Czechoslovakia to Hungary, and from there they tried to go to Palestine. Harboring illegal refugees was a highly punishable crime. In spite of the threat of spending years in jail, Zionist and left-wing organizations tried to shelter these unfortunate people until a way could be found to smuggle them out from Hungary to Palestine. I was working in a print shop when a complete stranger approached me and asked if I could hide some Jewish refugees. After talking to my roommate we agreed. After dark this same stranger escorted two Czech girls to our room and without further word or explanation left. They didn't speak Hungarian, and we didn't speak Czechoslovakian. We didn't ask questions about what had happened to them. We were too immature to understand their private agony. They were just available pretty girls, and we were young men. We spent the entire evening trying to make out with the two girls. The world's agony was still distant and not personal. In the morning both girls were gone. Now I wish I could talk with them and apologize. Was I less full of contradictions and opportunism than Vilmos? Again it was youth and exuberance instead of maturity which was leading me towards my destiny. I had no idea that my future would follow that of those frightened and homeless girls. My character was growing, but not without its scars and regrets. What would have happened had we been more sensitive? I wonder if sensitivity would have thwarted survival or enhanced it. I live now with my regrets about those two frightened, disenfranchised young women who bore the scars of war before we could fully recognize that we would be next.

At the end of the spring soccer season in nineteen thirty-nine, I received my first contract as a semi-pro. My salary was three dollars a week. It was a nice addition to my very meager earnings from my part-time job. More important than the money was the recognition by my coaches that I had a future in soccer. I gained self-respect and hoped for a brilliant sports career. I could only do this by blocking out the dark political future that loomed. I was seventeen. Kristallnacht, dismal political news, or even refugees like the two girls had not dampened my foolish optimism.

Then came September 1939, and Germany invaded Poland. World War II had begun! The Hungarian press started a vicious antisemitic campaign. Atrocities on streetcars and in public places became an everyday occurrence. I started to spend what little free time I had with my roommate Lajos and his Jewish friends. My non-Jewish soccer teammates were very supportive during this time. The coach changed the name on my player's certificate to Angyal. The sports paper always printed the line-ups after the games, and the coach tried to explain to me that Mandel was not a good-sounding soccer name. He didn't have to add the obvious, which was that it was a name associated with condemnation and vilification.

Once in a while fistfights broke out after the games. I was in them with everybody else. I got a really good bloody nose once. I was in the dressing room when a faintly familiar fellow helped me clean off. When I opened my eyes I recognized him. It was Ferenc Nagy, a famous center halfback for Vasas, a Division I team organized under the left-leaning steelworkers. Nagy was a bit short, but strong like a bull. Wiping off my bloody face, he urged me to hit first and harder the next time. In 1949 after I moved to Budapest, I took his advice. In this later time I fast-punched with a rapid speech, and I was rewarded by being given a job with him and being able to play soccer with him.

- *5* -

A year and a half passed by. A year and a half of independence and growth. I was eighteen. Then I received an urgent message from my parents to come home. My middle sister, Rozsi, had gotten engaged to a very religious Jewish boy, a printer. As a dowry my parents had bought him equipment for a small print shop. At this time it was very difficult for a Jew to get a license to operate a business. My parents had heard favorable news of their young son who was independently making a living for himself in Budapest. News also had spread in the city about my soccer-playing ability. They needed my reputation and my help.

So I came home, home to Kecskemét, and started to inquire about the possibility of acquiring a printing license. I was told that it was impossible for a Jew. A sports fan at the city hall advised me to try to find a *strohman*—a Christian partner whose signature would make it possible to obtain a business license under his name. This was a profitable business for the *strohman*, who received money for partnering with a Jew and lending his Christian name to the official papers. But the people who performed this function were not friends of the Jews; they were taking advantage of an immoral situation. Later on they were even more despised since they tried to retain the businesses in their own names, after the few fortunate Jews returned from labor battalions or death camps.

The city's best-known printer was an antisemite and an old drunk named Molnár. He was the first in the city to wear the Arrow Cross pin and armband. Naturally, decent people and all Jews avoided him as much as possible. This man made his living by printing anti-Jewish pamphlets and distributing them on the street corners. This person, however, represented the only hope my sister and brother-in-law had for an income. He would have to be their *strohman*. The only person who could talk to this despicable man was me.

Old Molnár was crazy about soccer. I was sure he had heard about me as a player. He might even have seen me playing. I bolstered my courage and went to him. I knew that I had to talk quickly and be effective before his native antisemitism took over. He looked at me in shock at my audacity to visit him. I started to talk to him about how everyone knew what a good printer he was, but that his shop was in need of new machinery. Then I continued that I had new equipment and a good printing press, but no license. He closed the doors and shutters, and started to talk to me. He asked about soccer and about Budapest. I realized that he was skirting the issue, so I spelled it out.

"Mr. Molnár, you have a license. I have the machinery. Let's form a partnership."

He agreed. I did not mention anything about my Orthodox brother-in-law at this point. I would have been thrown out.

He agreed on a fifty-fifty arrangement on one condition—that no one would know that he was working with me. I agreed. I figured that as long as he got his profits, he wouldn't need to visit his partner's shop and see my brother-in-law, the Orthodox Jew, who was now his partner.

So "good old Mr. Nazi Molnár" continued printing his anti-Jewish materials at his old shop, and we printed other materials in the converted basement. Whenever I confronted Mr. Molnár about the lies and half-truths in his pamphlets, he always had a ready answer that varied with the degree of his drunkenness.

"I don't believe any of this, but my friends pay me well to print it."

"Every half-lie is also a half-truth."

"I will stop printing this soon."

The "soon" came when the Soviet troops occupied Kecskemét.

The wedding day of Rozsi and her betrothed arrived. Relatives and friends came. A day before the ceremony my father was informed that the wedding would have to be canceled, as Lajos's blood test was positive for syphilis. Rozsi became hysterical, and the family was shocked. My father called his almost-son-in-law in. Lajos said, "It is not true. I have never had sexual intercourse with anybody. It would be against my religious beliefs."

He was thirty-four years old. It was the truth. Jewish Orthodoxy dictated abstinence until marriage. This confirmed my conviction that religious Orthodoxy with thirty-four years of celibacy would never be part of my religion.

A well-known person with connections at city hall promised to look into the faulty laboratory results. We paid bribes, which was part of the daily fabric, to get the test "corrected." With unwarranted angst, some money, and high anxiety the wedding was finally a reality.

The family needed me, and I felt their necessity, so I stayed home to run Molnár's second print shop with my new relative. Life was not delightful, but it was not unbearable either. I went out to solicit printing orders and then went back to the shop to help produce them. Within months after the marriage, with my sister pregnant, my brother-in-law, Lajos Preisz, was called up into a labor battalion.

A son, Miklós, was born to them while Lajos was away. He was a wonderful little kid. Miklós was two years old when, together with the whole Jewish population of Kecskemét, he was deported to Auschwitz. My sister Sara told me the rest of the story when we were reunited after the war. During the selection process at the death camp, my sister Sara held the baby. At the last moment, just before our family as a group got in front of the S.S. officer who, by pointing his finger left or right, determined who would live for a short while and who would die instantly in the gas chambers, my sister Rozsi took Miklós in her arms.

"I want to share the fate of my son," were the last words she uttered.

She and Miklós died in the Auschwitz gas chambers that very day.

My brother-in-law never saw his son. When little Miklós was born, he was already serving in the doomed labor battalion somewhere near the river Don, where he died in the winter of 1941. My sister and her son perished with my mother, while Sara and Iren were spared. So little Miklós, age two, ascended as smoke from a crematorium. The smoke of his mother and grandmother joined his small trace. Joining them were my aunt, my uncle, my cousin Klara, age seven, and my cousin Marta, age nine. Dare I hope that Miklós's spirit was commingled with that of his father, Lajos Preisz, who died in the labor battalion, his grandfather, who died as a horse, and with my brother József, who was shot trying to escape the labor battalion?

- *6* -

In 1940 laws restricting Jews came into effect. These laws slowly stripped us of our Hungarian and human rights. The first law, called the *Numerus Clausus*, was a quota system limiting the number of Jews who could go to the university. Some Jews said, "Not so bad, not everybody has to go to the university."

This law had been more or less in effect since 1920, but now was again in high fashion. Hungary could claim to be the first country to establish anti-Jewish laws. Stricter new laws superseded the old ones, copied the Nazis, and even outdid the masters. Almost every month more and more restrictive regulations were enacted, curbing Jewish economic and social life.

The 1940 laws stated that Jews could not be teachers. A Jew could not be a judge. A Jewish doctor could only treat Jews. Then others came, canceling out opportunities of becoming a civil servant.

"That's not so bad. One can try another job," was the answer to pessimism and despair.

All of us waited for a return to the old order, a change, a miracle. Maybe tomorrow, or next week, or next month, the trumpet would be heard over the radio to proclaim that this nightmare was over. We yearned to hear that this odd temporary episode was over, and that we were still regular Hungarian citizens.

Very few of us had the courage to try to get out of Hungary. Very few of us understood the insidious poison which we were being made to drink. We were young. We could accommodate. This was only a temporary hitch in our lives. We did not know that staying would seal our destiny. This was the year I was running my sister's little print shop, earning a little money for our simple needs. My major concern was to keep Molnár happy and drunk. This was not a difficult job. He was not a bad *strohman* after all. He was satisfied with half the profit without making additional demands and didn't resort to further blackmail. At the end of the war, after I had managed to get home, I walked over to Mr. Molnár's shop on the main street and then to ours in a sidestreet cellar. I later heard that Mr. Molnár had escaped Kecskemét with other fascists prior to the Soviet occupation of our town.

I was eighteen years old. I was independent and free to do what I liked, within the limits of Jewish law. My parents overlooked my so-called "goyishness," this love I had for the secular. Being Jewish, though still very precious to them, was becoming a heavy burden to carry.

Jewish education classes were organized to combat the exclusionary rules. Poetry was read and studied. Shows were arranged. Political discussions took place within a small circle. Most of us leaned to the far left, partly due to our upbringing and partly in reaction to the reactionary politics of fascism. We felt that the West had forgotten us. We thought Stalin would save us. Some of us looked to Palestine as a safe haven.

It was during this time that my brother József tried to get out of Hungary through Rumania to Palestine. The border patrol caught him. After two days of interrogation and beatings, he was shipped back to Hungary. For a week he could not wear shoes because of the beatings on the soles of his feet. We admired him for his courage. While most of us discussed politics and listened and tried to bide our time, gentle-tempered József had taken action.

I remember a political meeting put on by the Jewish education classes which ended with a very heated argument. The main speaker was Pista Krausz. In replying to an accusation that he was a Communist, he retorted that his love for Communism had something to do with his hatred of the world for allowing racist laws to be in force. Others answered that to be anti-fascist did not automatically mean becoming a Communist. Most of us sided with Krausz. The hope and the rescue we dreamed of would come from the East. The West was too silent.

We wrote essays about different subjects. My assignment was to read part of Thornton Wilder's *Our Town*. We learned about new poets. I remember one poem a ten-year-old chose to read. I don't remember the actual poem, but the meaning of it is as clear to me now as it was to me then:

I am a Hungarian.
I was born a Hungarian.
My nurse sang me Hungarian songs.
My mother taught me to pray in Hungarian.
I love you, beautiful Fatherland.

We were all tearful and shaky after hearing that verse. We still felt deep in our hearts that we were, and would always be, Hungarians. The heartbreaking part of this recitation was that the boy's father was in a labor camp wearing the yellow armband of dehumanization.

Then the exclusionary rule came that no Jew could play any team sports with Gentiles. This definitely hit closer to home. But I adjusted. We organized a Jewish soccer league. My friend Pista Virag's parents had a small farm outside of the city, and they arranged soccer practices on the field between harvests. Pista's father was called in by the police. He was told that Jews were not allowed to play or gather without permit. That was the end of the soccer club. We then got a permit and arranged track meets in a lumber yard owned by a Jewish merchant. This was a lumber yard with no lumber, as the merchandise had already been confiscated. We were able to have running and jumping events in a quasi-competitive fashion. I won the triple jump and one or two running events. We tried to lead a life which looked near normal, but it was not.

Now there were more racial laws. Sex between Jews and Gentiles became a punishable offense. It was definitely dangerous, but love would not recognize racial laws. If you met a decent girl who saw beyond racist policy, there was no dilemma unless you were discovered. The problem was that there was such a law to begin with.

Around this time I met Aranka. She was a sixteen-year-old Gentile girl who was already divorced. Her father was an old-time Communist who was jailed in 1920 for his political beliefs. They had a bakery ten kilometers from the city in a place called Rendor Falu. Aranka had gotten pregnant at age fourteen by a helper her father used in the bakery. The irate and volatile father made the helper marry her. She lost the baby, and they were divorced. She was not pretty by others' standards, but to me she was feminine and handsome. I think all the neighborhood Gentile boys were afraid of her father, Mr. Petnehazy. That may have been the reason she allowed me to become her boyfriend.

One day, I walked her home. Coming back a gang of local Jew-hating thugs surrounded me. One of them recognized me from soccer. He said to the others, "Don't touch him. I know him."

They didn't rough me up. My soccer-playing ability gave me a little respect, notoriety, and some protection. Years before, my name had been mentioned in the papers as a good Jewish soccer player. Soccer was so important that the group that had threatened me just a few minutes ago, followed me back to my neighborhood to protect me from other gangs. It was an uncomfortable position to be protected by thugs and for the shallowest of reasons. The racial laws were in effect and Aranka was Christian. This group knew that she was my girl-friend. I was being protected, not for humanitarian or moral reasons, but because I had agile feet and a good boot. At the same time this treatment fed the feeling that I was special and different enough to be optimistic about the direction of my life.

My parents and the rest of the family slept in the main house. On the opposite side of the yard was a small room which had once been a tool shed. That became my room. It was my choice to stay in this separate section and totally in keeping with my relationship with my family. In the middle of the yard was an old-fashioned well. Aranka and I used to lay blankets in the garden near the well on warm nights while the rest of my family slept. Escaping from the privacy of my hot room, Aranka and I moved out to the cooler garden. There was a moon. It was not too dark as we lay on our backs talking and counting the stars and doing the things that young boys and girls do. One night, my father, because of the heat, walked out into the yard towards the well to get some water. We noticed him and were apprehensive as to his feelings on finding us in scandalous familiarity. He must have seen us as we lay undressed on our blanket. My father pretended not to see us and walked away. This was the way he handled emotional sit-uations. I was too young then and distant from him to ask him about his feelings that day, as I would do as an adult had we been given that luxury. Maybe my father was less oblivious than I realized, and perhaps even understood me and my needs. Maybe if circumstances and times had been different—maybe we could have bridged that emotional valley and talked. I still wonder about all the sentences cut short, and all the missed understanding.

My relationship with Aranka lasted until I was called into the labor battalion. To my great surprise and against my desire she came to the railway station to say goodbye. She put herself in great danger by hugging me, a despised Jew with a yellow armband, before the train left, in front of police and others.

The departing Jews were treated with malice and mockery. At the last possible second she put her wristwatch in my hand as I leaned out the window. She then disappeared into the crowd. That brave, courageous act would have additional consequences for another later on.

There were bad days and good days, but now mainly bad days predominated. When would we get good news? Sometimes I thought I would hear only bad news the rest of my life. Would it be too much to get something more from life? Something beautiful, something surprising, and unexpected! I wondered what would become of me, and what would become of the whole world. During these dark times I stopped thinking of the future and stopped planning even a day ahead. I knew I had to survive. Today's animals who dressed in Hungarian and German uniforms were trying to make us disappear from the earth. I would not disappear, not because life in its present form was so beautiful, but because I knew it could be better. I had to form my own plan and try to live accordingly.

By this time we were completely separated from Gentile Hungarian friends and schoolmates. We organized ourselves so we could still be playful and young. We did not want to relinquish our youth. We organized bicycle trips. We traveled in youth groups to neighboring villages to visit friends and relatives.

Our favorite city was Nagykoros. It was a city of small but prominent Jewish population. We stayed at their houses, danced, and had a little fun with boys and girls of our same age. Our bicycle group loved to visit a small village called Agasegyhaza. This village had a very friendly couple who were farmers. I cannot recall their names; but I remember the farm, the friendly, childless middle-aged couple, and the way they made us feel very welcome and almost carefree. They received us with open hearts. The farmer had a small lake on his farm that he allowed us to use for swimming. We felt free and unchained. We had no social restraints here.

Another reason to go to this village was to stop at Aush's grocery store. It was in the middle of the village, and we would always stop and listen to his stories. We called them "the famous Aush stories." First we would go into his store to buy a sweet or have a glass of water, then we would go out to his yard. We would sit under the shade of his fruit trees waiting for him to emerge from the store and join us. His stories took us back to happier times. I recall he spoke of inner discipline. He talked about his war experiences in World War I. He had been a hussar, or horse soldier.

"Imagine me, the only Jew, on horseback," he used to tell us proudly.

I visualized him dignified and heroic, riding his horse. He showed us his medals and retold the deeds that he felt did him and the Jews proud. He told us several times, always by request, how he had lost his foot at the battle of Verdun. We did not feel sorry for him, in fact we envied his pride and daring.

I have fond memories of Aush and his family. The Aush stories were the legacy of a people, a culture, and a country. This was a legacy passed to me and others by Aush. This was the same Aush who limped behind the buggy to his death, wearing his medals, his stories, and his Hungarian pride.

- 7 -

Constant harassment now became part of our everyday life. My father and I had been frequent visitors to a tobacco shop. We felt the shopowner's attitude change. She stood behind her counter, looking gray and pale with unkempt hair. Cartons of Hungarian cigarettes, matches, stamps, envelopes, and newspapers surrounded her. Despite evidence to the contrary, she started to not have anything that we wanted to buy. Her last carton of cigarettes was for someone else. Stamps were never the right denominations for us. Newspapers were pushed on us which had fascist editorials and sentiments. If not those papers, she would only have very outdated papers for me to buy. I used to buy the daily sports papers, which she stopped having whenever I was around.

In the spring of 1941, the German army marched through the city of Kecskemét on its way to occupy Yugoslavia. They camped in the main square. Our rabbi said, "Stay in the shadows. Don't show yourselves. It is too dangerous."

We couldn't stop ourselves from watching these golden soldiers. The Germans looked invincible. They were so well-dressed in their pressed uniforms. They looked so strong, blond, and beautiful. They ate chocolate and oranges. Everybody surrounded them. In spite of our feelings they looked like young lions—so strong, perfect physically, perfect in discipline—perfect!

The restrictive anti-Jewish laws would lessen for a while only to have the screws tightened again. The strictness or the leniency of the application of the laws depended on the war news. If the German offensive stopped, no new laws were enacted, and there was an easing of the application of the old laws. Jews could not help but be very ecstatic at war news which was diametrically opposed to the national welfare of the now fascist Hungarian state.

In the Hungarian Parliament a few brave politicians dared to express moderate policies. They were usually members of the Hungarian Liberal Party. In 1944 they ended up in concentration camps or had to go underground, an arrest warrant or worst awaiting them.

During a period of some easing of the laws, several individuals got a permit to organize an unofficial Jewish soccer tournament. Kecskemét, Nagykoros, Cegled, Szentes, Szolnok, and Kiskunfélegyháza were the participating cities. The championship final was played in the city of Szolnok. This city was sixty kilometers northeast of Kecskemét. We were permitted to use a Division I team's field, the stadium of Szolnoki M.A.V. (Hungarian National Railroad). This fed my dream of playing in a first-division stadium. The dream was that I would do so as a first-division player, not as a member of a sometimes-outlawed Jewish team. But I was there, and the coach of the first-division team was there also to fuel the dream.

After we won the game, the first-division team's coach took me aside and said that if I would change my name to something "more Hungarian or Christian," he would get me an established Christian identity, and I could play in the reserve squad professionally. I was overwhelmed by his offer. I talked it over with my friends and coach. They said it was very dangerous because I might be recognized. I dropped the idea. I did not just drop it because it was dangerous. I dropped it because I needed to affirm who I was. Some dreams are worth danger, but rarely are dreams worth disowning one's own identity. I don't know if it was the right path or the left one I took at that moment, but it certainly sealed my fate and closed the chapter on my professional soccer playing.

- 8 -

Although the anti-Jewish laws effectively separated Gentiles and Jews in their daily lives, the Hungarian Army did not finish this separation until January 1942. The army was mainly pro-German and antisemitic. In spite of this, Jews were in the fighting units until the end of 1941. A few months later the fighting Jews were divested of their weapons and uniforms. They gave them yellow armbands identifying them as Jews, and almost certain death in the labor battalions.

The original idea of the labor battalion was to keep the Hungarian Jews from foreign labor camps and to use them in Hungary. Whatever view was originally held in the higher echelons eroded slowly as the Jews came to be seen as slaves to be worked to death by whoever "owned" them.

In April 1941, before the Jewish divestiture, just a few weeks before German army attacked the Russians, my brother Sándor's artillery unit was shipped to Ujvidek, Yugoslavia. The Germans needed the road through Hungary and Yugoslavia to cover their southern flank. The Yugoslavians were a fiercely independent nation which resisted the Germans. The Hungarian army supported the Germans and occupied a part of northern Yugoslavia. Later they committed atrocities against Jews and Yugoslavians, especially in the city of Ujvidek. The captain of my brother's army unit kept my brother and the other Jews under him in the barracks and didn't let them out during these murderous rampages against innocent civilians. Captain Maklary did this to protect my brother and the other Jews.

In June Hungary declared war on Russia, and the order to transfer all Jews out of the army was strictly enforced. A few months later Captain Maklary came to our house. My parents were paralyzed in apprehension seeing a high-ranking officer in uniform at their door. He was on leave from the Russian front and had come to pick up warm clothes for my brother, who was now being transferred to a labor battalion. To be in a labor battalion was to be a prisoner and an enemy of the nation that he had called home. Captain Maklary showed the finest human decency that represented the best Hungary could offer. He traveled to a Jewish house during his leave out of concern for another's well-being. He was a protector. He was a lion.

During this time, about a year or so before I was called up into a labor battalion, we played a soccer game against a Jewish labor battalion squad. This was a group of middle-aged prisoners. They were a transport unit working mostly on the railroad station loading army equipment. How heartless we were. We didn't feel sorry for these mature men in their thirties who were virtual prisoners of the state. Why didn't we feed them or help them? Why did we think of it as just another soccer game? I think it was youth and a feeling of immortality that guided our thoughts then. I still had a year before it would be my turn to "serve," and I just didn't think that any horrors could apply to me or my life. I needed to compartmentalize my life in order to remain buoyant.

Even though sporadic frightening news came back to us that Jews were disappearing and dying in the labor battalions, we still lived almost a sheltered life in our city, believing that these events did not really apply to us or the people we knew. Surprisingly, I looked forward to the time I would be old enough to have the adventure of serving as a man in a labor battalion. To me it represented manhood. I remember that when it was my turn to go, I went with no fear and instead a kind of enthusiasm and bravura. I thought of it as freedom from the shunning antisemitic behavior of former friends who no longer greeted me. I thought it would be an opportunity to be more of myself. I was too right and too wrong.

Jews who foresaw what was going on tried to escape if they could. But I was young and naturally foolish enough to believe that life was an adventure which I could now participate in. Young men always dream of omnipotence and beating the odds. I was no different. I could change things. The world was mine.

People have asked me what, if anything, we knew of the atrocities happening to the Jews in Poland or other occupied countries. Despite the bigotry and racial laws that were our constant shadow, we didn't know a thing. Rumors abounded. When we talked to our elders about the horrors, our Jewish leaders always tried to pacify us.

"Don't worry, everything will be straightened out."

If the elders, who were the most reasonable, stable, and venerated, cautioned against paranoid fears, then maybe, we reasoned, we should feel safe. So we stayed where we were in fear of escaping prematurely. This paralysis, which was in part fear and in part optimism, eventually caused thousands to die. Thousands who might have been able to buy their way out didn't, because of this false hopefulness. But when is the time to leave your country? When is the moment people should say that their country has betrayed them and the situation can never be remedied?

$$- \textit{9} -$$

By 1941 both my brothers, Sándor and József, were in labor battalions somewhere in Ukrainia. Sándor had been put into the battalion from the army, József was put directly in. In the beginning, furloughs could be bought. József came home for a two-day furlough in June to get some clothing for himself. I walked with him to the railway station as we had walked to school together in the recent past. He was tall, good-looking, and strong. Love of life still exuded from this self-contained brother. This was the last time I saw him.

I remember that the military police were at the railroad station in great numbers. They were asking for documents from everyone. I remember the yellow armband on József's sleeve, his rucksack on this back. He was such a fine specimen of a man. Our goodbye was a short handshake due to all the confusion and commotion. He turned around once and saluted me. If I had known the future, there would have been words and an embrace. If I had known the future, I would have thanked him for being so full of life and offering me an alternative in the family. If I had known the future, I would have run from the railroad station with József and with my entire family. I would have run for our lives. If I had known the future— but I didn't.

Since 1930 a military law had been in effect that stated that every male on his sixteenth birthday had to register for the draft. There was a mandatory three-hour weekly session to prepare the Hungarian youth for their military service. The name of this premilitary organization was *Levente*. The premilitary training taught Hungarian males to march in formation and stand at attention. They were taught Hungarian military songs. Hungarian males were issued imitation rifles. It was a waste of time for everyone, but part of a passage. In the beginning Christians and Jews were not separated.

In 1941 the army discharged its Jewish soldiers from military service and sent them to the labor battalions. Now, instead of the *Levente*, every non-Christian boy of sixteen was ordered to the temple yard and issued a yellow ribbon to be fastened to the left armband. We also had to bring a spade or hoe. We got an instructor specially assigned to the Jewish group. Roll call was chaotic since our instructor, Fecske, was unable to pronounce the Jewish-sounding names. Not knowing what to expect, there was a little nervous laughter here and there from all the uneasiness. Finally Fecske ordered us into formation with spade or hoe held like a rifle on our shoulder for inspection.

There were forty of us. Everyone had a four-inch yellow armband fastened four inches under his left shoulder. We held our spades or hoes tightly against our right shoulders as we marched in the city's main streets, sometimes goose-stepping according to orders. We were ordered to march from the temple yard to the Catholic church, back to the railroad, and back again using another route. Our instructor ordered us to sing as we marched. Suitable to our pathetic situation his selections were profane and crass army songs. It was mental torture. It was a form of humiliation to take proud boys and make a mockery of their patriotism, equipping them with yellow armbands and garden tools. Instead of the rite of passage called *Levente* there was cruel caricature. I remember watching Christian former friends and neighbors, young and old, boys and girls, standing on the sidewalk watching us in a parody of what should have been a proud moment. Some laughed at us, others smiled, others just looked on detached. I saw girls whom I used to dance with a short time ago who were now separated in experience from us forever. Fecske ordered us back to the temple yard. He gave us instructions for the following week and dismissed us. We had a meeting and an election was held. Pista Augner, a tall handsome boy whose father was an attorney, was selected with me to be co-captain of the group. We secured the storage area for our "weapons," the tools. The group was then dismissed.

I knew a Christian boy who was a friend of Fecske's son. Without hesitation I walked over to his house. I started to tell him of our afternoon of humiliation and disgrace. He told me he had seen our march, and it had shamed him. I told him to accompany me to his friend Peter Fecske's house.

Fecske answered the door and for minutes we all pretended that we were visiting his son. The family lived in a one-room shack with a dirt floor. His wife, an invalid, was in bed. We sat in the kitchen of this one-room apartment. Fecske commented that he knew my father. The son told his father that he knew me from the soccer field. We all agreed to a glass of wine, but there was none to be had. We walked a few blocks and bought some wine. After the third glass conversation became very open, honest, and friendly.

Fecske said that he had received direct orders and specific instructions about this day.

"I was told where you were to march and even what songs you were to sing."

The humiliation was orchestrated from above! When I asked him what would happen next week, he replied that no one knew, but not to mention our conversation.

The next week, after roll call, I was ordered to visit a factory on my bicycle preparatory to the group's working there later that day. I was told to wait in front of the factory for the group to join me. I knew that Fecske's reason for sending me ahead was to save me from marching in the group with a yellow armband and work tools. He gave me similar scouting assignments for weeks upon weeks.

I remember one episode which occurred while I waited for the group in front of another factory. I was sitting on a park bench, having removed my yellow armband, as the Jewish group arrived. A citizen approached me, not knowing I was part of the group.

"The Jews must be committing sabotage."

I asked him how he knew that.

"Just watch them. They look contented and not suffering at all."

Ah, the logic of it all. If the Jews looked human, then they must be up to some malicious plot! My answer to my fellow citizen was to pull the yellow armband from my pocket and warn him that my sabotaging colleagues would exact a price for his remarks. I took him by surprise. He started to babble about his being a good Christian. Since this meeting with him I have always been cautious when someone evokes his religion as an excuse for irreligious thoughts and actions.

I have often wondered about his thoughts on his special brand of Christianity. Was his the Christianity of robbing the Jews of their homes and furniture? Was his the Christianity of rejecting licenses for Jews to run a business? Was his the Christianity of taking over the Jewish enterprises without paying for them? Did being Christian mean the taking away of the meager possessions of a poor Jew? No, this man and those like him were not true Christians. I know what being Christian means. Christian kindness is the Hungarian air force pilot who came to my sister when my family were shoved from their home into the ghetto. He had courted her years before. He came to our ghetto home openly in daytime in his uniform and offered her an escape to his parent's home. She refused to leave the family. He offered to take the whole family. Christian empathy was evidenced in Fecske, who in his small way tried to lessen hardships on a sixteen-year-old boy. Captain Maklary was certainly Christian in caring for the Jewish soldier in his Christian-Hungarian artillery unit.

After the war, in 1945, I tried to locate Fecske. He had moved to a small village. I found him in a desperate situation. His wife was dead, and he was penniless and could not even afford a little piglet that he could raise and fatten up for meat and lard. I bought him two and told him to fatten up one for me and one for himself. A half-year later I visited him again. He was in his yard. There was only one pig now, and he explained that some-one had stolen the other pig. Naturally the one stolen was mine! I didn't care. He had been decent to me in an indecent time and situation. I gave him money to buy another piglet. That was the last time I saw him.

- *10* -

In September of 1942, my age group was called up from the premilitary organization into the labor battalion. We were told to go to Hódmezövásárhely in the south of Hungary. The army supplied us only with hats and yellow armbands. We had to bring the rest. We arrived eager, not knowing what was waiting for us. The ten young men from Kecskemét had traveled the four hours by train together.

We had heard stories about other labor battalions, but thought that with our luck and strength, we would triumph. We had heard about the labor battalions that had been sent to the mines in Bor, with few returning. We had heard about labor battalions that had been ordered to march in front of the Hungarian front lines. Their job was to probe the no-man's land for camouflaged mines placed there by the retreating Soviet armies. We had heard that the officers were pleased with the result and joked about "a few less mines and a lot less Jews." In spite of mine explosions, hunger, frostbite, and mistreatment, a few from the thousands who began had managed to get as far as the Don River in the Stalingrad area. There those who did not perish, as did my brother-in-law, were captured and sent to prison camps along with their former guards and officers. We had heard about the labor battalions, but we had not understood.

We didn't have to wait long before we began to see that what we had imagined as a rite of manhood would be a grim adventure in survival. When we arrived at the staging area in southeastern Hungary, we were corraled into a barracks with one side facing an open field and the other side facing the road to the city. The district commander was a former teacher. Teachers had the worst reputation as being brutally antisemitic. This man, however, appeared sweet-talking and quiet. He never raised his voice. If a problem developed, his response would be, "Oh, my son, I'll take care of you."

Underneath this facade was a murderer. His name was Captain Katona. In 1945 Katona was put on trial as a war criminal. He was found guilty, and hung.

As the ten of us from the city of Kecskemét arrived in Hódmezövásárhely we found ourselves in the middle of hundreds of confused Jewish boy-men. We were surrounded by yelling, cursing, shoving soldiers. Our education had begun.

Good fortune or disaster began the minute assignment to units was made. The assignment determined one's fate. It was essential to be in a unit with the right officers and with the right friends. To be assigned otherwise would be death.

"Five" was the unit number given for the labor battalions from this whole area. Units consisting of two hundred cowed, anxious young men were counted and delineated into "five-per-one, five-per-two," etc. The number two hundred was reached in the middle of our small group from Kecskemét. We were divided. My group was five-per-two. Mr. Moto was right behind me and became five-per-three. Harsh reality came down that day because I had never anticipated that our small group would be divided. I realized at that moment that I would have to use all my powers, wit, and knowledge to survive.

Five-per-two had four sub-units of fifty men each. A white armband connoted the converted Jews who made up the first unit. Most of the converted Jews were rich boys from Budapest. Conversion seemed to be a luxury of the rich and sophisticated. The white armband delineated a kind of pseudo-protection for them. The rest of us wore the yellow armband of Judaism. I was in the second subunit, which had fifty members. It consisted of our group from Kecskemét and some Yugoslavian Jewish boys from the southern part of Hungary. These boys spoke Hungarian and Yugoslavian equally. We called them Chetniks after the Serbs, who were fierce fighters. The main unit of five-per-two were the boys from Budapest. The fourth unit was the very religious, poor Jews from the eastern part of Hungary, called Russinsko. They all spoke a mixture of Yiddish and Slavic. Most of them were used to hard manual labor as they worked in the forest felling trees in order to produce charcoal. They were a hard-working, hearty, although uneducated bunch. If you had a friend among the Russinkos, it was the greatest benefit. They were good workers. It meant everything to be surrounded by good workers because you were rewarded or punished as a unit.

My sense of survival began to emerge on this very first day. I put myself in the middle. I thought that if I stayed as "gray" as possible, I could survive. I didn't want to be the leader. I didn't want to be the best worker. I didn't want to be the worst worker. I didn't want to be the last man in the line-up, nor the first. There was a penalty for being distinctive here.

Unit leaders were always Jewish. Our unit leader was named Pali Kerekes. Our lifelong friendship started in this battalion. Our labor battalions were led by a lieutenant, a sergeant, and a corporal who were from the Hungarian military. There were also ten guards. These were the people who governed our lives. All these men were Christians. All had their own reasons for being relegated to lead the Jewish battalions. Some had volunteered. Unit five-per-two had a lieutenant who was formerly a teacher. His name was Lieutenant Szonyi. Although initially terrified by his profession and its allegiance to antisemitism, we ended up blessed. We all ended up with a warm and almost fatherly feeling toward him. Everybody in our unit felt initially that we had the worst fate awaiting us with the lieutenant being a teacher, but he was a superior person. In our group the majority survived.

In the first ten days life was not worse than the way I had imagined it might be. Besides a little work here and there and the getting ready for constant inspections, our main task was to stay clear of any trouble. This was not too difficult to achieve, and we kept busy most of the day. Certain signs, like a sudden outburst of violent beating for no other reason than being in the wrong place at the wrong time, made us see that life would not be a romantic adventure, and that-life threatening hardships and not heroic deeds were ahead of us.

The worst part of those early days came after lights-out. My sleeping spot on the straw was between Lajos and Pista. The three of us became a subgroup among the original unit from Kecskemét. Lajos was a slender boy, sensitive and literate. He was nurturing a moustache under his prominent nose and tried to convince himself of its maturing attributes. His ability to endure fatigue and hardships without complaint made him a wonderful friend. Pista was my classmate. He was an easygoing, honest, and loyal person. In our youth group he had been the best in poetry recitation. Back home we had all envied him for his curly blond hair. Soon he would be teased for his bald head and protruding ears.

To lie in the dark stable on a thin layer of straw, tightly placed between friends, and to listen to their sighs and occasional sobs was so very difficult. Our bodies were wherever we would be commanded to go, but our thoughts and hearts, especially at night, were free with family and friends. How often I felt Lajos's shaking body and heard his soundless cries! How often did I put my arms on his shoulders, not saying a word, but communicating in the gesture: "Hey buddy, you are not alone here in the dark. I am with you. We are all with you."

Finally we got our first orders. There would be a sixteen-mile forced march to Kakas-szek, a small village known for its mineral hot baths. We learned rapidly that it was impossible to carry all our belongings on our backs as ordered. One third of our possessions were discarded at the first stop, never to be retrieved. This was another of the many lessons we had to learn and learn fast. Walking back the next day with half-full rucksacks was easier, and we all realized the major importance of having friends. With a friend you trust you can discard a heavy coat and share your friend's sweater instead. Sharing like this meant a lighter load. A lighter load and a friend meant survival. With friends you could discard two flashlights and share amongst the four of you. (The flashlights would always be stolen anyway by our guards!) Friends and trust were the mortar that would allow optimism and survival. One had to learn fast in order to survive. In those few weeks I quickly began to adapt and change. Whatever belief I had that the labor battalion would be a vehicle for my manhood was discarded along with the belongings left on the trail. I realized quickly that it was my manhood which was at stake here.

At the very beginning our guards were not overtly brutal. The feelings were there but kept under control. The brutality grew as conditions changed. In the beginning the guards accepted presents from the richer boys. This bribery allowed some few luxuries which were shared around. Some were even allowed to visit home or the villages for a day or two. Our lieutenant treated us humanely, so that the corporal, sergeant, and guards had to follow suit. These days abruptly ended when our guards got drunk and a day of brutality would begin. The brutality grew as we weakened and appeared less human. The brutality grew as we traveled farther and farther from home. The brutality grew daily in small surges or huge cascades.

True racist and hate feelings were just under the surface and always ready to rise. The guards were specially selected or had asked for this assignment. This meant that they were thought to be unfit for fighting and were punished by this assignment, arousing their ire, or that they wished to be around and torment "kikes." Either way boded poorly for us. A great majority of the guards had been in Ukrainia or in Poland with previous labor battalions. The open secret was that there were orders that the guards could return home only after all the Jews were dead. We knew of their background and their hatred of everything we were. They also knew that we knew. In the beginning, while still in Hungary, the soldiers had an easy enough life, so that their brutality and anger was kept in abeyance. A few officers and soldiers were innately humane and kind, but they were in the vast minority. As conditions changed, brutality, callousness, and downright murderous rage were the order of our every day.

Right from the very beginning we all sensed that our world had changed. We were no longer strong, omnipotent young men, but were unsure and frightened. One day in the beginning of hell, the worst of the soldiers, Darazs, drunk, started to brag that he deserved this easy life because he had already helped eliminate another group of "Jewish traitors." I could only imagine what rewards he would feel he deserved if allowed to eliminate all of us.

From the onset we were always on edge, always wondering what would send someone into a rage. When the guards were not drunk, most of them acted tolerably. They would allow us our daily meal while sitting in the shade of trees. When they were drunk, it was different. The guards would order us to kneel with our hands in prayer thanking Hitler for our daily bread. We had mixed feelings about this abuse. While the guards were having their fun with us, the ridicule allowed us to have a couple of minutes more of rest. Even as we rested in prayer, we were burning with shame and humiliation. Under Jewish law one never kneels to anyone, including our God. In the labor battalion one knelt as ordered.

In unit five-per-two there was a cantor. He was a tall, bright, brave man. Officers and guards and fellow workers called him "Cantor" out of respect and honor. It was during one of these intolerable "praying sessions" that his leadership shone. In his kneeling position he began to sing, intermixing Jewish and Hungarian words. Our tormentors thought he was praying, but the cantor was cursing our torturers. We blessed him silently for his courage and the group feeling it fostered. These incidents of emotional torment were frequent, but were minor inconveniences in our lives compared to what would come.

In the early days we slept on straw in a converted stable. Our space was so tight that Sergeant Bimbo said, "Sleep well on one side. At midnight I'll get you up and you can turn to the other side."

It wasn't too bad yet. We had food and some of our personal belongings. There was the humiliation of being prisoners of our own country, but there was also the feeling, in the beginning, of being strong enough to take whatever we had to endure, since it would be temporary.

Conditions were primitive, but human. We had open latrines facing the highway. Farmers on foot and horsedrawn carts passing by could see us sitting in the open latrines. We thought that this would be as bad as it could get, hunkering pantless in the open latrines. We thought it would only be as bad as the sixteen-mile weighted hike. We thought it would only be as bad as drunken rages. We thought that we could tough out the few months of the war. We were wrong.

We spent evenings writing letters and reading letters. We talked and sat on the ground, which was covered with a thin layer of straw. Our barracks was a former stable. We even had one electric light. We had heated discussions. Most of us believed that in a few weeks the West would start an offensive or the Soviets would come from the East. We would then be free. The argument was about the time until our liberation—weeks or months. The other part of the discussion was about who would liberate us—the Americans or the Soviets. The question was always in which direction our deliverance lay and how soon it would come.

After lights-out, no one was allowed to leave the barracks. A guard was stationed outside the door. We had to ask permission to go to the latrine. Sometimes you would be allowed to go immediately. Sometimes the guards made you wait until the line was four persons long. I had another close friend, also called Pista, a newly married man, who spent all his free time writing letters to his wife. We all envied him. On mail day he received two or three letters from his wife. He was waiting in line for the latrine around midnight. I joined him. He was in agony and unable to hold back the natural urge any longer. Pista opened the door to see who was on guard duty. It was Private Darazs, the worst person under the circumstances. Darazs looked in an even more foul mood than usual. Still unable to wait, Pista politely asked him for permission to use the latrine.

"You fucking pigs! Close the door. I did not give you permission to open it."

His threatening gesture to the most innocent and natural of requests was unbelievable to us. Everyone was up now, but still lying on the straw, and aware that somehow Pista's fate was linked to their survival as human beings. We were just a few weeks into the labor battalion and already we were smelling the stench of servitude and dehumanization. We waited a few more minutes, and then I opened the door. I was angry and my temper flared.

"Private Darazs, sir. Do you want us to behave like pigs and relieve ourselves in our sleeping quarters?"

Darazs, to our surprise, opened the door and entered the barracks. His stupid face expressed nothing about his intentions. By now everyone was apprehensive. Everyone was up and alert, but lying motionless, knowing that something significant was happening. Darazs turned to Pista and in a falsely friendly voice, he asked, "Are you the married one?"

Pista confirmed his question.

"What is your wife's name?"

"Anna," Pista replied.

Darazs hesitated for a second and said, "Tell me, married man, how is your wife's cunt? Until you tell me you won't shit. You tell me or shit in your pants."

The barracks was in stunned silence. Pista turned pale. He could not answer.

Pista began shaking. I grabbed his arm, went to the door, pushed the soldier aside, and took him to the latrine. My anger was not a form of bravery, but more a vestige of my former personality. I still believed I had rights. I still believed I had a voice. I was wrong.

The five-per-two's would never forget or forgive this episode. It was pivotal to most of us. How much personal humiliation would it take before one began to sacrifice all one's values? This lesson of cruelty and humiliation was the one first posed by the stupid thug guard. It would not be the last. But it broke some of our spirit and stole some of our youth.

One Sunday before our first deployment, we were allowed a parental visit. I didn't write my parents about it. I did not want them to see me this way. I was no longer the irrepressible young boy who thought that the labor battalion would be another small but surmountable burden. The mother of one of my friends told my mother. While the other parents arrived and were eating homemade cookies, I sat alone. I then noticed my mother enter. I was so glad she was there. We talked about indifferent and inconsequential subjects. I guess she did not want to burden me about the worsening situation at home, and I did not want to sadden her with our conditions here. I loved her, even though we sat like strangers. I loved her so much that I carried her last postcard to me on my person for fifty years. I spent my first winter of the labor battalion on the road freezing. I was homesick and starving. I relived that visit from my mother. I played it over and over in my mind. It kept me sane and hopeful for my return to a normal home life.

- *11* -

*F*or our first assignment the authorities sent us by railroad to Kabol in the southern part of Hungary to build fortifications along the Danube River at the Yugoslavian frontier. Kabol was a farm settlement in the middle of nowhere. It had scattered farms of sheep and cows and didn't even have a cantina. It was a hundred yards from the Hungarian side of the Danube. We were housed in a former barn.

Yugoslavia was occupied by the Germans, but it also had partisans. The military was trying to fortify the Hungarian side of the Danube. Kabol was not too far from Ujvidék, where the Hungarian army had committed the infamous bloodbath against innocent Serbs and Jews. The Hungarian soldiers had reasons to fear the partisans, since Hungary had sided with Germany, and Hungarian troops, together with the German occupiers, had committed atrocities against the Yugoslavians. This was a dangerous assignment for Hungarians and, therefore, for us. We in the labor battalion kept hoping for a partisan attack. We feared the elements, the brutally hard work, and our own side. Being caught in a crossfire did not seem as dangerous to us.

It was constantly raining. We were always wet. For six weeks it rained every day, sometimes without interruption day and night. Our overcoats, shoes, and socks never dried out. In the evening we tried to dry them in the barracks, but it was impossible. The worst part of the constant deluge was the condition of our shoes. Sometimes by evening it was almost impossible to remove them. At wake-up call it was very difficult to put on the wet shoes. Walking in the mud was torture in itself. The mud was so thick that it impeded our march. It would suck the shoes off your feet. The person behind you would invariably march right into you and trample the shoes down into the mud. At best, you might be able to retrieve the lost shoes on the march out the next morning. I remember losing one shoe and retrieving it the next morning completely filled with water and mud. I had to put it on, water and all, in the midst of receiving kicks and remarks about my mother's virtue.

We didn't curse the rain too much. It was also our friend. The guards in their raincoats sought the cover of trees and did not push us as hard. We cleaned ourselves with the wet leaves of the trees. Except for the rain we never could clean ourselves. Athough we were working on the bank of the Danube, it was against strict orders to go down to the river to bathe. Border guard soldiers with machine guns were assigned to enforce this rule. We never had showers or even a dish large enough to collect water so we could wash. We had our daily work quota to finish. That was the only thing that mattered.

Part of our major work was to build tank traps ten yards deep, twenty yards long, six yards wide. The Danube was wide here, and there was no bridge in the area. We could not imagine how tanks could cross this deep river and could not see any reason for our task. For the officers, despite the rain and the possibility of partisan attack, this was a plum military assignment. They were far from the Russian front, and anything was better than the fighting.

We strung barbed wire in other areas. Two persons carried a heavy bundle of barbed wire on a long pole to the group whose job it was to fasten the wire on cross-legged poles placed deeply into the ground. The barbs were sharp, and sometimes the metal wire was twisted. Untwisting and handling the wire was done with ungloved hands. The boys whose job it was to bring the wire laid it down in the mud and turned back for the next load, taking back the carrying poles. The group whose job it was to fasten the wire to the fence had to carry the bundle of twisted shards fifteen yards with their bloody bare hands. Their coat sleeves were cut in shreds by the barbs. Although all assignments were harsh, some were downright torture.

Usually we were finished by nightfall. The long walk to our barracks was always the worst part of the terrible day. The guards rushed us, yelling curses and kicking. They always blamed us for the late hours we worked. They blamed us for being burdens because they had to guard us. We heard over and over the refrain, "You're making me do this to you," when we were struck for inconveniencing them by lateness. We seemed to make them do a lot to us. We were such burdens!

When we arrived home there was always the head count. We would then wait until the guards had eaten. Then we could eat and rest a bit.

- *12* -

We were soon reassigned to another task. We went wherever the work was. We went wherever expendable labor was needed. The officer of our next assignment was a madman. He was attached to the army engineers. None of my five-per-two comrades can recall his name. I think we have tried to banish him from our memories. His features and his large leather whip are, however, etched in my mind. He would walk amongst his "stinking Jewish slaves" with the whip in his hand. He made us run with our loads of cement sacks on our backs and run back for new supplies. Even with running all the time, we could not deflect the constant beatings. Our guards were brutal, because they were no longer held back by more humane commanders. Guards no longer were given orders by our own lieutenant, but by the madman who will never be remembered by name.

Every other Sunday was our rest day, and we would count the days down until that one precious day arrived. This day was the only chance we would have in two weeks to try to dry our clothes and mend them. It was the only time to try to wash at the well. This was the time to become human again.

On a miserable Saturday night right before our torturous walk home, the commander came with his whip in his hand. Even more enraged than usual, he told us that we would lose our free Sunday because of the lack of progress on the wall fortification. Our walk home that evening was even more dreadful than usual. Our spirits were as dampened as the weather. Hope of finding our own humanness in the personal chores done on Sunday had been removed. The commander looked energized at the opportunity to wield his power over our Sunday as he did the other days of the week.

For a change that Sunday was sunny and warm. For some unexplainable reason, our wake-up call was two hours late. More surprises followed. For breakfast we got a large bowl of barley and sausage. We were allowed second helpings! The food was so good that fifty years later, I still tease my wife that she has not come close to preparing that wonderful dish.

Around eleven Sergeant Bimbo came out in his dress uniform. He entered theatrically on our Sunday of punishment, looking like he had stepped out of an operetta. He lined us up and ordered us to sit in a relaxed position. He greeted us with his "Hey, cigars." This was the joking term he would call us, and it made us believe that things would be all right this Sunday. He entertained us with stories for a half-hour and then ordered us, as part of the prescribed punishment, to do a few push-ups. He had given us back our one-day-a-fortnight of human decency. Sergeant Bimbo remained human no matter who the commander was.

Sergeant Bimbo was from our city of Kecskemét. His family owned Kecskemét's largest hardware store. He never indicated that he recognized us. We were sure he did. We waited for him to indicate his willingness to talk to us. This would be the right path—to wait. We waited and waited, and he never recognized us. Later we realized his dilemma. If he recognized and talked to us, perhaps his commanders would have stopped his kindness, feeling that he was showing favoritism to his "hometown Jews." In that case he would have to prove that he was a "true Hungarian" by becoming more violent or even murderous towards us. If he were a murderous person, we, his hometown witnesses, would have been his first victims. So we waited until after the war, when he told me that not demanding any recognition from him had been the right way.

The work assignment in Kabol was not life-threatening, but it was threatening in other ways. There were no cities or villages nearby. There were no taverns where our guards could get drunk. As frightening as it was when the guards were drunk and their brutality emerged full-blown, it was not less frightening when there was boredom in their ranks. It was almost natural that these uneducated and untalented soldiers who were not good enough to serve in the fighting units used us for entertainment by inventing new and more humiliating punishments for us without reason. The true face of fascism and primitive hatred would emerge. We were in a very bad situation.

A few people from this sparsely populated area just looked at us. They looked and pretended that they did not understand what they were seeing. We, the strange Jews, were now invisible to them. We were nonexistent. A secret sympathetic look or gesture would have strengthened our belief in humanity. We received none. I wondered if they were ashamed once they got behind closed doors. I hoped that they feared for their own lives and therefore were afraid to intervene for us who were doomed to disappear from this world. I dared hope that there was kindness beneath the stares that hostilely looked right through us. I disguised the truth because it was too hard to bear. As we later learned, the Bulgarians and Rumanians, our neighbors in southern Europe, did not follow antisemitic orders so willingly. In Hungary they seemed to be embraced with a passion.

One morning, while we lined up for the morning coffee, the guards pulled four of us out. I was one of the four. The rest of the group left for the work assignments. We waited uneasily, not knowing our fate. When we found out that we had to walk with only one soldier guarding us about ten kilometers to the nearest railway station to unload supplies for the army, we were overwhelmed with relief. We realized that we were being given a choice assignment. We would be able to hear real news, not just the short, censored letters from home.

Rain came down softly, and we walked leisurely ten kilometers to the railway station. My assignment was to shovel coal from the train car into the army trucks. One guard climbed with me into the car and stood in the corner smoking. We were unable to get cigarettes at that time. He casually tossed it unfinished near me. It was almost a whole cigarette. I did not pick it up. I didn't want to seem less than human, groveling in the coal for a cigarette butt in front of the soldier. He watched me curiously as he lit another cigarette for himself.

At noontime he marched us to the nearby army post for our meal. This was a real meal, a full army ration, and a double portion of bread. There we were free to walk around and listen to the soldiers' talk. The soldiers were talking about mass murders of Jews and about crematoriums. We did not understand what they were talking about at first, although the horror slowly began to filter through our denial. I remember a very young soldier looking at our faces, saying, "This will be your fate, too."

The Hungarian soldiers stared into our faces and tried to read our reaction. We stared back, trying to ascertain their feelings. All our faces were masks. I myself felt stunned with disbelief. These soldiers had been in Poland, where they had witnessed such atrocities. I believed they were telling the truth, and yet it was a truth no one could believe.

We returned to the railway station to continue to unload the railroad car. We were left alone in an empty railroad car. We tried to digest some of the truth we had just heard. I seriously thought of running and escaping at that moment. We did not have soldiers around us. I should go. I should get away right now. But I faltered. Where could I go? Who would hide me? Perhaps the coach in the city of Szolnok who had offered me a Christian identity would hide me. Could I reach him? Would he still be there? Would he turn me in? I thought some more. Maybe I could reach Aranka. I was sure of her. But their home was behind a small bakery, and the bakery had workers. Someone might see me or overhear something. Since her father was a former Communist from the 1919 revolution, he probably was under special surveillance. Would he hide the Jewish boyfriend of his Christian daughter? How long would I have to hide? Where were the Soviet forces? I needed more time to think this through, and the moment was lost. I was afraid I would bring danger to my family and friends. Escape was hopeless.

From the railroad car a distant segment of the Danube was visible. The water looked smooth and blue. I visualized the beautiful bridges which spanned the river in Budapest. I remembered crossing the bridges in the yellow streetcar surrounded by my teammates. We had just finished a soccer game. I had scored the winning goal. I remembered every detail. I remembered the feel of the ball and the moment I released my kick. It landed next to the left goalpost. What a goal it was!

"Get out of the car, pig-Jews!" Back to reality in a second! A new railroad car never materialized, and we left before dark to return to the barracks. I picked up a discarded newspaper on the way and put it in my pocket. Later I shared it with my friends.

On our way back to the barracks we saw two gendarmes marching behind three crying women. One of the women carried a little baby in her arms. Were they Hungarians? Were they Yugoslavs? Were they Jews? We passed them, exchanging glances. We felt a kinship with them and whatever their pain and their fate was. People in the street averted their glance from this sight. The women were invisible too. I thought again about concentration camps and crematoriums.

- *13* -

The work, the naked hatred of our guards, and the physical conditions were beginning to take their toll. Our energy was becoming so fragile that additional cruelties could sap all our vitality, and small acts on our behalf could maintain us. One dark evening after work we returned to the stables. A few candles burned. After returning from forced labor we were supposed to clean our work tools and shovels. It had been very muddy, and we were beyond exhaustion. A few of us just couldn't clean up.

The time in the barracks was usually the beginning of a safe period which lasted until the next morning. This evening there was an inspection by another brutal guard, Randovitch. He picked one of us and found a shovel that was muddy. He started to yell, slap, and kick the worker with the telling shovel. He began to beat the worker with his own shovel. Death and murder were in the air. Someone had the courage to run to the officers' quarters and tell Lieutenant Szonyi.

Lieutenant Szonyi, who was already undressed in his quarters, ran in wearing only his boots and his officer's overcoat without his breeches. It was extraordinary to see our officer in this condition. He saw Randovitch beating this Jewish fellow with the shovel.

Candles flickered as we watched what we knew would signify the path our lives would take next.

"Guard, what is your name?"

"Private Randovitch, sir."

"Guard, what is your religion?"

"Catholic, sir."

The lieutenant slapped the private resoundingly and snarled, "Do you know what the Bible teaches? Do not touch the face of human beings."

I'm not sure what Bible passage he was quoting. I'm not even sure I understood what the lieutenant was saying, since his own slap seemed to be a contradiction of his message. But I did know that it was a slap in our behalf. Finally, someone was doing something in our behalf. It was an unforgettable episode in our lives. It was an act of decency and courage.

We sat on the straw overwhelmed by what we had just witnessed. Szonyi and Randovitch left. We started to sing. Pista and Lajos, my friends, took an oath to write a show about this in great detail. When they started to argue about a detail, I told them to let me dream my own dreams about this miracle. My dream was that I would put the medal of honor on Szonyi's uniform one day. We fell asleep as the candles slowly burned. These were the kind of people we would meet. The human and the inhuman. This is where one choice, a path taken, could spell death or life. This is where a wrong guard or a right commander spelled salvation or hell.

One of the soldiers must have reported Lieutenant Szonyi after the slapping incident. He was replaced. The new commander, nicknamed Motley, was a small man in word and deed. The first thing he inquired about was the kitchen. He told the soldiers that he would improve their food. He was a harmless fool who was only interested in his daily food and wine. We always saw him half-drunk. In his wanting only to get through his assignment, we were left to the mercies of others. Our situation went from bad to worse, and from worse to desperate, after Lieutenant Szonyi left. Before we'd had a good commander in a bad situation. Now we had a fool for a commander instead of a human being, and the guards had no one to control them.

One of the first free Sundays after Lieutenant Szonyi left, we were ordered out of the barracks with all of our belongings. First we thought that we were to get fresh straw or disinfectant with which to clean the place. Then the soldiers ordered us to remove all our clothes and put everything from our pockets on the ground. We would be searched and robbed. We had heard about these searches from an occasional lucky member of a labor battalion who had managed to get home. The alleged intention of these searches was to find secret materials that we could give to the enemies of the Hungarian state. The real purpose was to rob us of whatever valuables we had. We would be degraded, disrobed, and humiliated so that a guard could get a better watch or a ring.

Personally I didn't have much to lose. I tried to distance myself from the humiliation of the search by thinking about it coldly and rationally. Rich boys now would have nothing to barter and nothing to share. I was trying to convince myself that this was not so bad when I remembered the watch Aranka had given me as a going-away present. All of a sudden I had no emotional distance, I had to save the watch. It represented love, normalcy, and loyalty. It represented home.

I looked quickly at my situation. Eight soldiers were doing all the searching. They could not search every pocket. I put the watch in the most obvious outside pocket, figuring that they would look for small treasures in more hidden places. I was right. They overlooked the watch, and I won a small victory that day. The watch would later buy freedom for another. Other boys tried to hide valuables in small holes they surreptitiously dug in the ground or by putting them in their shoes. They were beaten mercilessly if their treasure was discovered. Their treasure was usually valuable only for the sentimental reason which tied the boy to home.

In the meantime, in the middle of this robbery it started to rain, as it did almost every day. Darazs was in charge, and he wore his usual idiotic grin. Behind him was a blanket filled with our confiscated personal belongings. All this occurred during unrelenting intimidation and cursing. We must have looked funny, all standing naked in the freezing rain. Standing naked in the rain with meager belongings no longer ours, I felt ashamed and disgraced. Strong athletic boys started to cry. We didn't feel we belonged to the human race. Somehow I recovered and realized that we belonged, and the assaulters did not. We were the human beings.

In the distance a group of soldiers approached, singing. We were two hundred yards from them. Suddenly our soldiers began to look hesitant. Now there were witnesses to their barbarism. They started kicking and cursing us. We were ordered to dress. The rain thickened, mixing with our tears. Today's humiliation had finished.

- *14* -

Sunday morning we were lined up as usual for breakfast. The soldiers and officers were already lined up, which was very unusual. It was announced that our company would get a new assignment. This announcement was made by "Motley," the officer who had replaced beloved Lieutenant Szonyi. We had nicknamed him with that moniker because he had large blotches on his face. He also behaved in a motley manner because he had many contrasting elements in his personality. He was good and bad, mellow and angry, kind and generous one moment and cruel and pitiless the next.

We were given three days rest and cleanup, and we then would be moving. We didn't know the details, but the three days rest was the best news yet. The cooks started to boil hot water in the kettles. We washed our underwear. We went to the well to draw cool water to wash ourselves. Interestingly the weather sided with us. The rain stopped. The sun was ours. Our bodies and clothes dried. We sat in front of the barracks enjoying the sunshine and rest. We felt like we were on vacation. These small moments reminded us that we were men, not animals and not slaves. These small moments were like a transfusion of sunshine.

We marched to the railway station. Our good fortune continued. We had ten cars to move us to our new destination. Thirty men and two soldiers per car was a luxury. Officers were in one car and our wagon and horse in another. This was a two hundred and fifty kilometer, three-day trip to Nagykoros. Most of the time the train doors were open, and we sang and played as a fresh cold wind cooled us.

We became foolish. We became boisterous and rambunctious. During those three days we reentered the world of normal young men. We played a joke on Lajos. While he was asleep on his back, we unzipped his pants and put shoe polish on his genitals. We all crowded around Lajos during this precise operation, betting whether his prized organ would move or change position during our application. Whoever bet it would remain still won. He then awoke. He laughed louder than we did on awakening. We were again like boys. Things were in proportion here, and horseplay had its place. We could move around and talk to one another.

We felt new hope here. We believed that the Soviet summer attacks had been successful. We felt that the newspapers were still spreading lies, but noted a milder tone in them. We felt that since our lot had improved, freedom would shortly follow. The rumor was that the Hungarian government would surrender and try to make a separate peace with the Allies. During the three days rest and the train ride, we could believe again in whatever good news we could find.

From the railroad people we learned that our destination was Nagykoros. In order to get there we would have to pass through Kecskemét. Two friendly railroad men sent a message to my father and a few other parents about this. When our convoy stopped for a few minutes in the Kecskemét railroad station, my father was waiting. I jumped off, hugged my father, and exchanged a few words until the guards chased me back onto the train. Finally we arrived at our destination.

Nagykoros had been one of our favorite bicycle destinations in less life-threatening times. Perhaps because of that memory and because of the lighthearted feeling on the train, we were a happy, rested group now, joking and kidding, and waiting for our orders. We sat down in the shade of some large trees near the station while awaiting our orders.

An army car stopped in front of us. An engineer officer alighted, looking formidable and angry. Before his feet hit the ground he was screaming and cursing, "You stinking Jews, I have been waiting for you for three days! You are sitting in the shade while good Hungarian soldiers are dying at the front."

We lined up and started to march from the railway station, realizing that the end had come to a carefree moment in our history. We walked five kilometers and noticed the forest slowly engulfing us. On closer scrutiny we noticed barbed wire intermingled with the green fir trees. We had entered the forest of Csemo. There was a camouflaged army ammunition depot in the forest.

Loading and unloading ammunition was hard work. There were lots of soldiers there, and we had the same ration of food as the soldiers, except that we had to labor and they only had to watch us. We worked six or seven days, with Sunday sometimes off. Five-per-two had a good sleeping and resting area in a former ammunition warehouse which was dry and wind-proof. It was a fairly warm winter, and we had plenty of straw all the time. The ground was soft, and we could get comfortable.

Our sergeant, Bimbo, took almost complete charge of our group. Commander Motley was away most of the time. When present, he was drunk. With Sergeant Bimbo's help we received clothing from the Jews from Nagykoros, Kecskemét, and Budapest. With his unofficial understanding a third of us sneaked home for a few days. He was a source of strength and stability during a time when we were owned by weak and brutal men.

One morning at the wake-up one of the Chetniks refused to jump up. Darazs started to kick him. The Chetnik got up and punched out the soldier. Naturally, he was reported and called in front of Bimbo to explain what had happened. We were sure he would be court-martialed.

Our sergeant Bimbo was not a big man, but he was strong. First he beat up the Hungarian soldier, Darazs, screaming, "How could you let a Jew beat you?"

Then our Chetnik got his share of the beating, and a strong warning. He was also ordered to do ten pushups! Justice was served, and Bimbo made sure no one lost face.

After the war Bimbo was accused of war crimes. He was accused of having committed violent acts in another Jewish battalion. His trial was in Budapest. He asked a few of us from five-per-two to be his witnesses. We were happy to try to help him. At his trial, in front of the tribunal, fights broke out between his Jewish character witnesses from the five-per-two and his Jewish accusers from the other group. I was unable to believe that Bimbo was capable of doing the atrocities that the remainder of his former group attested to. Could he have changed so much? He had certainly been fair and humane to us. He was sentenced to three years.

Did we do the right thing to defend him? The only thing one could do was to state the truth, but that truth hurt others who had been brutalized by the same man who had been consistently responsive to us. The right path?

- *15* -

At this time the war situation slowly started to shift against the Hungarians and Germans. It was no longer assumed that the Germans would win the war in one year. They didn't talk, though, about losing. From our guards' behavior we could surmise the way the war was going. Good news for them was always bad news for us. When the fascists and the Nazis were winning, then the Jewish prisoners were scum and less than animals. When the war news turned bad for them, the situation became tentative for the soldiers guarding us. They were less sure of themselves. They were in the minority, and they had brutalized us. What would happen if the tide turned?

Even though survival was based on the comradeship of one's fellow laborers and the luck of one's battalion leaders, when it came down to it, one's survival depended on oneself. Sometimes by being physically fit, sometimes by being clever, sometimes by being opportunistic, sometimes by being anonymous, and sometimes by speaking out. One used whatever means one had to find a way to rest, eat, and remain hopeful. Everyone tried to find ways to save himself. Sometimes those ways worked, and sometimes they spelled death.

When anyone in the battalion was sick, he had to go to a Jewish doctor. Ours was a dentist. His name was Gyetwai, and he was from Kiskunfélegyháza. He looked ancient to us. He was probably in his mid-forties. He was married and always looked gloomy and preoccupied. He did what he could to help us with our medical needs without having the needed expertise, equipment, drugs, or training. I decided to use him and the system to try to get rest by feigning illness. I knew that I needed to regain strength sapped by inadequate food, deprivation, and brutality. I also knew that I ran a risk of being caught as a malingerer with a terrible outcome awaiting me.

I complained about pain, and Dr. Gyetwai told me, "Go see the sergeant. I don't know what to make of your pain."

Sergeant Bimbo looked at me and said, "Good luck to you. Go to the army sickroom in Nagykoros. If the army doctor finds you sick, he'll send you to the hospital in Kecskemét."

At the army sickroom, a high-ranking officer in a white coat over his uniform gave me a short examination. He looked at me angrily and confronted me. "Have you ever really been kicked in your ass?"

I thought my ruse was over, but answered, "Yes, sir."

That apparently was the Jewish humility he wanted to hear, and he sent me to the hospital.

I worried about being found out. I thought I would be kicked out in two days. I worried about being punished for my deception. I worried about the Hungarian soldiers and officers there. I was the only Jew in the hospital. I was put in a big room holding twenty-eight beds. There I found a former schoolmate. He greeted me warmly. He was a corporal, and his friendly attitude towards me assuaged the others in the room. He told me he could send a message to my parents that I was all right. What worried me was that the doctors would find out that I was malingering. I was concerned about what punishment would await me as I tried to rest and eat.

My friendly schoolmate told me that one of the officers in a private room wanted to see me. I sneaked into his private room. He asked me to get him a bottle of schnapps; and that if I did, he could arrange to have me kept there longer. Ah, bribery still had its place! I sent a message to my father, who smuggled in a bottle of schnapps. After sharing a drink, the officer said that alcohol would hopefully ruin the medication he was on. He had gonorrhea and wanted to remain sick enough to stay in the safety of the hospital. The drinking would allow his weekly test to remain positive for gonococci. The young officer blessed the Polish lady who had infected him and thereby saved him from front-line duty. So there were at least two of us trying to save ourselves! His friend was the examining doctor. One word from the officer allowed me to remain in the hospital for three weeks. The schnapps made sure his weekly gonococcal test remained positive.

Along with my constant anxiety of being discovered, the hospital stay had other unpleasant moments. During my soccer-playing time I had met and played with Miklós Rozsa. He had a sister, Boske. She was a beautiful girl. She was slender, friendly, and quite splendid. She was friendly to all her brother's teammates, including myself. One day Boske took me aside and told me a shocking story. Although Christian, she had contracted a venereal disease from a prominent Jewish boy. She asked me to talk to the boy. I was not aware that Boske's father was aware of his daughter's illness or my involvement in it. Old Mr. Rozsa was now the hospital's maintenance man.

One day, when I was assigned to cleaning the toilets, Mr. Rozsa walked in to check on something. I'm sure he recognized me. There were cigarette butts in the urinal. He yelled at me not to use the broom, but to use my hands to remove the butts. I obeyed. I wondered if he was attempting to regain the equilibrium he had lost years ago when I was a witness to his daughter's transgression and shame. Now he would be a witness to mine. I imagined that in his mind we were now even.

The good food and rest in the hospital helped me regain full strength. During my stay there, my conscience bothered me. My friends were suffering while I was relaxing. Perhaps I should be suffering with them? Would my suffering lessen theirs? These thoughts played in my mind continuously.

- *16* -

My three-week hospital vacation ended. I received my hospital discharge paper and had to return to my group. I had been sent a message previously from Lajos that the five-per-two had been shipped to Körösmezö and Tiszaborkut in the eastern part of Hungary, which is nested in the Carpathian Mountains. This was an area of small poor villages in the high mountains. It was the last military post before leaving Hungarian territory. Neither Lieutenant Motley nor Sergeant Bimbo went with our unit. My discharge orders were to return to Csemo. This allowed me to gain a few more days of freedom.

Sergeant Bimbo was in Csemo. Although we both knew where the five-per-two was stationed, he agreed to send me back to Hódmezövásárhely to gain a few more days. I asked him a day's leave to visit my parents. I needed to refurbish my equipment. He gave me one extra day.

I had already been over a year in the labor battalion. In a few months after this first visit home the Jews of Kecskemét and the surrounding villages, would be rounded up for extermination. My father would be rounded up first and used as a farm animal until he died in harness. Later my sisters, my nephew, my mother, and all the relatives would be sent to Auschwitz as part of the Final Solution.

I reached home in the late afternoon on a Friday. At the railroad station was a group of raggedy-looking Jews who looked strangely alike in their shared misery. Soldiers with bayonets were guarding them. My papers were checked. They let me pass without a word.

My father was ready to leave for the synagogue when I got home. He asked me to join him. Walking there we talked about family and friends. The subject of our future was never mentioned. We arrived in the middle of the Friday evening service. The familiar members of the congregation looked at me for a second and then continued reading from their books with the familiar rhythmic swaying of their bodies. Surrounded by the prayers, the swaying bodies, the familiarity, I felt at peace and wondered what I had run away from all the years of my adolescence.

I had a restless night in my old room on the other side of the yard. The solitude was strange. This was the first time in over a year I had any privacy. I thought about my brothers. I wondered about them. I prayed they were still alive somewhere in the Soviet Union. I knew they were serving their country as slaves, but I fervently hoped that they were alive.

In the morning I visited Pista's parents. I wanted to tell them how Pista was doing. They had become so old. That same day the parents of others visited me to ask about their sons. I got letters and small packages to carry back to their sons even though they were in a different labor group and even though I was not sure I would be reassigned to my old unit. My mother cried a lot.

For some reason I thought a lot about my shoes. They were in poor shape. Poor shoes could mean infection, amputation, and death. I did not have money to buy new shoes. I did not ask my parents, and they did not seem to notice, nor did they offer to replace them. My shoes became some sort of symbol for what was faulty between my parents and myself. They didn't really notice the important things about me, and I couldn't tell them. I knew that they meant well, but they didn't notice my shoes, my needs, and therefore failed me. I hoped that they were just too preoccupied to notice, yet I was deeply hurt that they were oblivious to my shoes and my condition. Even among the memories of that last visit home, this nagging hurt remains. It curdles my last memory of my parents. No one knows what his last memories will be of his loved ones, but one hopes for soft and loving memories. Mine are clothed in blame and sadness.

The distance back to the railway station was short. Now I was totally alone. My rucksack was heavy with packages. The Gyorfi family, our Christian neighbors, sent me bacon and sausages. My Orthodox Jewish parents gladly let me have these forbidden foods, which indicated some inner knowledge on their part about what was happening. Taking the last hundred meters to the station I heard an unstoppable cry of grief. It was my own. I covered my mouth with a handkerchief and looking straight ahead said farewell to my family, to my city, and to almost all I believed in.

After this last visit home, I had an uneventful train ride back to the original assembly point, Hódmezövásárhely. There I presented my written orders received in Csemo from Sergeant Bimbo. I was overjoyed when I learned that my assignment would reunite me with my original unit. This was pure luck. If they had shipped me somewhere else, I would have been lost without my comrades. They were my life-blood. I had gambled that taking all the extra days would advantage me, and it had.

I felt well rested and relieved as I walked to the railway station to catch the train back to my unit in the easternmost part of Hungary. My peaceful walk was interrupted by the sudden shriek of an air-raid siren. Everyone ran for cover. I walked into the nearest yard and tried to enter a cellar for protection. The owner pushed me away from the cellar door, shouting, "This is all because of the Jews. The vengeance of the Jews is what is causing this bombing. They targeted us for bombing runs because they know that this city is as assembly station for Jews going into forced labor."

I screamed back obscenities at him as he slammed the door in my face, leaving me vulnerable to the "Jewish bombing raids."

What logic! The Jews were to be blamed for everything. I had been blamed for the long working hours which kept the guards away from dinner. Now I was being blamed for being in a labor battalion against my wishes and being stationed in someone's village.

I remained in the open yard under the tree. I heard the whistling noise of the bombs. The citizen who had locked me out of the cellar ran into the yard yelling, "My horses! What will happen to my horses? My pigs! What will happen to my pigs?"

Another person from the cellar came out to the yard, checking the stables. I was less than the farm animals. Bombs continued to drop, closer now. The ground started to shake. After the bombardment the family climbed out of cellar frightened. Dust and noise was everywhere. The owner who had locked me out appeared shaken and fearful. His wife came out in the yard, making the sign of the cross. She then started to curse "the Negroes and Jews who sit in the airplanes and aim for hospitals and schools." She knew this to be true because she had read it in the paper. She screamed at me that these monsters gave toys to children with explosive devices that would maim and kill them. She said that Jews gave the pilots orders. I wanted to answer, but by then her attention was turned to her horse as it galloped towards us, blood gushing out of its many wounds caused by flying glass from the stable window. I continued towards the railway station without a word, now knowing that whatever I had gained in my hospital stay was very temporary.

It was nighttime when my train left for Tiszaborkut. Military police checked my papers twice. The train was unheated and dreadfully cold. I was the only passenger with a yellow armband on this military train. Drinks were being passed around. It smelled like vodka or palinka. When the bottle came to me, I didn't know what to do.

"Take it," the soldier next to me said.

I took a gulp. It felt good. What felt the best was that it was offered me man to man, not man to subhuman. It was pitch dark when the train stopped at Tiszaborkut. The snow was high. I started walking, not having any idea where my unit was. Guards stepped out from their guardhouse with their weapons trained at me.

"Halt!"

"Papers."

The moon was out. The snow was deep. The dogs were barking. The whole landscape had an eerie, frightening quality to it. I was traveling backwards, reeling. I was back to a primitiveness of conditions and attitude. Finally a soldier directed me to my group.

It was winter cold in the high Carpathian Mountains. It was dark when I stepped into the barracks—my home. The straw on the floor was tightly packed with sleeping men. A stale smell permeated everything. I shook the nearest boy,

"Where is Lajos?"

He was my closest friend, and I needed him especially. I found him. We had always bunked together, using our blankets together. I woke him, "Lajos, I'm back."

He replied listlessly, "I have lice."

He fell back into an exhausted, cold sleep. We were best friends, and he had no strength to say a few words of welcome to me. His only words were a warning. It was a warning about how bad everything was for him. It was a warning about living under conditions where only survival counted. Forget being human, just survive.

During the several weeks while I had been away rebuilding myself, the situation had worsened for the group. I was sheltered in the hospital. I had not been worked half to death or beaten so that I no longer felt like a human being. The group had been so abused that they felt brutality was normal and even deserved. "I have lice" meant "I am no longer a man. I am a nonperson."

It was a confusing transition from the normalcy of the hospital to the near-death situation which awaited me. Here I was laying on the straw next to my buddy. He was hungry. He was infected with lice. I tried to gauge my feelings as I went off to sleep. I had the feeling that my emotions were already blunted as a kind of protection in the war called survival. All I knew, and all I would ever know, was that I had to get free. We would all have to get free. But how could I get free without outside help?

Freedom would have to come. The idea of freedom would keep me spiritually alive! Of this turmoil, of this cruelty, of this illness, of this death, I was an unwilling participant. I was a witness to this madness. But I would survive and become free. Then I would tell the world.

I thought, as I drifted to sleep, that I was a young man, lying in the straw next to my lice-infested friend, while our Hungarian guards, our former fellow citizens, must remain drunk to feed their craziness and brutality and then to drink more to erase their conscience. I prayed for these soldiers to be in our place and to smell the stink of disease, abuse, and fear. I also knew, deep inside, that we were better off spiritually than they were. We had not given in to the basest of feelings.

Wake-up call came at five. Everyone was morosely quiet. The members of my unit, like automatons, removed the thin blankets that they had slept in. They wordlessly picked up their threadbare coats. They walked out silently and lined up for the morning coffee. This was a different group of young men than the ones I had left weeks ago. These men were beaten. These men were lost. These young men were now old.

I reported to the duty officer. I tried to adjust myself to the surroundings. The kitchen was open and next to the stable. The group's only horse was silently eating. I looked from the horse to my comrades and could not tell the difference.

I went to the shoemaker and began to ask questions about what had happened to the unit. He briefly painted a dark, stark situation. He told me about the new sergeant who had replaced Bimbo. His name was Vida. He had a problem writing and counting. When he got drunk he would seclude himself in his office and cry. He was weak, and he could not help himself. He certainly could not control the guards. It was certain that he could not help us.

The shoemaker told me that our food rations were being sold by the soldiers on the black market. This was not new. It happened sporadically everywhere, but now it was done more openly and more universally, and the men were always hungry. Bread, sugar, and our occasional meat were taken out of our mouths and sold to black marketeers. The new officer did not have the energy, the strength, or the willingness to try to stop the stealing. Maybe he believed that the Jews deserved this fate. The Jewish laborers were being worked without enough food, while profit was being made by the soldiers.

Donath, the Jewish clerk, sat in his makeshift office. Long long ago in Hódmezővásárhely, he had been able to arrange or buy privileges for the wealthier boys—a few days off, a special visit from a girlfriend or wife. Even for those not rich these special privileges usually filtered down with sharing or gifts of food or clothing.

"That time is over," he told me solemnly.

The ordeal was now in earnest.

The five-per-two group got ready for the march to the mountains. We had been ordered to the eastern front. New tools were issued. My section became the wheelbarrow group. Forty-five wheelbarrows were to be pushed towards the high mountains. We were to push our wheelbarrows towards Russia. Could they really order us to push wheelbarrows up higher and higher in the mountains all the way to Ukrainia? Yes, Yes! This was the Hungarian Army's Jewish labor battalion, and everything was possible here.

The wheelbarrow section fell behind. We pushed the wheelbarrows filled with our own equipment up the hill. Szabados, the gypsy soldier who was assigned as a guard to the wheelbarrow group, had been the chief black marketeer during the more normal times months ago. He started screaming and beating us.

"Hurry, you Jewish pigs! Hurry, you lazy dogs!"

I still felt empowered by the humane treatment at the hospital, where I had been treated almost as an equal. I was not as broken-spirited as the rest. I reacted automatically, screaming curses back at him. No one in the five-per-two felt human anymore. My outburst was incredible to them. I again screamed back the same threats which had been screamed at me.

"You dirty pig! You ass-kisser! You motherfucker!"

Our section was spread out over several miles. Szabados was the only soldier around. He was alone with the Jews of our section, one of whom was challenging him. He looked around for help, there was none. I stepped closer to him, daring him to do anything by my manner and stance. I kept my eyes locked on his as I threw the wheelbarrow into a ravine. Several of my fellow laborers stepped around me. Szabados kept his mouth shut and walked away. Everything stopped as the members of the battalion wondered why he hadn't killed me on the spot. Lajos said, "He will kill you when we get back to the base."

We arrived back at the base almost two hours late without wheelbarrows because the section had followed my lead, and all the wheelbarrows were at the bottom of the ravine. By the time we got to the gathering point, new assignments had been issued. The gypsy soldier, Szabados, had been moved somewhere else, the same day. He could not kill me. That is the luck or fate that makes or breaks a person. That was enough luck for me to expect. I now had to readjust myself to the group and fit back in.

The little food I had brought with me from home was stolen by someone hungrier than I was. We marched thirty or forty kilometers each day, most of the time without food or water. Our sacks were heavy, no matter how little was in them, and they pulled and crushed our shoulders. The weight on our shoulders both physically and emotionally twisted our insides. I felt constant pressure in my throat. And I had just returned from rejuvenation. Others must have felt much worse.

It was very cold in the mountains. The snow had been cleaned from the road by another labor force. We had seen them on the way to Delatyn. Their fate must have been worse than ours. They were older than us, and therefore did not have the reserves of energy that the younger have. They moved slower, saving their energy. We watched them slowly transfer their weight from one foot to another as they trudged the mountain road. We watched and tried to learn from them in order to survive. Our conditions, considering the circumstances, were more tolerable. We were hungry all the time, but very seldom actually starved. Our chief cook, Pista Goli, and his helpers were decent fellows. They tried to see to it that the workers were fed something.

When we arrived we were given our work assignments. Assignments were now even more critical as our physical condition worsened. The best assignment was the railroad detail. We would load supplies from the railroad cars to the army trucks. Inside the cars we were protected from the wind. The best assignment in the railroad detail was to be a trucker. One would load the truck and ride with the supplies to the destination and then unload the truck and return to the railroad yard. During rest periods we would be allowed to eat something from the army rations. Fortification work was much worse. To be assigned to a German group was even better, although we were more afraid of the Germans.

All these hierarchies of work assignments were based on the basics of survival: was there protection from the elements, time to rest, and some food to eat? To be treated as a laborer instead of a slave was also of considerable importance in the ranking of the various details. To our continuous surprise the Germans treated us better than our fellow Hungarians.

During this time we worked at our own pace. There was no rush. To finish the job meant a new assignment nearer the front lines, so both the laborers and the soldiers agreed wordlessly on a slower pace. Inspection time was different. When we heard from the distance the voices of our guards, cursing and loudly yelling to get the work done faster, we knew then that inspection time was approaching.

When we first arrived at Delatyn, a small city on the Ukrainian side of the mountains, we realized that something was terribly wrong. We were billeted in vacant Jewish homes. Soon we realized that there were no Jews left in the entire city. Where were the Jews from this city? Were they guilty of something? I vaguely remembered that old farmer and his wife shouting about Jewish saboteurs leading the Jewish and

Negro bombers. But how could a whole city of Jews be guilty? Horrifying stories circulated about atrocities, cruelties, and merciless acts perpetrated on the Jewish population. We could not and felt we should not believe these stories. The stories about gas chambers were impossible. But the question still nagged us: Where were the Jewish people from this city? We had hours on our hands. As we marched through the city we saw mezuzahs on the doors, remnants of a Jewish life, but no Jews anywhere. A nagging, terrifying pressure settled around my heart.

- *18* -

Springtime came slowly. The winter cold and the work assignments had taken their toll on our spirits and our bodies. The sun shone on the distant Carpathian Mountains. Our desire, made more painful by the contrast of spring, was to see and make contact with our loved ones. We had a chance to talk with one another in our spare time, but we grew tired of the same stories of long ago and hungered for messages or letters from those at home.

We were assigned to abandoned homes in groups of ten and fifteen. There was water in the homes and a stream to wash our clothing. We agreed among ourselves that the Germans were magicians to be waging and winning this war. No one talked anymore about the capitalist countries, since those had failed us by not coming to our aid. We wished only for the Bolshevik armies to come and save us.

We were more on our own here. If we needed firewood, we tore down fences. If we needed potatoes, we removed them from the neighboring fields. If a farmer complained, we threatened to burn his farm down. At this time we received a new corporal named Magony. He took complete charge from our former leader, Vida, who was always drunk. Our new corporal tried to make our lives less miserable. If nothing else, he restrained the roughest soldiers. The black marketing of food rations stopped under his jurisdiction. A few weeks after his arrival we received our new assignments.

We marched a few days and arrived at the river Prut. The Prut runs north and south and flows into the Black Sea. The bridges had been blown and pontoon bridges had been built across the river. The original bridge had crossed forty yards above the river. The pontoon bridge had been built in the deep valley of the riverbed. The supplies and equipment would have to be carried up and down the steep grade to the pontoon bridges and back by the labor battalion. The downgrade to the bridge was tremendous. The upgrade was horrifying. The passing army units with their equipment had to manage the steep incline of the mountain to get down to the pontoon bridge and the steep incline up to return. The solution was "Jewish horses"—us.

The traffic on the roads leading to the bridges was extremely heavy. There was a constant bottleneck at the bridge. Our job was to get the armies and supplies east when the Germans were winning, or get the armies and supplies west when the Red Army was chasing the Germans and their Hungarian allies the other way. The worst for the Jewish "horses" was ironically what was best for the Jewish prisoners, the retreat of the fascist armies. The fascist armies were always in a panic to escape and not to be taken prisoner by the Red Army, so the work load on us and the chaos were unbelievable. The pressure was on us, sick and hungry as we were, to superhumanly carry wagons and supplies down the river bank, running towards the west. Going east was done at a slower pace, as the enthusiasm for engaging the enemy was never very high.

On one section of the mountaintop there was a crucifix. Our job was to run up the steep mountain to the waiting group of soldiers and then return on the run with the supplies. Trucks, artillery pieces, supply wagons, and horses were lined up for miles waiting for our shoulders and backs. That cross was in front of me all the time as I ran up the mountain towards the supplies. I kept my eye on it as it willed me up the mountain. For this Jewish boy that cross became a beacon. It was what I aimed for as I tried to make the upgrade. I unswervingly kept my eye and my will on that cross. I kept repeating silently some prayer which would stop the pain of my arms and legs and slow my breath. We had to pull and push the rolling army equipment. My shoes went the first day. I put a piece of my blanket around my feet. Which was worse, coming down or going up? Which was worst, getting a Hungarian army through or a German army through? The latter question was easier, the Hungarian army was much worse. But the worst is not to have hope. The cross was my hope, my spirit, and my will. I would not be broken!

One day a small German artillery piece fell out of our eight-man team's grasp and into the river. We thought this would be the end of us. A German sergeant, following his officer's orders, came with us into the chest-high water and instructed us on how to retrieve the artillery piece.

"Hold here. Hold there. Don't touch this part."

All of this done in a quiet professional tone. If it were a Hungarian sergeant, we would have been at the bottom of the river.

The Germans, if in a hurry, would ask the Jewish section leader for our help and reward us with bread or cigarettes if we did the work at their time schedule. I have to admit that they gave us reasonable time for the job and always kept their promises.

To the Hungarians, our fellow countrymen, we were only beasts of burden. In reciprocation we didn't steal from the Germans, but we stole everything we could from the Hungarians. When a wagon came, and we couldn't steal from it because the driver was on one side and his helper on the other with weapons trained on us, we turned it over. The needed food landed in the mud. On our way back we salvaged the loot by hiding it in our pockets or throwing it into the bushes to be retrieved at an even later time. If one of the wagons carried sugar and lard, we pushed our hand first into the lard and then into the sugar. We put our bounty into our pockets. We had a few seconds to steal while the soldier with a carbine trained on us looked away.

There were times when rumors were rampant that the Soviets were near and attacking. Partisans would start to shoot down at the people on the pontoons. Partisans never shot at any of us. When we worked on the bridge itself, the soldiers took off their uniforms and tried to camouflage themselves to look like us, the Jews. There was something both amusing and heartrending about that.

The officer in charge of the bridge and its comings and goings was a ruthless, heartless person. The Prut is a very fast river. One day the rail I was using for support broke off, and I fell into the water. I could not swim, so I hung on to the rail, which was still connected to the bridge by a nail. The officer came over, "I need some Jews like this guy. He wanted to save a piece of Hungarian wood, so he jumped into the river to save it."

He amazingly believed what he had said. The Hungarian wood was more important than my life, but I had proven my bravery by recognizing this fact and acting on it. Because I was so "heroic," he sent me to my living quarters to dry off. I didn't have to do any more work that day. I gained one week of rest with this "heroic" act because every day I said to different soldiers who were assigned to guard duty at our base, "I don't have to work. The captain sent me in to dry myself. I saved some Hungarian wood, and this is my reward."

The extending of my time drying out was not without considerable difficulty. I had to be as invisible as possible. I found myself wandering closer and closer to the forest which surrounded our camp. Without even consciously noting it, I was attempting to get nearer to the source of sporadic gunfire which seemed aimed at the Hungarian and German convoys and our guards. I wondered what nationality these partisans were. I wondered whether they were civilians or soldiers. I wondered if they were antisemitic, as we had heard the Polish partisans were.

As I took this "drying off" time to rest, I thought about my chances of survival. I realized that, more than food and shelter, my friends were essential to my survival. I thought about each person who worked hand-and-hand with me and what made him special to me.

Gyuri Berger was very good-looking and always smiling. He bunked with Pali Kerekes, our group leader. Both of them survived, and Gyuri became a very famous heart specialist. I still wonder how he maintained his good humor through all the horror.

Gyuri Schon was another friend who was a very great help to the group. He was a blacksmith with one horse to shoe. He was later assigned to the kitchen area. He always managed to have a little extra food which he shared with our group. He usually didn't keep any for himself, saying that we labored, and he had the easy job and didn't need it.

Lajos Kolin and Pista Zilzer were my two closest buddies. A friend's closeness could prevent the breakdown of morale and spirit which was as dangerous as malnutrition or frostbite.

By the end of the six weeks of working as transport horses on the pontoon bridge to support the armies crossing, the group was exhausted. Many had lost shoes. My left foot was constantly bleeding. I wrapped my foot daily, but the water

and mud always permeated my exposed and vulnerable foot. I
was literally on my last leg.

- *19* -

By 1943 Soviet pressure was pushing the Germans back.
The Germans needed fortifications and a road for a possible
retreat into Hungary through Ruthenia and the Carpathian
Mountains. We were about to became their road builders. We
were in bad shape, exhausted, and not able to take any more
of this backbreaking, spirit-shredding hard work. More and
more accidents occurred, caused by our exhaustion.

From the river Prut in Ukrainia we walked to our next destination to build roads alongside the other Jewish battalions
that were also becoming road builders. Because of our condition, what was usually three days walk became ten excruciat-
ing days. We arrived in the city of Körösmezö, near Ruthenia. It
was a sizable village. We were moving slowly westward and
passed other groups of Jews in labor battalions that were
trudging towards the front, perhaps to replace us at the
bridge. I will never forget one group. They were staggering on
unsteady legs. They were a mixed age group of seventeen-year-
old boys turned old and men of thirty who looked ancient.

They had no overcoats, and they were shaking from the cold, exhaustion, or fear. Perhaps they visualized what was waiting for them. They never looked up. Their eyes were blank and already dead. They were emptied of spirit. It was obvious that this group would not last more than a week.

At Körösmezö a pleasant surprise awaited us. Sixty Budapest parents had sent packages to their sons in the battalion. All of the packages had been broken into and looted by the soldiers. Whatever was left was up to the boys from Budapest to recognize and take. But the booty was too enticing, and two hundred starved and ragged men surrounded the loot. I saw shoes. I shouted, "Those shoes are mine!"

Simultaneously, a fellow from Budapest shouted, "They're my shoes."

He started to grab one of them. Magony came over and said, "They're Mandel's shoes."

He had noticed the state of my feet earlier and knew that my feet could not last much longer. Unfortunately, the shoes were a little small. So my feet was now covered, but my toes were cramped and curled.

We regrouped in a little Ruthenian village for two days' rest period to recuperate, find clothes, and get medical help.

What we found was an empty village with scattered furniture in the streets. This former Jewish village was empty. Prayer shawls and prayer books were desecrated in the mud. The wind blew the pages of the sacred Torah. My mind started to race. Where were these people? What had happened to this entire community?

These Jewish homes had been vandalized by neighbors. The neighbors had desecrated the holy and the secular. These simple and unassuming neighbors, now installed in the formerly Jewish homes, were surprised to see Jews again. They were wise to play good samaritans to us. Magony gave us two hours to get back to camp with tools. We each had to find an ax, shovel, hammer, anything. During our march from the bridge, we had "lost" all the battalion's tools.

We followed his orders, and also helped ourselves to whatever we could without asking permission from the same people who had usurped their Jewish neighbors' homes and possessions. We were proud of our revenging acts. These acts in some way validated the spirit that we still retained. We were men and could take things back. We could still right wrongs. But there were certain things we could never regain. We could never replace our lost years. We could never bring the missing Jews back to their homes and give them back their furniture, prayer shawls, and prayer books. By this time we had seen too much and been hurt too much.

We were reassigned again, unexpectedly, to go east, and not west towards home. We were rushed to the nearest train station, but there was no train available for us. We camped next to the tracks. On the other side of the railway line, in an open field, a few hundred Russian prisoners were sitting on the grass. They were surrounded by armed soldiers. All in the battalion watched them. These dirty, unshaven Russians did not have shoes or entire uniforms. Could this be the Soviet Army that we had prayed for all these years? Were these the men from whom we dreamed of salvation?

We watched the Russians, as did our guards. Only the tracks separated us, but no one could cross over. The populace of this small town where we waited for the train was of mostly Slavic origin. The villagers started to gather and watch the Russian prisoners. Some of the villagers had tears in their eyes, seeing their Slavic brothers as prisoners. Others, the Hungarian-speaking folk, watched the Russian prisoners with open malice and mockery. We heard them say, "Our soldiers will be able to finish them off easily."

Since the civilians were able to cross the train tracks, we collected our bread rations and had the civilians deliver them to the prisoners. No guards objected.

We didn't know what to think. We wondered what they made of us, fellow prisoners. Did we look as threadbare and desperate as they? Had they any knowledge of the Jewish battalions?

Our train finally arrived. We entered windowless freight cars and traveled east for two days. It was late afternoon when we arrived at the edge of Ivano-Frankovski. We were in the middle of nowhere. Our belongings were thrown to the side of the road. From an army engineer truck, hammers and pickaxes were thrown to us. The engineer officer took charge. The work started immediately even though it was almost totally dark.

All army personnel including clerks were drafted into the work force. It was a rotten beginning. We tried to position ourselves to get easier-appearing assignments. Would getting a hammer be better or a getting a pickax? These types of choices could spell death or survival. We tried to guess what would be an easier assignment.

Now we were road builders. One group had to take big pieces of rocks from the mountains. The other group broke the rocks into little pieces with hammers. The third group spread out the small stones and pushed them into the ground. On that first evening engineering soldiers showed us how and what to do. It was past midnight when we got our food rations. We collapsed in utter exhaustion.

The next day there was the early wake-up call. Our bodies were racked with pain. There was no time for complaints or laments. We had to hurry to line up for bread and coffee. Suddenly, as we waited, a heavenly baritone voice sounded. Our cantor started to pray:

"God give us strength—to die or live. Give strength to the Jews to be able to take this persecution. God give us strength to be strong and worthy of You."

He then began another song of joy and happiness. It was amazing and wonderful. We felt better.

I was in the rock-breaking group. This wasn't the worst part of the work, though constant blisters were a hazard. The work group was spread out more than a mile. We had a quota to finish. Soldiers came and went, coercing us to work faster.

One day, a group of soldiers went by. A soldier on horseback stopped in front of me. I was sitting on the ground, hammer in my hand, breaking up a good-sized rock. He was a former classmate. He was a soccer player older than myself and a bully. I had always tried to get out of his way whenever possible. In peacetime I considered him a dangerous person. What would it be like with three stars on his uniform? He asked what he could do to help. In wartime, it appears that bullies can become empathetic. I said we were hungry. Fifteen minutes later he came back with a sack full of bread for the whole group. So this peacetime bully was really a caring person when it counted! When this benefactor, Pista Kokeny, came home in 1946, I had already told my friends about him. He got the headwaiter job in the Beretvas Coffee House. He received well-deserved support from all of us. The bread server during the war also became our bread server during peace.

In the mountains above the road work were little huts where peasants lived. It was strictly forbidden to leave the area where we were bunking after work. But we had to get some extra food. I volunteered to sneak out of the camp, climb up to the mountain cabins, and try to exchange a shirt for food. For my risk, half of the food was shared with our Kecskemét group; the other half was split by the whole group. This added supplementation helped a lot, since for breakfast we only had black coffee and a slice of hardened marmalade.

We never had time to sit and eat. We shoved the sweet things into our dirty pockets and ate on the march to work. In the evening, if we had boiled potatoes, I would eat one for dinner and save one for breakfast. We were hungry all the time. In normal times we had regular army dark bread. We never knew how long the normal time would last. Up at dark, back at dark, days merged into one another and into the weeks which followed.

One day the engineers looked for masons among us. Two of us, one of them me, were selected to be masons. Our job was to bring the stones down from the mountains and build the retaining walls which were to hold up the road. It was a very good assignment.

I had a partner on this road work. He was an uneducated, crude fellow. He was also amazingly shrewd. Instead of the heavy rocks, Farkas taught me how to get the light, soft, friable stones. They looked strong, but were not. Use of these stones would guarantee that the wall would collapse when the first car or truck tried to pass by. The wall looked massive and impressive. When the retaining wall was inspected from below, the officers who were ten yards away looking up were so impressed that they ordered double soup for us for three weeks. We were rewarded for laziness and sabotage. I rewarded each of my friends by sharing my extra soup with each of them. This is how survival occurs.

One major drawback in road building was that we never had a place to sleep. We dug a hole, cut a few pieces of wood, slanted them down to the ground, tried to cover the front with leaves, and used it for shelter. If it rained, this was no shelter at all.

The things that sustained us during this time were friendship, a little extra food, and news that would allow us to hope. The capture of Mussolini was greeted with joy by us. So was the summer offensive of the Red Army. How the news filtered down to us was a miracle and a mystery at the same time. Somehow we were all aware of the war news. This news kept us going with the hope of liberation. After one good news release, several bad ones usually followed. We constantly saw and heard planes overhead. Once in a great while pamphlets came from the planes. It was strictly forbidden for us to pick up these leaflets. On one of my outings to exchange one of our meager possessions for food, I noticed a leaflet lying on the ground. It held a message from President Roosevelt of the United States of America. In Hungarian it said, "Live without fear." I suddenly realized that his premise could only be fulfilled if all of us were free. I whispered the message to my friends. We did not know if we would ever be free again—free not to fear; but for a few hours a message from six thousand miles away gave us hope.

- *20* -

The summer was over. It was the least unpleasant time, and now the worst time began. A cold front came in with snow and ice. We had neither winter clothes nor warm shelter. I had a raincoat which we hung over the entrance of our bunker to stop the snow from entering. In the morning, the coat was like metal; it was frozen stiff. Now I dreamed of sleeping in a warm bed with a loved one. I dreamed of warm days and cool watermelon. I dreamed of soccer. I dreamed of seeing places not torn by war and torment. I lay on a thin layer of straw, tightly pressed to my brothers, covered by a flimsy blanket, and listened to the sighs, moans, and cries which filled the night. I transported myself back to my home, and I was in my own bed. It was summer and the air was warm. I walked with Aranka outside to get water from the well. Am I dreaming? Yes, it is cold, and I am without my love. No, it is really Aranka holding my hand. My sister Sara just offered me money to deliver a love letter. I can feel the letter in my hand. No, that's the edge of my thin blanket. The distant sound of the bouncing soccer ball is real. The ball is in the air, perfectly positioned for a header. I try to jump for it. I cannot move.

"Mother, help me. Please, help me mother."

I am being shaken awake,

"Try to get some sleep." Lajos says.

Before wake-up call I will have to sneak out again with a shirt to try to make an exchange. Will they catch me this time? I promised myself that when I was free I would never set foot on a mountain again.

Our new assignment was to clear the snow from the roads. It was unbearably cold. With my tight left shoe, I thought I would lose my foot from frostbite. Soldiers on trucks passed us. No one paid attention. We were the invisible. We tried to get as close to each other as possible to keep warm. Physical and emotional closeness was the only barrier to the freezing weather and even more barren emotional climate.

During the winter months, the Russian army completed a full breakthrough. The German retreat started, and the Hungarian and German armies started to run. It was a disorganized group of soldiers who had lost their leaders, had lost their courage, and had lost their spirit. The main desire of the soldiers was to try to get away from the advancing Soviet forces. This was a panicked, unorganized run from the front, with artillery pieces and trucks left behind. The labor battalion was caught in the retreat. We witnessed only the end of the retreat, but seeing it made us feel that if we were strong, we would survive. We had to survive the retreat and somehow survive the Russian assault. But if we hung on, perhaps, just perhaps, we could live.

The wounded came back in horsedrawn carts if Hungarian, and in open trucks if German. I remember hearing their screams and their cries for help. We had no pity. They were the enemy who mocked and tortured us. They were the ones who had imprisoned us and our families. The stronger wounded were marching. The weaker sat down. Once you stopped moving you were doomed. The Russians wouldn't find the stranglers until the spring thaw.

Our guards suddenly became frightened little boys looking for help and forgiveness and asking for our favor. We outnumbered them, and if the Russians won, they would need us. We felt that our turn had come. The most sadistic guards, Randovitch, Szucs, and Darazs, tried their utmost to demonstrate their newfound friendship towards us. For a few weeks, maybe a month or so, our spirits rose higher. Although the cold was the same as before and our food ration was less, there was a feeling of hopefulness. We would soon be saved. I remember the soldiers made promises.

"If we get out of this alive, we'll start afresh. We treated you badly only on the orders of our officers."

The retreat lasted to the river Prut. We were routed back in a great rush to our nightmare again—the Prut!

Our job now became that of building bridges on the Prut for the retreat. We had to get the retreating forces down with all their supplies and then pull them up on the other side, just like before only in reverse. We were now helping the retreat.

A section officer lost his jeep during the retreat. He was given two horses and a wagon. His job was to go back and forth across the river and try to organize his forces in the retreat. When he got to our station, he unhitched his horses, and staying on the wagon said, "My Jewish horses, take me down the ravine. If you do, no harm will come to you."

We were his Jewish horses. He thought he was being kind, comparing us to horses. He didn't really abuse us, but he felt he had to save the horses and use our labor instead. The horses were more important than our humanity and our lives.

The Soviet advance stopped. The Hungarian and German armies gathered strength on the west side of the river. Spring came in 1944. The German-Hungarian army tried to reorganize and gather strength for another attack towards the east. The Hungarian soldiers were not anxious to cross east. They were unsure how the tide was going. Sometimes we were pushed to work hard. Other times slowing down was the order of the day.

The guards again became wild animals, perhaps fueled by their own recent embarrassment at showing us their fear. Suddenly they forgot the four weeks when they had been nice to us. Work now became more unbearable, as their harshness and cruelty sapped us further. They now saw the tide going their way again.

The trucks, artillery pieces, ammunition, supplies, and troops were lined up at ten different places along the river waiting for us. A week or two later we had to blow up the bridge. Again the panic returned to the soldiers. They were in the path of the Russians. Whoever had crossed east now tried to get back. This bridge was blown and rebuilt four times. We got only a few hours of sleep at night, working seven days a week in that confusing spring of 1944.

- *21* -

The Red Army gained strength and began its attack. We were moved back to Ruthenia, to the eastern part of Hungary. We were of two minds. We liked to hear the sound of Soviet warfare and its promise of finally freeing us. At the same time it was dangerous near the eastern front, and we wanted to be back in our own homeland again. We were Hungarians who could not ally with our own people and looked to strangers for salvation.

We entered the first large Hungarian village since leaving for the eastern front. Our group was stretched out almost a mile.

Everybody was tired and exhausted. The first fellows slowed down to get reorganized, and by the time we had all caught up we had been energized by a new force. As we entered this township of our homeland, somebody from the battalion had started to sing. This village had been made *Judenrein;* all its Jews had become part of the Final Solution. Now the remaining Gentile villagers were standing on the street watching the first Hungarian Jews return to Hungary.

We felt so overwhelmed that we had come this far alive. We had to voice, in song, our joy of life and our pride at being Jewish and of having survived. The feeling was so exhilarating that we sang beautifully with all our hearts. We were singing to life and to show these people and ourselves that we were alive. We had come back. We had returned. I remember their faces watching us, the whispers around us.

"The Jews are back."

We needed to show physical and spiritual group strength. The song that erupted from our lips was pure spontaneity. The whole group felt that we had to show our resilience, our strength and our courage.

One member of our unit, Tamas Balassa, was a musician from Budapest. He had created to the tune of "Anchors Aweigh" a song that was the special song of the five-per-two. That song was sung over and over again going through the village.

Months ago in a friend's house, we were waiting for a visitor and his brother from Canada. When he arrived, the conversation turned to the past. He started to tell a story that was very familiar. I stopped him and started to sing the group song. I hadn't recognized him. He hadn't recognized me. It turned out that he was Pista Goli, the cook of the labor battalion. Two survivors reunited through a song.

- *22* -

Rumors spread that the Rumanians would ask for a separate peace and severe their ties with the Germans. The German army needed roads to move troops and supplies out from or into Rumania. Again, the labor battalion was called on to build roads and fortifications for them. We noticed Allied airplanes above our heads daily, and behind them, shiny little pieces of paper flying. We had long discussions about these luminous flying objects. We didn't know why those specks were there, but we knew somehow that it was good for us.

Our orders changed again. We were loaded into a narrow-gauge freight train. The cars didn't have sides. The small locomotive moved very slowly higher and higher into the mountains. We traveled almost a full day. The night in the open car was bitterly cold. At dawn the train stopped. We saw a sign over the train station which read Viso.

It was dawn when we arrived. There was the smell of clean cut grass. The sky was reddish. The panorama, the high mountains, the reddish sky was like a travel brochure. We had arrived at the edge of a clearing surrounded by high vertical mountains. We camped in the clearing and had our morning coffee. Behind us we heard the water of a small spring rushing down from the mountains.

There was a trail which led down from the mountains to this clearing. A low-ranking officer entered the clearing from the mountains, riding a mule, and came towards the middle of our group. Before coming to a full stop, he announced, "My name is Lieutenant Dudas."

He was elegant and immaculately clean. Sitting sideways on his mule he spoke to us briefly, and ended by saying, "You will all die here!"

So much for the picturesque setting. He lined us up in single file, and we followed him and his mule. I will remember all my life walking towards my promised burial place watching the rear end of a mule.

Our backpacks, although half-empty now, felt like a ton, as we climbed higher and higher. To our left was the deep valley; to our right was the mountain wall. All of us clung close to the mountainside as we were afraid that we might fall off the trail into oblivion. The mountain was beautiful with the sun shining, even to us frightened, sweat-stained men.

Finally we arrived at our destination completely exhausted. We were ordered to build our own shelters. A few huts for the officers and staff had already been erected on this plateau. The eight men from Kecskemét decided that we would build one bunker for all of us. Two of the boys dug the trench. The rest of us went into the forest to cut tree branches. With one end of the branch in the ground and the other across the trench to the other side, we made a bunker with a slanted roof. Unfortunately, when it rained, which it did continuously, we got soaking wet.

When we were in the forest we noticed an abandoned hut hidden in the mountains. Later we went back and took the shingle roof from the hut and laid it on top of our makeshift roof. Ours was the best shelter on the plateau. We were proud and satisfied.

The trouble started at daybreak. The five workers who occupied the "abandoned" hut came down to our area armed with axes and their righteous indignation. Excitedly they started talking to our Sergeant Vida, who was already half-drunk. They complained that the Jews had taken the roof from their quarters. Vida sent Corporal Magony with the armed workers to our bunker.

We were aware of our visitors and were in the process of hiding the shingles. Our sleeping area was disassembled as we stood in front of our bunker. One of the workers angrily pointed to the poorly hidden shingles and demanded a document from Magony allowing them to beat the Jews up and recoup their shingles. Magony replied that they were free to beat us up, but he wouldn't supply documentation for it. The workers insisted on written permission, which they did not get, so they walked away cursing under their mustaches, apparently wanting official sanction for their acts more than the act itself. We kept the shingles.

Our job was to cut down tree trunks and carry them several kilometers up or down, depending on the location of the fortified bunkers. Tank traps also had to be dug and camouflaged. Every fifteen kilometers or so another group of unfortunate prison laborers like us had a similar job to do. It was hard work because the ground was uneven and the tree trunks heavy. We had to learn how to cooperate in order to navigate the rough surface full of shallow holes and elevations.

The eight of us from Kecskemét worked together as a unit. We were friends; we were workmates. We carried tree trunks which were ten yards long and ten to twelve inches thick. Naturally the bottom root part was much heavier than the top part. In order to do this work required cooperation and practice. Did the taller boys do better at the front, middle, or end? Was the road upward or downward, and what did that do to positioning? Where should we position the strongest amongst us? With time we worked this out almost to a science. Four of us carried the trunk on our right shoulders and four of us on our left. We could manage on level ground. But on an uneven surface it became a very severe physics problem to solve. The boys in the middle carried no weight when going over a depression, yet the trunk was too huge to be carried by less than eight men. An elevation was more than a physics problem. It could, and often did, become deadly. A crushed foot or a broken arm meant almost certain death in a German concentration camp.

One day an officer from the engineering unit came to our section to supervise our progress. The officer surprised us and found us resting after negotiating a very difficult part of the ground while carrying a heavy tree.

"Who told you to rest?"

We were standing next to a tree trunk ten yards long that we couldn't carry anymore. He methodically slapped all eight of us. He walked by each prison laborer and slapped each young man in turn. Methodical degradation! He did this unhurriedly, slapping one of us and leisurely strolling another two yards to slap the next. On and on he walked, slapping the life and manhood of each person. When he was finished, he walked away looking proud. He had done his job and was a brave Hungarian officer. I am sure he was self-satisfied, a pleasure which was constantly denied us. We picked up the tree and continued our labor. This was terribly humiliating for all of us. We were exhausted, pushed beyond endurance, and yet we resented our pride being slapped away.

Shortly after the slapping incident we were reassigned to a new job. We had to select and mark with a saw trees of certain proportions. We then had to saw down these trees. This was a wonderful assignment. Under the pretense of finding the right-size trees, we could wander and rest. One day Lajos and I were making a grand gesture of theater in marking and felling a tree. For an hour our saw made only a slight dent as we went through the motions of this labor. The forest around us was thick. It was impossible to see an approaching guard. Sometimes that worked in our behalf, as we could lose ourselves in the wilderness. Sometimes it backfired. During this hour of faked work, sometimes we became so engrossed in conversation that we were oblivious to any danger. There was a danger here of being found being human.

Lajos was telling me about his parents, his brother, and his neighbors. Suddenly the poignancy of the memories made him cry. He dropped the handle of the saw and leaned on my shoulder. This took place only seconds before he was aware of the peril of our position. He took the handle and worked again. It was very difficult to listen to a friend in pain and not be able to embrace him or look into his face. The last sentences of his quiet monologue will stay with me forever.

"I always wanted to sit in Gyene's Pastry Shop in Kecskemét and order eight slices of chocolate cake. I wanted to order every different flavor of ice cream. I never had enough money to order more than one. Now I fear that I will never get to eat even one ever again."

Lajos survived. He was in the group that escaped with me. He married twice. He now lives in Israel and works as an accountant in a large bank. I wish him a rainbow of ice creams and pastries.

- *23* -

We had to use wisely any opportunities which arose. We had to conserve our strength and our energy when on easier work assignments to be able to survive the tougher assignments. Doing heavy labor on our food rations was near impossible. On the other hand, beatings would occur if we didn't work at a top speed. If someone was found resting, the punishment was to lift him off the ground by his shackled hands, which were behind his back, and let him dangle with his toes barely touching the ground. We learned high theater performing the easier assignments, so as to appear to be doing more labor while rejuvenating, all the while escaping beatings.

We all got our share of beatings, but one beating in particular will remain with me always. Whenever he could, Gyuri Schon, who was the group's blacksmith, shared his meal with one of us. He was seen handing over his bowl by one of the guards. As punishment for "stealing food" two soldiers tied Gyuri's wrists to his ankles and then lifted him by a carbine between his arms and legs so that his buttocks was facing us. We were ordered to go one by one and strike Gyuri's buttocks. The first few boys imitated a blow, but were beaten senseless by the guards, who were now drunk and boisterous and wanted our blood. To spare themselves the boys now beat Gyuri.

I was in the middle of this group. I was horrified at the notion that I, or any of us, would be capable of hitting a comrade whose sin was in feeding us. I knew that I could not hit him, no matter what.

"We have feelings," I said loudly to the air.

"We should remain human beings," I said, softer this time.

"I will not touch him," I whispered.

My turn came. I stepped next to Gyuri and positioned myself in the same stance as he, readying myself for the blows which were sure to follow.

Suddenly the beatings stopped. Next to me was Lajos assuming the same humiliating position. Others followed.

"We are still human beings!"

"Yes!" "Yes!" "Yes!"

Magony, our decent "Papa," came forward in a great rush. He ordered the guards to untie Gyuri. We did not know what to expect or what might follow, but nothing happened. Gyuri, after a few days on the work detail, got back his blacksmith's position. He continued to carefully share his rations with us.

A few of our boys were beaten without reason no matter what they did. It was done as a demonstration to all of us of our slave status. This usually happened to the same boys over and over. They were the ones who had lost hope and self-respect early. Their victim status left them able to be further humiliated. They were usually dirtier than the others and weaker. It was as if they held a sign which said "Victim." These were boys who did not have friends to support and help them, and whose victim status further distanced any succor.

If we finished a section of work, we moved our camp forward. Most of the time we did not have the time and strength to build shelters for ourselves. On such occasions we tried to find shelter under heavy big trees with lots of leaves and branches. Trying to find grassy smooth ground without sharp stones was a prime task. When the rain began at night, the tree leaves kept us dry for awhile. When the rain drops overburdened the leaves, the water poured down upon us. In our half-sleep we moved over. For minutes, sometimes a half-hour, we were dry. Then there would be another downpour. No matter how many moves we made during the night, we got wetter and wetter. Usually we ended up standing leaning against the tree with the blankets over our head to protect us. We always hoped for a sunny day and the opportunity to dry out.

Many times our food supply did not arrive at all. Sometimes only a small portion reached the kitchen, the rest having been confiscated by the guards for themselves or to sell on the black market. This was the starving time.

We had small streams everywhere around us, but seldom had the strength, time, or the needed permission to go down to the stream and bathe. Our soap bars were long gone without any possibility of new ones being issued. This was a time of degradation.

The group was infected with lice. Our clothing started to shred and become rags. We had boys who came for their morning coffee in freezing weather dressed only in undershorts with a blanket as their only cover and protection from the elements. We were a pitiful bunch! This was a time of death.

I could barely remember that I had once been the young man who felt empowered enough to defy Darazs. I could barely remember that I had once been the young man who cursed the gypsy black marketeer. I could barely remember that I had once dreamed of playing soccer in front of a cheering crowd.

As we deteriorated in body and spirit, the Hungarian soldiers increasingly acted barbarously towards us. They had food, clothing, and shelter. They lived like kings among us. Their anger came from a deeper source than personal hardship. They blamed us for the war, for the separation from their families, and for their hardships. We were used to being blamed for everything. It even began to make sense.

The army engineers assigned to us demanded quotas for everything. To build a small bridge across a stream, hours would be allowed. A tank trap required a quota, independent of its location. A stretch of road demanded a certain deadline. Stone breakers needed to break a certain amount of stones in the allotted time. We were constantly threatened with severe consequences for not fulfilling our quotas.

Ultimately, as threatened, the order came down that every tenth man would be shot for sabotaging the war effort by not reaching our quotas. We were ordered to a large clearing. Soldiers surrounded us, weapons drawn. The soldiers added to our terror by yelling and cursing as they lined up everyone— the kitchen staff, the office staff, the shoemakers, and the sick.

We were ordered to form two lines facing each other. Twenty meters separated the two lines. We had to stand at attention with shoulder touching shoulder. Soldiers with their weapons trained on us were stationed between and behind the two lines. It became deathly quiet.

Corporal Klinovsky, one of the kinder soldiers, was ordered to start the count. Every tenth man was pulled out of the line. The men pulled out looked resigned or terrorized depending on how much of their personality was left. As Klinovsky neared me, I counted in my head, "Twenty-eight, twenty-nine, thirty."

I was the thirtieth man. I would be shot! Klinovsky walked past me and pulled out thirty-one. Number thirty-one started to scream in protest, "I am thirty-one."

Other soldiers rushed in to kick and shove him to the center where each tenth man cowered. It was frightening! It was terrifying! It was unbelievable what men could do to other men! Twenty men-boys facing execution, facing death. Death for not being good-enough slaves. Death for not meeting quotas which made no sense. I should have been one of the twenty, but I was not. My left leg was shaking uncontrollably when, with great fanfare, the commanding officer marched into the center and announced, "Next time, if you do not finish your quota, my order will be carried out!"

So this was just a lesson, a dress rehearsal for madness! No one was executed that day.

A few days later, we were digging tank traps. I was at the bottom of a huge hole digging when Klinovsky looked down. I whispered, "Thank you."

Klinovsky started to scream at me like a madman. He pulled me up and administered one of the worst beatings and cursings I had ever received. After that he pretended that he didn't know me.

- *24* -

A short time after the mock-execution incident, the battalion had to work later than usual to finish our quota. It was dark by the time the soldiers started to march us towards our sleeping area. We were blindly tired. Anger and hatred towards us was building. We were being blamed for the guards having to stay out late to watch us. They blamed us for our rags, our lethargy, and our fatigue from malnutrition. All these conditions meant that we were working less and reaching our quota later in the evening. As revenge for their being out late in order to watch us finish our inhuman quota, the guards organized a terrifying lesson to get us home rapidly.

We were stampeded! With threats, pushes, screams, and gunfire we became a running herd, stampeding in mindless terror. The guards were going to run us to death or else kill whoever did not move fast enough. We ran out of control down a narrow road filled with rocks. Quite a few of us had no shoes. We were running madly in an animal panic while soldiers shot their pistols, shouting and hitting whoever slowed down. We were running for our lives. If one fell, it meant being run over. If one didn't run, it meant death. Death was all around us that evening. We ran sucking air, voiceless screams emanating from our throats as our bleeding feet pounded the rocks.

On the run we crossed a small temporary bridge. A guard stood at the edge of the narrow bridge. One of us with enough guts and plenty of desperation pushed the guard into the water as he fired into the air with his rifle. He screamed for help, adding to the confusion and din of the moment. Now, for a change, the soldiers became frightened and started to scream, "Stop! Halt!"

In the dark and outnumbered, the guards became visibly afraid that we would turn against them. We did not stop. We could not stop. We were now going on pure adrenaline, our rational minds dormant. We saw, on the narrow, half-finished road made of our sweat and tears, headlights coming towards us. Some of us who saw the headlights tried to stop. Others behind yelled to keep going, fearing reprisals.

"Don't stop! Keep running!"

"Stop! Stop! We'll be killed!"

We kept running into the headlights. We ran around the car, surrounding it. We stopped. For some reason the headlights now represented civilization and sanity to our savage minds on this dark uncivilized night.

In the car was a high-ranking general coming for inspection. His jeep could not move because of all of us had encircled it. The general must have been frightened, too, surrounded by blind running madness. Rising from his stationary car, he asked us, "Why are you running? Who is your officer? What is your group?"

He said something to one of the Hungarian guards very harshly. We became quiet and docile again. We walked back to our base camp bitter, exhausted, and spent, not knowing what to expect. We knew that despite the fact that we had suffered every indignity, we had suffered yet one more. The embarrassment of being ruled by pure stampeding fear would steal sleep from all of us forever. The humiliation of behaving like a frightened dumb animal rather than the humans we still tried to be would hound us. The next day we didn't have to come out to work, and our food ration started to improve. But this cattle drive (and the time I stopped being human) will stay with me forever.

- *25* -

As is usual in situations of deprivation, most thoughts were on the basics of life. Our discussions were always about food. We talked about what we liked and how to prepare it. Boys who had never cooked talked about how to fry chicken, cook sausage, and beat eggs. There were arguments among us discussing this subject. We argued about what was the best way to prepare food. We argued about what food tasted the best. It was an absolute necessity to try to get, somewhere, somehow, a little extra food to try to fill our stomachs. Sometimes we could only do it in fantasy.

Before the distribution of the evening meal there was a half an hour of standing in line waiting for our turn. This was the time that the soldiers came in first and ordered the cooks to give them extra rations. We also knew that they stole extra bacon, marmalade, and bread for the black market. We were less than work animals, and our lives meant nothing.

The cooks worked around the kettle with two hundred hungry men standing staring, waiting for their turn. We were always ravenous. When the time for the food distribution came, everybody tried to position himself according to his private ritual. Was it better to be at the front of the line, where the cook might give a little more? Was it better to be at the end, where the food is thicker? We dreamed what it would be like to be a cook and to be around food. No matter how nice or how decent the cooks were, and they were all decent fellows, they had to endure our jealousy. They had a better life.

To be assigned as a cook was like winning the lottery. To be assigned as a tailor or a shoemaker was also very fortunate. The shoemaker's job was to repair shoes, but he never had material. He should have had a few extra pairs for those of us who needed shoes, but there were no spares. The tailors also had no supplies to work with and, therefore, had an easier life.

The prime position was to be a servant to one of the officers. If you served an officer, you had extra food. You didn't have to work except in extremely urgent situations. Ah, the right choice, the right luck! Of two hundred men in the battalion, only ten had choice positions; the rest of us did hard labor.

From our campsite we woke up at dawn to walk miles to reach our work area. The narrow half-finished road wound through the high mountains and forests. Occasionally one of us managed to jump into the forest and become invisible within a second. Friends of the temporary escapee would cover for the one who found temporary refuge in the wilderness.

It was an absolutely unreal feeling to leave the hardships of a forced-labor camp and enter the trees of another world. Animals would wander freely, birds would sing. Though one planned to escape permanently, there was nowhere to go.

It was a wonderful feeling to be in the forest. Somehow you felt that you were free. You felt relaxed, although still hungry and tired. The problem of missing the noon meal was nothing because most importantly you felt human. You had a chance to dream. Most of our dreams were about food, homes, parents, and girlfriends. I always dreamed of soccer. On the battalion's march back to the camp, you had to jump back to your marching group without the soldiers noticing the reentry.

Once when my turn came up I spent a hungry but wonderfully peaceful day in the forest. As I was resting and dreaming about food and in half-sleep, I saw myself playing soccer in a stadium. A smile came into my heart when the huge crowd applauded me and cheered me on and on. Me, Odon Mandel, home from the labor battalion! The oncoming noise of walking feet brought me back to reality.

"No, I am not at home playing soccer. I am here alone hiding behind trees. What is that noise? Who is coming? Are they looking for me? If so, what can I do? If they are soldiers, where am I to hide? Should I run, or should I hide? Am I a rabbit or a man? What would a man do?"

My mind raced for answers. A choice was made. I did not run. It was not a soldier. It was another Jewish boy from another battalion doing the same thing. He was very scared when I stepped out from behind the tree. We started to talk.

I told him my name, and he told me that a Sándor Mandel was in his unit. That was the name of my brother. I had to go with him and try to find my brother. I would try to get back to my own battalion during the night. It was dark when we got to his camp. The Sándor he had mentioned was not my brother. I stayed that night since it was impossible now to return to my unit. The next day I returned to the area where my unit was working. I tried to sneak down from the mountain unnoticed.

This time my luck had run out. I was caught. The guards knew I was missing since they had done head counts that evening, as they did every evening. They locked me in the office overnight to await whatever punishment would be mine.

In the morning a guard took me to the nearby army headquarters. A young, tall, nervous army captain started to swear at me. He called me a "nobody," a "stinking Jew." "My mother, the whore," was mentioned in his rage two or three times in the first minute.

In the course of the interrogation, while the officer wrote his report about my escape attempt, I had to stand at attention in front of a shaky kitchen table which served as for his desk. I brazenly observed my inquisitor. He was not much older than I was. From his use of arcane phrases I could tell that he was a well-educated person. So he was a Hungarian officer with a good education safely positioned behind the front lines! He would be free from anxiety about his immediate well-being. I thought that it would be nice to change positions with him, just for an hour or so. I would also have liked to see his reaction if he were in my place.

He dismissed the guard who had accompanied me and told him to go to the kitchen and eat something. As soon as we were alone the expression on his face became friendlier. He told me to sit down, offered me a cigarette, and begged me to forget and forgive all that had happened.

"How was life in Kecskemét?" he asked. "How is life in the labor battalion?"

I answered as best I could.

A short time later he called back the guard and in a cold official voice said that I would have to stand trial for attempting to escape. He dismissed us, ordering the guard to take me to the kitchen and feed me before escorting me back to my battalion. I couldn't understand which army captain to believe, the one who had cursed me or the one who told me to forget and forgive.

For two delicious days of escape, I would now be on trial for my life. The trial never came about. I never learned why. I had already learned not to try to understand that which no rationality could explain. No explanations were offered to people like me.

- 26 -

On March 19, 1944, the German army occupied Hungary without resistance from the army or the public. Now Hungary became a country strongly supervised by the Germans rather than independently allied to Germany. Now, even more than before, Hungary became a willing tool for the Germans.

A few weeks after the occupation, Jews were rounded up from large cities and small villages. Every Jewish boy sixteen or older was drafted into a labor battalion. If you could not aid fascism that way, you were carried off to the ghetto and then to a death camp. This was the time that Aush and the rest of my family were exterminated.

By May, the five-per-two labor battalion had a new supply of substitute boys from the round-up after the occupation. Two boys from Kecskemét were assigned to our group.

The new boys were so green. One of them, Gyurka, was a short fat boy with a constant grin on his face. He was so inept and clumsy that I could not help but watch out for him. Were we this innocent months ago? They threw away their dirty socks with holes. I picked up the dirty socks and either darned them with yarn or unraveled them for thread. Another set of socks when one was wet could save a foot. Thread for darning could keep out the elements. If they found a rusty nail, the new recruits would overlook this treasure. A nail was a very important part of your life. With a nail you were able to hang your cap, sock, or shoes, and the next morning they would be dry. With a nail you had the rudiments of a home. When the wake-up call came at dark, you knew, if you had a nail on the wall, where your belongings were. With a nail you were civilized. One's dignity hinged on such trappings.

The new recruits offered us a chance to hear the news from home. When I asked them about my parents, they suddenly became very quiet. They talked about everybody else. I said, "How is my father?"

I saw that they couldn't talk to me about him. Finally, I was told by Gyurka that my father had been taken by the Gestapo, together with thirty-five other prominent Jews of Kecskemét. How my father came to be counted as a prominent Jew mystified me. Who reported him to the Gestapo and for what reason?

The boys brought the news that from April fifth on all Jews had to wear a yellow Star of David. Shortly after this decree was enacted, they told us, all the Jews had been forcibly moved to the temporary ghetto. By order of the authorities, the Jews had to turn in their real and personal property. Radios, bicycles, money, and jewelry were all confiscated. I wondered about my family and their safety. The boys said that presently the safest place for a Jew was to be in a labor battalion. How lucky we were!

When the new boys came, their rucksacks were almost full. I had a chance, with their "surplus" shirts, underwear, and razor blades, to go quite often to the forest people to barter for food. I had my own territory and my own families who had become my suppliers. Other boys from other groups had their own group of forest families to barter with. We respected each other's territories.

It was very difficult to predict how the forest people in their scattered huts would receive us. They knew we were Jews. But partisan Jews were a threat to them. They thought we were partisans, and we let them believe this. We asked for food. They gave us little. We realized how little they themselves had.

For a shirt or thread we got a bucket of cooked potatoes. We let it cool and carried it back to camp. For one razor blade we got a half-wheel of homemade sheep's-milk cheese. We felt that we were together with their deep misery of poverty. That made us brothers in suffering. That did not make them brothers in feelings. They were against us.

Two nationalities lived in the forest in these mountains. The lumberjacks were mainly Hungarians and Rumanians. We avoided them. They constantly moved from location to location. They were openly hostile to us. The other group was friendlier. Their job was to produce charcoal. These people cut hardwood into firewood-size pieces. They buried them in pits in the ground and ignited fires in the pits. The wood did not burn, but became a soft coal which was used to heat the irons for housewives. These forest people were always decent.

In June 1944, great news came from passing soldiers. The Americans had occupied Rome. This was a cause for celebrations. The new boys from the labor battalion got together a good assortment of goods to barter. I climbed up early that morning to the furthest hut. These early-morning trips meant that I had to get away before the morning line-up for coffee. In the morning it was still dark, and I had to rush. It was dangerous, but not too difficult to disappear.

I reached the hut of the people with whom I had dealt before and found the door open and nobody home. I lay down on their cot, waiting and dreaming. I knew that in a month or so I would either die from this desperate life or be liberated and live. There was nothing I could do about it. I spent the time dreaming about going home. I would talk and talk. I would eat. I would talk and eat ten pounds of chicken paprika with a gallon of milk. I would have thick slices of my mother's coffee cakes. I would play soccer. I would make the National Team and then celebrate my victories with food. Food! Talk! Soccer! They were good dreams.

When the forest people returned, I tried to talk them into hiding me, but their language was different. It seemed to me that they did not understand or perhaps did not want to understand my pleas. I had no way out. Meantime the boys were waiting for me eagerly for their share of the exchange. It was time to return to them and put my dreams on hold.

Next to the road was a narrow-gauge railroad. It ran the thirty kilometers up and down the mountain. The two cars carried supplies to the soldiers in the mountains. The railway men had seen us working daily. They were aware of our sorry situation. One day they threw us a sack of moldy army bread. The taste was bitter. Someone had the idea of spreading a little toothpaste on the top to disguise the taste of the mold, but we didn't have enough toothpaste. Toothpaste and moldy bread, what a combination; but when one is really hungry, it is food.

This was the time when Friedlander, one of our comrades from Budapest, managed to jump on the train going down towards the city and tried to escape. The gendarmes found him and brought him back in two days. They threatened to court-martial him, but we were so far into the mountains that nothing happened. They built him a shed and shackled his legs. He was able to walk only eight yards with that chain around his leg. Someone always had to bring him food. He was imprisoned, so he didn't work. In a week he got so fat, by our sickly standards, that everyone envied him. He was fat and not doing anything. We were working and starving.

- 27 -

In late summer rumors abounded that the Red Army was mounting an attack through Yugoslavia towards Hungary. If this were true and the attack succeeded, the German army would be trapped in Rumania and in eastern Hungary. To the labor battalion this meant that we had a chance to be captured and then be freed. All signs pointed to the rumors being true. From the distance we could see civilian younger boys assembled in groups with officers who were trying to teach them the rudiments of fighting. We felt this to be proof of the desperation of the Hungarian and German armies and proof of the truth of the rumors.

We heard from the railroad men that these youngsters were being shipped south to Yugoslavia. Hope and jubilation gave us new strength. We began to show open resentment towards our oppressors. We might make it!

Our hope and joy were short-lived. We were assigned to road building. The Hungarians were now in a reckless rush to finish the roads. German army cars soon appeared on the new roads, including the feared S.S. units. We learned the reason for the big rush. The Soviet army had entered Bucharest at the end of August. So while the Soviets marched to liberate us, we still were being worked to death in the panic of the German-Hungarian dilemma.

The overflights of Allied planes increased. More and more good war news came to us, but our plight remained the same. The Rumanian army had joined in support of the Soviet forces. Together with the Soviet armored groups they had crossed the Carpathian Mountains and had entered Hungarian territory. When we heard this news we thought that our time would come shortly. All we had to do was to manage to stay together and stay alive. It was just a matter of time! The Germans started to issue desperate orders.

"Achtung! Achtung!"

Now there was death by hanging for the slightest offense.

Yes! Yes! Yes! *Achtung* for ourselves! Yes, the end of our suffering was near. We just had to hang on and live a little longer.

Our hope was too early, but it gave us a thin ray of confidence shining from total darkness. It allowed us to muster the strength to endure a little longer. It allowed us to feel that there would be an end of this madness very soon. How many times had we felt that the time had come just to be disappointed once again.

The Hungarian soldiers who guarded us began to show fear and tried to cover it by behaving even more brutally towards us. Their desperate behavior was evidence that our suspicious about their imminent defeat were justified. This put us at greater risk. Our hope of the changing situation unleashed our captors' fears. With their fears about defeat came an additional chance of their murdering us.

Our section of the road was finally finished. We abandoned our campsite again and moved south ten kilometers. We had no shelter. We were depleted; the rain and wind were unrelenting. We were terrified that we would die before the war ended.

I recall one unusually clear and warm day. Two of us were sent a few hundred yards ahead of the group on a digging assignment. The section of road where we were working was at a bend so we were invisible to the guards. We put our shovels in the ground and talked while pretending to be working. Such intervals were magic moments of human renewal and interaction. From nowhere, Darazs, the most brutal soldier, came upon us. He had hardly begun to scream and pummel us when another labor battalion came into sight. They could hardly lift their feet. They moved slowly, tediously, painfully. It was our brother battalion, the five-per-three.

All of our attention riveted onto this group. They might bring both the guard and us information which would be essential to survival. They looked worse off than we did, and in fact were. I recognized someone and started to talk to him, and Darazs forgot about us and started to listen to the conversation. Another tragedy averted by luck!

The story of the five-per-three was a horror story. The Hungarian command ran them through areas where live mines were placed. One-third of them died that way—for the Motherland! Among them had been my good friend from Kecskemét, Mr. Moto. Mr. Moto had died being a mine detector.

The five-per-three were exhausted and malnourished. Lajos Berger, my former roommate from Budapest, was among them. It was with him that I'd had the misadventure with the two Czechoslovakian girls. He was now near death. I managed to give him half of my bread ration. He whispered that he had seen the Hungarian gendarmes shoot and kill my brother József during a retreat.

My brother had tried to cross over to the Russians instead of running west with the retreating fascist German and Hungarian armies. So this was the tragic termination of my favorite brother, József. The same brother who used to let me intimidate him on the way to school. Well, his last act was one of courage as he tried to march bravely towards what he felt would be salvation. He had been shot in the back facing liberation.

Lajos and I said goodbye to each other. That was the last time I saw him. He was twenty-two. He looked like he was ninety-two. It was a day of goodbyes.

Our days continued to follow a pattern. Work, a bit of food, work, a bit of food, a little sleep. Work, work, work! It was too cold or too warm. Days followed days with bone-aching, empty-stomach monotony. Our minds and personalities became as numbed as our feet.

A group of us were assigned to work in a German depot. This was a small warehouse hidden in the mountain caves. The Germans were surprisingly efficient, compared to our experience with fellow Hungarians. Even more surprisingly, they were nice to us. They gave us enough to eat. We were never hungry when we worked there. Their officers told us that if somebody was caught stealing he would be shot immediately. Saying this in a calm voice was completely convincing. None of us tried to steal. The Hungarians we worked under tended to terrorize us, threaten us more, and make each moment brutal, but there was more threat and intimidation than murder. The Germans were more humane in their interaction, but murder would be done if there was a problem. There would be no false executions, only real ones.

Our work for the Germans was hard. We were not mistreated. We regained some of our strength. We felt almost human among the Germans. There is a strange irony in the fact that the Germans never mistreated me personally. Yet it was their policies of hatred and genocide that snuffed out all I loved. Although always fair to me, man to man, they had no conflict in putting people to death in hordes. My Christian roommate in Budapest years before had the same dichotomy.

After a few weeks, we were reassigned to the Hungarians to unload the narrow-gauge railroad cars. It entailed loading and unloading ammunition, wagons, and horses. It was bone-crushingly heavy work. We would unload, load, and carry heavy weights on our shoulders the entire time without a break. We had to do it running. We lost the extra pounds we had gained with the Germans in a very short time.

Our senior officer was reassigned. A new lieutenant was assigned to us. In the beginning we watched him very carefully and fearfully. Our lives depended on his goodwill. He was a young man. He just wanted to play soldier with us. Sometimes he let us run up the mountainside, and then had us come down making somersaults. He liked ordering us around. We were his little toy soldiers, his toys.

Other times we would walk to work, get to the spring, and he would let us bathe. It was a very nice gesture from him, but one not necessarily made for humane reasons. He was smart enough to see that the end of the war was approaching, and we were, therefore, seen as possible dangers. We were never sure of his humanity. We could not read his true character. He was young, educated, and behaved decently towards us when he wasn't surrounded by other officers. We could never figure out whether he was simple and humane or expedient and manipulative.

- *28* -

We spent the early part of September on the roads. We received new orders to move west, away from the front—location unknown. In the distance we heard the sound of heavy cannons. Were they German or Russian? Was this death or salvation? Were they thirty or sixty kilometers away?

I still had a winter coat, although threadbare by now, as did my bunkmate, Lajos. Together we had three blankets. We knew we should carry warm clothing. Without it we could not survive another winter. We also knew we could not survive the march carrying them. My friend Lajos and I wordlessly left one blanket and our heavy coats at the camp. We also discarded our spades, against strict orders. We were going now on instinct.

We marched without our supplies, hoping, feeling that the end was near. We made the silent commitment that it would end for us soon one way or another. The surrounding mountains were very high. We didn't know where we were—Poland, Rumania, or Hungary. We never knew where we were, but now it seemed more important, since the end was so near. I suffered from a tremendous toothache. I knew that I didn't want to suffer anymore. My tooth seemed to ache in cadence to our disorderly march to our new destination.

Our group marched in a unruly fashion. We staggered from total exhaustion. We now looked like the groups from other labor battalions which had appeared doomed to us. Days passed without having any food other than our bread rations. We passed a cornfield. I'd had enough. Enough of pain, hardship, and difficulty. All I could think was, "Enough of this toothache!"

Almost automatically and without conscious thought or plan of what I would do or where I would go, I jumped into the cornfield. I landed, knees bent, close to the ground, ready to pounce in attack or ready to run. Within seconds, six others followed.

"Don't move. Stay low. Don't talk."

The used-up, worn-out battalion with its scattered soldiers vanished from our sight as they marched past a curve in the highway. When the dust from their shuffling feet settled, I whistled, indicating that the immediate danger was over. This was not a heroic plan for an escape, but the natural instinct to suffer no more abuse. I jumped because I was cold, hungry, and my tooth ached. Among the escapees were Friedlander, who had once escaped and had been fattened by his imprisonment; two new boys from Kecskemét; and my best friend, Lajos. Because of a feeling that I couldn't last much longer, because of a stupid toothache, because of luck or karma or choosing the left or right path, my fate was sealed.

As the five-per-two left us we stared at one another silently and nodded at the course we had chosen. The five-per-two had been my life for almost two years. Most of us had survived the elements, the starvation, and the brutality because of some humane officers, personal stamina, and enduring relationships.

We learned long after the fate of the rest of our comrades. Weeks after our escape another large group did the same and was liberated by the Soviet army. Others who remained in the labor battalion died in Germany in concentration camps. Now, in the middle of the cornfield, neither we nor they knew what lay ahead. Our destiny was now different than that of the rest of our battalion. Now we were on our own. I had chosen it, for better or for worse, because of a toothache. We waited for awhile in the cornfield. When we felt with reasonable certainty that our guards had not noticed our disappearance, we cautiously and quietly turned from the road and walked towards the mountains.

Now we heard the constant sound of artillery duels which seemed closer. For days we listened to their deadly music as we marched in the forest. Two different sounds were differentiated. One had to be that of the Red Army. Later we learned that this sound was that of the Katyusha, the Soviet missiles which were mounted on trucks. They fired for a few minutes, then were suddenly silent. Then their eerie high-pitched sound began again. Then as quickly as they began there was silence and just the sounds of the forest. What was happening? Were the Soviets being pushed back? Were they succeeding? Later we learned that the Soviets constantly moved these truck-borne missiles since they did not want German artillery ever to mark its location. But to us each silence was an omen and each lull increased our anxiety.

Although we looked on the Soviets as liberators, we knew that we would be the Hungarian enemy to them. They might not make the distinction that our yellow arm band broadcasted. We marched never knowing whose hands we might fall into and what our fate would be. We knew what was behind us. We could not go back. We could only march on, forward. In reality moving forward was moving us further east, further from home. What else could we do? Where else could we go?

We decided to try to join the partisans. We had heard that they were in the mountains. We had to cross a river to get to the mountains. It was a very wild area. A peasant woman showed up and we shouted, "*Partisansky, partisansky.*"

We tried to indicate to her that we wanted to cross the river in order to join the partisans. She showed us a place to cross the river on foot, where it was shallow. If we stepped out of the sandy area, the swift current would take us away.

One of the boys translated her language. We were in the middle of this narrow river, when Gyurka, who was one of the new boys from Kecskemét, let himself be carried off by the current. We formed a human chain and pulled him back. In the middle of the chest-high water, in a second of anger at his risking himself and us, I slapped him on the face. I think that slap made me the unofficial leader of the group.

"Don't try to be a hero! Just follow us," I warned him.

From that slap on I felt total responsibility for him. I eventually returned to Kecskemét with this boy.

We crossed the river with the rucksacks on our heads and our shoes tied around our necks. It was very cold. Snow coated the grass. We found a haystack on the other side of the river, dug holes in it, and buried ourselves inside. It was almost dark. The wind was blowing through the straw. I thought we would be dead by morning, frozen solid like my old raincoat. I awoke at dawn wondering whether I was really alive or dead. When we discovered that we were still alive, we rejoiced and felt nearly free. Although we were aware of our dangerous situation, this was finally a path of our own choosing. Our life, our fate, and our freedom were now in our own hands.

We continued towards the mountains and towards the partisans. We ran into a young peasant lad of fourteen or fifteen. He told us that this region was called Russinsko. In a mixed and heated discussion filled with mutual suspicions, we offered him a blanket if he would guide us towards the partisans. He took the blanket and rolled it with experienced hands. He started to lead us higher and still higher up in the mountains. He was used to it and climbed like a mountain goat. We were not. At sundown we camped in an abandoned hut. We felt unimaginably good eating stale bread around the earthen stove instead of waiting in line for the cooks to ladle out food.

The second day, we continued our forced march higher and higher until we arrived at a plateau surrounded by even higher mountains. In the middle of the plateau was a barn and hut. Around the barn, shepherd dogs guarded the sheep. In front of the hut, the shepherd waited for us. His dogs were barking; the wind was blowing fiercely. Our young guide shook hands with the shepherd as we were surrounded by the fierce-looking dogs. The shepherd invited us into his hut. He gave us goat's milk and cornbread. He told us that if we kept going this way, we would run into German patrols.

We found ourselves between the retreating Germans in front of us and the Hungarian and German armies behind us. Our only luck was that we were up high, away from passable roads.

Our guide, whom we now looked at as a trusted friend, after a brief private talk with the shepherd, advised us to turn back to his village. It is amazing how much we trusted this adolescent. We knew our lives were in his hands. Going down this goat path was not easier at all. There was an air of ominousness due to the proximity of the German and Hungarian armies. Many times the guide scouted ahead and led us in wide circles to avoid communities. A few times he came back within an hour or so. Many times, when he was away for almost a half-day, we felt that he had abandoned us. Once he returned with a robust-looking stranger. The stranger stayed with us briefly. He never tried to talk to us. He talked only to our guide in a low, soft-sounding strange language. Who was he? Our guide pretended that he did not understand our questions about the stranger. Finally we reached the village.

In order to get down to the village from the forest and mountain area, we had to cross a wide-open grassy area used for grazing. We considered what to do. The sun was behind us and would spotlight us. We knew that the villagers would notice us if we left the cover of the forest. We debated and decided to go forward. We were starving, as all our supplies were depleted.

We crossed the grassy area and walked to the first house. We noted the lack of people. From the distance we had seen farmers coming back, but now that we were in the village, not a person was visible. It appeared that nobody had noticed us, but we later found out the whole village had been watching as we crossed the meadow. Our guide told us hurriedly to climb up into the attic of the first house. We were anxious and slept fitfully. It was dark shortly, and then the villagers started to gather in our yard, bringing us bread, cheese, milk, and eggs. This was the first time that people had showed us kindness in a year and a half.

The villagers told us that this village and the others were still patrolled by the militia. Everyone had seen us cross the meadow, but they had to wait until it was safe and dark to meet us. We fell asleep with full stomachs in fresh straw while one of us stood watch.

We spent the next week meandering between small villages and hamlets, looking for the elusive partisans. We went up to the mountains and down again at night, but we never found the partisans. Cautiously one of us walked ahead to look for signs of friendliness or danger. Always out of sight during the daytime, we never found the partisans. The partisans might have been around us, or might not have been. They might have avoided us, not knowing who we were, or they might have left the place for safer environs.

We were sure that the people around us in this relatively narrow area between the river and the mountains had heard about the Jews hiding and wandering in their neighborhood. Sooner or later someone would report us. Not having any other choice, we decided to cross back to the west side, the Hungarian side, of the river. We decided to wait for the old fisherman. His boat was there. We could have untied his boat to go to the other side with it. But we didn't want to do that. So we waited for a day until he returned. We trusted him, for he had tried to guide us into the hands of the partisans and away from danger. When he returned, we told him what had occurred. He opened his small knapsack and shared slabs of bacon and bread. He let us eat silently. He told us he had heard that we were still around and that he wanted to help us. He knew we were afraid of being caught and dying, and that we wanted to run. He said that a long time ago he had been afraid to die also. He said that as a going-away present he would give this advice: "Don't run away. Have faith. Stand up and face whatever life has to offer. Go forward."

His last sentence was said in a quiet, emotionless voice. It seemed like he had lost all of his strength in this sharing of himself. I knew he had finished his speech. I also knew that he was right. He told us to take his boat to the other side and that somehow he would get it back. We waved goodbye from the middle of the river.

Our group ended up on the side of the river where we had begun. We were now on the Hungarian side of the river, facing towards the highway. We faced the east, where we hoped our liberators would come from. As soon as we got to the narrow half-paved side road, Hungarian soldiers caught us.

We were again in Hungarian hands, far from liberation. The soldiers who had captured us contemplated what to do with us. They told us to sit down and wait. Their world was in an upheaval, and they had more to deal with than just us. So we sat side by side with our captors, all Hungarians, with very different visions of what we wished to happen next.

- *29* -

As we were being detained, a group of soldiers herding hundreds of cows came into view. The officer in charge of the cows stopped and questioned our guards. No one knew what to do. Everyone was nervous. The artillery sounded nearer. The war was coming in our direction. The officer in charge of the herd assigned all of us, the prisoners and the guards, to help his unit herd the cattle westward. Not having any choice we became cowboys for the army. The destination of the cattle drive was the Hungarian city of Nagyszöllös. Being a cowboy was much better than being a member of the labor battalion. Being a cowboy was much better than being a stampeded cow.

At night we slept in tents. We had warm food and plenty of milk. A few days later the cows, the soldiers, and the Jewish cowboys arrived in Nagyszöllös. Friedlander, our escape artist, again disappeared without a hint to anyone about his plan. An hour or two passed, and he reappeared. He went up to the officer in charge of us and the cows. After saluting in a perfect military fashion, he withdrew from his pocket a document and handed it to the officer. We watched him in great wonder. He saluted again and ordered us to line up. He executed a soldierly about-face and with marching stride walked to our group. He then ordered us to march. We left in formation, heading west.

When we were out of the city Friedlander told us that he had gone to the military center and reported to an officer. He stated that he had delivered the cows as ordered and now needed open orders to return to our original group. The military was in chaos, and the officer, not knowing what to do with us or the cows, issued an open order for Friedlander to lead us to our group. So we had our document. We were no longer prisoners or escapees. We were legal.

The problem was that we didn't know where to go. We wanted to wait for the Russians. We wanted to be liberated by them, but we had to march westerly, away from them. We marched in single file on the edge of the road, leaving room in the center for the retreating unorganized army. They were rushing towards the west. We did not rush.

We were resting at a roadside well when we ran into some of the army engineers who had worked us so mercilessly in the past. Now that the tide of war had changed, they had a "business proposition" for us. They would guide us through the dangers of the retreating Hungarian army; we would act as their "prisoners" during that period. We would be protected, and in return they would have "prisoners" and, therefore, an alibi for not being with their unit. They did not want to be in the fighting unit and were afraid being captured by the Red Army. This way both sides would get safe passage. They were part-deserters, and we were part-escapees. Together we could forge an alliance based only on necessity.

We seemed to need each other for the moment; and, therefore, a wobbly union was formed. As long as they needed us, they were civil to us. Within two days we began to hear their old antisemitic remarks. We left them immediately. Our freedom had allowed that much. So much for business propositions made for expediency only.

While we were with these Jew-hating engineers we got encouraging war news. We heard that the Soviet army was advancing rapidly from Yugoslavia northerly towards southern Hungary. This was the most encouraging news we had heard so far, The Soviet southern front was only a few hundred kilometers west of our present locality. We listened for the sound of the advancing Red Army's artillery. Where were they? How long would we have to wait? At night, when we tried to sleep in an abandoned hut, we fell into a gloomy mood. With the absolute quiet, we never knew what our future held.

One night, sleeping fitfully and hungry, we woke to the music of the Soviet Katyusha. I knew at that moment that the war would be over soon. This knowing was different than the hoping, the longing, and the wishing which I had done for years. I just knew. The artillery duel began. For five days the ground trembled, and we felt as if Judgment Day had arrived. All the heavy gunfire was not more than a few kilometers from our hiding place. At night it was quiet, and at dawn the duel began anew. On the fifth day it was quiet. Were the Russians coming? Had the Russians been defeated? We didn't know the answers to any of these questions, and yet our lives depended on them.

We spent many days between villages in abandoned fields. There we picked vegetables and potatoes, and cooked them in the open. At one farmhouse the family ran away when we arrived. I'm not sure what they were afraid of or what they thought of us. Their flight caused us fear because they might report us to the authorities. We had to move on. The situation of living like this was becoming more desperate.

We decided to return to the city of Nagyszöllös. We seemed to be constantly going around in larger and larger circles, leading nowhere. Reaching the edge of the city, we climbed into an attic of an abandoned house. We pulled up the stepladder and looked out through a small window.

Before the Jewish tragedy, the city had a large Jewish community. It was famous for its rabbis and Chassidic community. Now seven lone Jews were hiding in an attic. None of us dared to speculate on the others' fate.

It was early October. From our vantage point we saw abandoned houses with their doors and windows boarded. Their yards and the little orchards attached to the homes were unattended. The grapes were not harvested and the fruit on the fruit trees was unpicked. There were no Jewish owners of these orchards anymore. Some of the Christian Hungarian owners, who had usurped their neighbors' lands, had also fled, fearing reprisals from the approaching Russians.

During the first two days one of us at a time stole out to the orchard to pick some grapes and fruit. It would not be enough to sustain us. Not having any other choices we had to forage or beg for food. We recognized the danger to us. We only left our hiding place when it was absolutely necessary. We would never go out at the same time of the day or night, nor would we forage or beg at the same locations. At night we entered the unoccupied house below our attic. There we could do some cooking. We were cut off from the world. We could not ascertain the direction the war was taking.

There came a day when we realized that the city had been abandoned by the Hungarian and German armies. From our vantage point we saw a few Rumanian jeeps enter the city. This military group gathered around the well in the yard below our attic. As we watched from our attic, we noticed soldiers among the Rumanians who wore a uniform we did not recognize. We heard someone speak to the unrecognized soldiers in broken English. We knew then that these were either British or American flyers.

We left the attic, and with the Rumanian guns trained on us, tried to explain who we were. But they were in a hurry, or they did not understand, or they had other more pressing business and left almost immediately. We climbed again into our attic.

Later Hungarian soldiers reentered the city. This time they came back in strength. We saw and heard soldiers in the city reveling, drunk. This was the time when Horthy, the leader of Hungary, severed ties with the Germans. He wished to ally with the West. It was October 15, 1944. Everyone was in a state of limbo. No one knew who their alliance was to or what their future would be, except the Jews. We knew that our alliance was with our liberators.

The next day Hungarian soldiers set up machine guns. We saw them switch from the temporary alliance with the Allies and swear undying loyalty to the new leaders of Hungary. These leaders were fascistic and more committed to the Germans than before. Life now became even more dangerous as people made their last stand.

- *30* -

It was still dark when, early the next morning, we came down from the attic that had hidden us for days. We had to move towards freedom. We could not remain immobilized and imprisoned any longer. We headed again towards the mountains. The sounds of the Russian artillery came closer.

Around a bend in the road, we were caught by the gendarmes. They were even more fascistic and brutal than the army. József, my brother, had been shot by this barbaric outfit when he had tried to escape. We were ordered to sit in a group with other escapees. Perhaps because I knew my brother's fate, or perhaps by instinct, I knew we had to get away. We had to do it now, and quickly. There were only two gendarmes. One was around the bend in the road looking for more "bandits" like us. The other was thirty yards away. I got up and started walking. My six "bandit" partners followed me. No one stopped us. The lone gendarme did not see us, or maybe he looked the other way. Was this another choice that saved our lives?

For about a week we hid, subsisting on nuts, plums, and grapes from unharvested trees. Sometimes there was food in the abandoned farms. We did not starve. We got a little stronger.

We found abandoned weapons in the fields. Soldiers had discarded them and were hiding in the area or trying to merge anonymously with the citizenry. We armed ourselves. We had pistols and rifles. What could seven men do, even if armed? It meant we would not be caught, or robbed, or made into slaves again. It meant that we were men again.

We arrived at a little village called Nagybegany. We came across an old woman, the village's midwife, who was willing to hide us. Cornstalks had been set up in her yard to dry out. She put three of us in this cornstalk tent and four of us in her small attic, which faced the small railway station. We spent a very desperate two days there in hiding. We wondered if we had miscalculated the distance of the Russian artillery sounds. The hours passed very slowly, filled with anxiety due to our not knowing what might happen in the next minute. During the second night I told Lajos that I had to go scout the area. The inactivity and my active imagination made rest impossible. Lajos joined me. We left the shelter together and started to circle the village in total darkness. In the distance we observed a huge fireball lighting the sky.

"Perhaps another warehouse torched by the Nazis," Lajos said.

"Listen! Listen!"

The light breeze carried to us the sound of Jew's harps. The melody was strange—both peaceful and frightening at the same time. Our hearts started to pump faster.

"They're here. The Russians are here."

We turned back to share the news with our friends. At dawn the sound of machine-gun fire reached our hiding place. We ran to the window and saw the little railway station blow up; we knew that rescue had come.

Lajos and I decided to get out again and scout the railway area. We moved slowly on our hands and knees. We heard bullets whistle past us, and were caught in a crossfire between the Hungarians and the Soviets. Danger seemed to surround us here.

We noticed two half-tracks and some motorbikes abandoned along the side of the highway. We saw Hungarian soldiers running towards their vehicles, holding chickens and pigs they had appropriated from the farm. During this crossfire incident, I got hit by shrapnel in my shoulder. I hardly noticed the impact or the pain. It wasn't serious. To this day I carry as a reminder of my liberation the mark of that small piece of metal in my left shoulder.

We returned to the attic and told our group what we had witnessed. We picked up the weapons from the attic and marched as a unit towards the village center. We were anxious, not knowing what was awaiting us there. We decided to carry our guns, remembering that this was how my brother had been shot, by attempting to cross over to the Russian side. We felt that the Russians would not mistake us for Hungarian soldiers as we looked more like prisoners and partisans than anything else. Further, we felt that they would instinctively know our hearts. Our minds were set.

On the way to the village center, a very hysterical woman ran towards us screaming, "The Russians are here!"

We found out from her that six Soviet soldiers had appeared in front of her on her farm. They had asked questions which she didn't understand. To her the Russians brought realistic fear. For us there was only hopeful anticipation.

The seven of us, with army hats and our yellow armbands, and with the rifles on our shoulders, marched into the village square to greet the Soviet forces. We stopped across the road in precise linear order in front of the church, hoping to be the first to greet the Russians.

Across from our line, the elders of the village had set up a table with a lace tablecloth. Upon the tablecloth was a loaf of bread, salt, and wine set out to greet the Russians. What a scene this was! Villagers, terrified of the Russians, stood ready in formal greeting. Seven starved, ragged, yellow-armbanded Jews stood in front of a church anticipating the dream that had kept them alive for two years.

A lone Russian soldier on horeback approached the church. He stopped in front of us. From our vantage point, looking up into his face, this silent soldier looked majestically tall. As he slowly marched his horse past us, he removed the army hats one by one from our heads and threw them on the ground. He then demonstrated, in sign language that we were to throw our weapons down. It is impossible to describe the emotions of this scene. The war was finally over for us after so many years. We had met the liberators finally. The emotions were of disbelief and joy that finally seven of us from the five-per-two labor battalion had survived and would be free. Our hearts had been torn apart by our own country which had betrayed us, and we were now welcoming another country's liberators to free us.

After the moment with our lone liberator on horseback, the Russians came in horsedrawn wagons, half-drunk. They appeared so disorganized. They were a conglomeration of women and men soldiers, old soldiers and young ones. What a contrast this was to the German troops I had seen and feared in my youth. These soldiers entered drunkenly singing. The German soldiers, who had looked like gods in my youth, had brought genocide. These soldiers, the first Russians I had ever seen, in their disheveled, inebriated state brought freedom for so many of us. They were our liberators. We prayed that the problem of being Jewish had ended. We knew we were not home yet, but were alive and human again. We were not healthy, but we were free.

The Russians stopped at the makeshift greeting table set by the elders at the center of the road. They took the bread and the wine, and they went quickly on their way. The ceremony, long awaited and anticipated and dreamed of in the cold nights sleeping in the barracks, took less than five minutes. The village was liberated and occupied in a matter of hours. In these few hours everything for me had changed. Now I could try to get home and find my family.

The next hours testified to our being free and there being a new order. The village elder approached us and politely invited us to his house. Other older, respected people came along with us. They wanted us to witness the fact that they harbored no Hungarian and German soldiers. They wanted us to assure the Russians that they were friendly towards them. The villagers knew that we were more trustworthy in Russian eyes than they were. We were now a valuable commodity. They asked the first Russian officer who noticed them to issue instructions. The villagers had no idea what was allowed or not.

There were shouts and shooting in the street. Two Cossacks on horseback were turning the city into chaos. The reason for all the generosity of the village elders towards us was obviously to prevent such plunder and rape. They had not fundamentally changed their attitude about us Jews, but they thought we might defend them from Russian atrocities. We did not want to save them from anything. Who had stood up for us? Who had been our go-between?

Some higher-ranking Russian officers came to the village office which now housed us and the village elders. One of the

Soviet officers spoke to us in broken German, asking who we were. I explained that we were Jewish survivors of the labor battalion. Did the officer understand me? Slowly the village office emptied. The officers left.

The village elders, not knowing their fate, walked home. The village was liberated and terrified. The Russian army had stopped for only a few hours in this small village off the main road. They then continued their march towards the West. In the process they had freed seven men with yellow armbands.

- *31* -

After the first Soviet troops left the village, we walked back to the brave midwife's house. We were without our yellow arm-bands, weapons, and hats. We did not question her motives. We just had good feelings about her. She had helped us during a dangerous time for her, and she took risks doing so. What if the Soviet offensive had been contained? What would have happened to her? She had acted humanly towards us, and we accepted it at face value.

She greeted us with a smile and told us about an abandoned house where a fascist policeman, who had fled to the west, had lived. As our first act of liberation, we broke into his house. I took a beautiful pair of shoes and a winter coat. The shoes were two sizes larger than my need, but they were heaven-sent. We also found in the house pictures of Hitler and his Hungarian ally, Szálasi.

We returned with our booty and found that the midwife had prepared boiling water for us in an outdoor kettle. In the outside trough we had a real bath with plenty of soap. How feeble-looking we were, standing naked in front of the trough, washing each other's backs. We were laughing over each other's boniness, while curious neighbors watched the seven naked Jews through the openings in the fence. As a thank-you to her and her generosity, we returned at night to the policeman's house and took every object of his that could be carried and brought them to her home.

That night we slept well as freed men. We were clean and had some clothes. After breakfast we said goodbye to the midwife and began our leisurely walk towards the nearest city, Beregszasz.

We left the village with our heads held high, our spirits mended, and fearless. We had entered as frightened escaped Jewish slaves. Now we looked forward to our first day of freedom. Maybe now we would have the "freedom from fear" that Roosevelt had written and sent to us by airplane. People of the village were in the street. They were standing in small groups talking. We could not tell whether they were relieved that the war was over or whether they were waiting for the triumphant return of the Hungarian army.

It was a beautiful day, and the sun shone. There was a sense that something immense and historic was occurring. At we passed people they would stop talking and look at us in an inexplicable way. Some of them turned away. Others looked at the ground or their shoes. Perhaps we reminded them of their own Jews from their own village. Some stopped and asked questions:

"Where are you from? What have you seen?"

Some offered us a glass of wine. Some inquired if we were hungry. Mostly they just wanted to talk. They talked about the faith of the Jews, and they talked about the Soviet soldiers. They needed our reassurance.

"They are human, too. They won't hurt us, will they?"

They talked about having suffered from the Germans. Here and there some would talk about the Hungarian soldiers. Others would say, "Don't say such a thing about our soldiers. The Germans did the looting and plundering, not our soldiers."

We observed and watched them as they tried to sort our their own history in order to predict their own future. But part of our being free was now being able to be angry at these people who had turned their backs on us. We listened and observed and did not care about their future.

We were stopped again. This time by a group with other questions.

"Is it true that Jews were made slaves? Is it true that Jews were put to death? Is it true that Germans made Jews into human mine detectors?"

"Oh, yes, all true. And, dear people, not just the Germans. It was your Hungarian sons and husbands that perpetrated slavery on a people also."

"No," They answered, "Not true. Everyone suffered. Our soldiers suffered. We all suffered like the Jews."

Again and again. We watched them with bitterness in our hearts and continued our slow walk.

No one knew what was happening. There was an air of anticipation. Everyone knew that there were Hungarian soldiers hiding in the neighborhood around the village, but the sense was that the Germans and Hungarian armies far away. The war was now behind us.

On the road to Beregszasz, an older fellow approached us. He was a Gentile refugee fleeing from the city we were marching towards. He had followed the German retreat out of the city and had now turned back towards home. He joined us in our unhurried walk and started to talk to whoever would listen.

"I was an idiot. I fell for the German propaganda."

I wasn't sure which part of the propaganda he was alluding to. Had he believed that the Germans were winning the war and followed them, thinking this would be his salvation? Or had he believed that the Jews were to be blamed for everything, and now he had to deal with us? Had he believed in German secret weaponry and German invincibility?

After a while, in a shy, frightened voice he explained his real dilemma. "I have two acres of Jewish land with a small house on it. What do you think? Can I keep them? Do you think the owners will return?"

I was now being asked to be a judge. A Jewish judge, no less. He wanted me to absolve him from quilt and let him keep the land he had confiscated from a Jewish neighbor. I told him to go to hell, but I knew also that my problem had just begun in earnest. I had survived, but what about my family? Had someone confiscated our home? Is someone in Kecskemét praying that we will not return so that our home will remain in his hands? Well, this Mandel is returning to take back what is his!

The city of Beregszasz was six kilometers away. We wanted to rest, sleep in a bed, and eat a decent meal. For these simple needs we needed a house to stay in for all seven of us.

We searched for signs of any Jewish life. There were none. Before the war, this had been a city in which a flourishing Jewish population had lived. Wealthy and poor, observant and secular, educated and not, the Jews had lived together in harmony. We walked up to a well-kept house. On its doorframe was a color change where the mezuzah had been. The mezuzah was a centuries-old sign of a Jewish home. Now we seven stood focused on the place where the mezuzah had been. Our eyes were on the doorframe, but our hearts were hundred of kilometers away. My thoughts were on a small house in Kecskemét. I shook off these thoughts, which were an unbearable burden on my body and soul and knocked on the door. A man answered, opening the door halfway. Through the half-opened door, I saw the big, nicely kept yard.

"We need shelter."

"Nothing is available here."

"Who lived in this house before you moved in?"

I couldn't help but make this strong retort. At the same second I pulled the right side of my coat open. On my belt I still had the holster which I was now using as an accessory pocket. The man became rightly afraid that I was threatening him. I was in no joking frame of mind. I was free now and here to reclaim what was mine or my brothers'. He reluctantly let us in. One section of the house was furnished, but not in use. We occupied it.

The metal shrapnel in my shoulder started to become infected. I had chills, and then I became feverish. I became septic and violently sick. My friends put triple blankets on me, but I could not stop shivering. I became delirious. I thought I was dying. Once I opened my eyes and listened to my friends whispering. I sat up in bed and told my friends, "Don't plan my funeral yet. I've been through too much to die now!"

A Russian medic removed the piece of shrapnel. I recovered in a day or two. My fate was to continue and endure.

The family who occupied this former Jewish house had a beautiful sixteen-year-old girl. Four other men from the labor battalion joined us, having been liberated; one of them Gyuri Berger. She fell in love with Gyuri. It was amazing to watch a boy and a girl fall in love. It was such a natural thing that we had been deprived of. I had not been thinking about girls. A potato was much more important. The subject of girls never came up in the labor camp. We thought about our loved ones, but not with the sexual luxury that normal young men in normal situations have. I watched Gyuri and his girlfriend affirm normalcy under our watchful eyes.

Gradually other survivors reached the city of Beregszasz. We learned of their arrival within hours from the locals. Most were in worse condition than we were. They tottered hesitantly on the streets, looking for a sign of Jewish life just as we had done days before. They arrived exhausted and demoralized, not knowing what to expect. We listened to each other's stories. We were all hungry to hear some news about family and friends.

Within the week perhaps nine other Jewish survivors had arrived in the city. Among them was a very religious boy of nineteen. This city was his home. He was the first Jewish returnee from this city. He persuaded us to gather some firewood and heat up the water for the ritual bath, or mikveh, to consecrate himself. He wanted to have a Friday-night service in his hometown.

The water was steaming hot. We were all soaking our emaciated and wasted bodies while talking to each other through the steam. Suddenly the door opened. The draft pulled the steam out. In the entrance stood a Soviet officer with two soldiers who trained their machine guns on us. Some of the neighbors must have reported our gathering. The soldiers entered.

"Who are you? Do you have a permit for a meeting? Do you have weapons?"

"We are survivors of the Jewish labor battalion. No, we do not have a permit to take a ritual bath. No, we do not have weapons."

We must have looked comical with our skinny bodies halfway out of the water. After a few more official questions the soldiers put their weapons down and the officer asked our permission to join us in the water. It was granted. Here we bathed—a group of ten Bar Mitzvahed men who constituted a minimal religious quorum and three Soviets. As we bathed we talked. I told the Soviets that in Kecskemét Jews had not been allowed to walk on the main street on Sundays because the right side of the street was for officers and their families and the left side was for soldiers and their families. The officer listed and then stated that from now we would be free to go with our family and girlfriends on either side of the street. We all nodded solemnly, each silently wondering whether we would ever see our families or our girlfriends again.

After a few minutes of absolute quiet, the local religious boy asked if he could help the Soviets move their horses from the synagogue so he could have a Jewish service. Everyone got quiet after this request. The Soviets appeared to visualize what might be happening in their own ruined homeland.

Two high-ranking Soviet officers ordered us in for questioning. The older officer asked us questions in fluent Hungarian. I stood at attention and tried to answer the best I could. I wanted to know him better, this man who was part of my freedom. I wanted to ask him where he had learned Hungarian. I asked instead when we could go home.

"Soon," he answered.

He asked about the labor battalion. He asked why we had endured the slavery of the battalion without rebellion and hadn't risen up to fight the Hungarians and the Germans. I didn't know how to answer. How could I explain to him what it means to be treated as a beast of burden? How could I explain to him that you cannot fight without weapons when you are starving and brutalized? How could I explain that you cannot fight without health? How could I explain that only when one feels human can one demand human treatment? My explanations fell short.

"If you didn't fight them, then you and your group worked for the Germans and their Hungarian allies."

I looked at my friends, but none of us had an answer. We could not explain our predicament to this officer even though he spoke our language. How could I explain that our greatest act of protest was bearing witness and staying alive. How could I explain that if I remained a person and did not become an animal I won? How could I explain to a victor what it was to be a captive and a slave?

I have pondered my answers to this officer for decades. How can I explain the condition of mind and body that was perpetrated on millions? Forty years later I took fifteen American boys to Hungary to play soccer. After telling them a few incidents about the labor battalion, they asked me the same questions: "How did it happen? Why didn't you fight back? Why did you let it happen to you when there were more of you?"

I had the voice and words to try to explain to these boys what I could not to the Russian commander. After my attempt at explanation, most of the boys stayed near me and managed to touch my shoulder or lean against me. Maybe their youth put them nearer to my feelings of helplessness than a commander of a victorious army. Maybe forty years of thinking had given me better words. Maybe time and terrorists and hostages had given everyone some thoughts.

We spent about a week in this house, resting, eating, and feeling better and better about ourselves. We had begun to feel and look like men in their youth again. The Soviet occupation was strong, and with that strength was risks. They were looking for German and Hungarian soldiers disguised in civilian clothing. They needed workers. They desired women. Being a Jew might make little difference if a Russian was ordered to pick up civilian for their labor needs. A few Jewish boys ended up on trains going to the Soviet mines. I was stopped twice, but I managed to show self-confidence and an image that I was very important and could not be stopped. All the roadblocks were haphazard, and so much depended on luck. Whether the solider was in good spirits or angry or homesick could mean the difference in your fate. It also depended on your willingness to argue or resist him or to find the right way to pacify him. The right path was taken by me, since I was never detained for long.

Our group from the labor battalion needed to get home. Friedlander got us a free pass in three languages that would allow us to leave the city and try to get back to our home. This paper was issued by a Jewish clerk without formal authorization. He took it upon himself to get us home.

We didn't know which way to go. Should we turn west, which was the shortest distance home? Should we go south towards Rumania, which was the safest way home? We could not find an unanimous answer, so we spent a few days in the city debating the merits of each plan. These choices were not casual, as the wrong choice could put one in Germany and a death camp. Many Jews were liberated only to be found by Germans and killed.

The same evening there was a knock on our door. A pale, frightened man entered. He introduced himself as a Jewish merchant from Munkács. He had been hidden in a cellar throughout the war years by a village woman. He was afraid to completely trust the woman when she told him that it was finally safe. He came to us for confirmation. We advised him to go and kiss the lady who had saved him and head home.

We had one more reason for delaying the setting of our time of leaving and our direction. We were not strong or healthy enough. I had my shoulder problem; others had injured feet. Almost all of us had abscesses. So we waited and observed the people around us.We waited for the right moment.

- *32* -

*T*he family that occupied the former Jewish house where we now were staying started to invite the Russian officers in. Many villagers hoped that by inviting in officers they would be saved grief during the occupation. The officers came and got drunk. Sometimes they left peacefully and sometimes not. We were sure that weeks previously the same family had entertained the Germans with the same eagerness. The Hungarians thought that peace of mind could be bought with liquor. Now that General Malinovsky's Soviet army was in their city, many would pound their chests with great vigor in the middle of drinking bouts with the Russians, declaring their newly held antifascist leanings. Their beliefs shifted with the wind.

Neighbors started to tell us about other neighbors.

"He was a member of the Arrow Cross."

"She was a thief."

"He was a black marketeer."

We bided our time. We kept quiet. We enjoyed their discomfort. We were being courted with the same expediency that Russians were given free rein to homes and liquor. We would not absolve anyone. Some crimes cannot be absolved. Judgment Day would come to the perpetrators. We were now sure of that.

Daily we saw a group of Hungarian and German prisoners in a poor state of health being led towards the edge of the city. They were guarded by a few Russian soldiers. We were not unhappy about this. The sight became an everyday occurrence. It made us feel vindicated to see them in our former servile position.

One day among the prisoners I noticed Klinovsky, the soldier who had pulled out number thirty-one instead of me, number thirty, for execution. He was visibly exhausted, dirty, and unshaven. I followed the prisoners to their campsite a few kilometers outside the city center.

I still had Aranka's watch in my pocket. This was the watch I had risked myself for by trying to hide it from our guards' robbery. With a little sign language and a bit of bargaining, the guards let Klinovsky go free in exchange for Aranka's watch. I thought back to the time of risk-taking when I had hidden her watch. I felt satisfied that it had been worth the risk. I was glad for the exchange, as was Klinovsky and the Russian soldier. I was sure Aranka would have also agreed. Her gift of love to me became a gift of life for another. It was not without danger for me, since I was negotiating the fate of a sworn enemy of the Russians and therefore potentially condemning myself. But this was the man who had tried to save me from execution. He deserved the risk.

I took Klinovsky to our place. I began to talk with him about what had transpired between the two of us. He was finally able to tell me his side of that frightful incident. The minute he had exerted his choice in not selecting me, his conscience had been sent reeling by his potentially murderous act. He could isolate himself from blame when he selected those who were condemned to be executed because of their order in line; since he, too, felt himself a prisoner at someone else's bidding. When he stepped out of that role to consciously save me, he was in fact, at that point, committing murder in choosing another. He could not face me or himself after that.

Our group of seven started to become restless. We decided that the time to leave was now and decided on our direction. We left westward towards Szolnok, a city on the river Tisza. This should have been the fastest way home. Szolnok was the place where I had turned down the offer to change my name to a Gentile one in order to play soccer on the Division I team. I retold the story as we marched towards Szolnok, overemphasizing my soccer skills. Debating whether I had done the right thing in refusing the offer took even more time. Talking about soccer took our minds off what might be waiting for us when we managed to get home. This became our consuming thought by day and our nightmare at night. Any distraction was essential to pass the hours, which were otherwise filled with anxiety and anticipation.

The roads leading west were jammed with tanks, trucks, and wagons moving the Soviet troops to their new staging area further west. There were constant air raids. Patrols started to check our papers constantly. It seemed to us that the shortest way towards Kecskemét was not the safest. A stranger stopped us.

"Don't continue this way."

He disappeared before we could question him. After a short meeting we decided to turn south towards Rumania and from there, if the situation permitted, to cross northwest towards Kecskemét.

Friedlander, who was from Budapest, decided to take the shortest route home, which was west via Szolnok, across the Tisza River. He left us there. He got home in 1947, a broken man. He, who had escaped so many times and had used his ingenuity to get us papers when none were to be had, was made a Soviet prisoner and put into a Soviet prisoner-of-war camp. He had suffered so much, only to exchange the country of his labor battalion. But he survived.

The remaining six of us started to walk village by village towards Rumania proper. As we progressed slowly we surveyed the war damage, which in some places were substantial. Besides the expected war damage we were unprepared to witness the Russian soldiers looting and raping. While repulsed by the brutality, it was not entirely undesirable to us. We wanted vengeance on the Hungarians. We still did not know what condition our home and our families were in. Our need for vengeance demonstrated both how brutally we had been treated and our consciously denied knowledge of the fate of our loved ones. In other times and situations we would have been horrified, but limping home without any news of our families, we were satisfied that crimes were now being perpetrated on the criminals.

Walking home at our own pace was almost like a daily pleasure walk. We did not plan our route, we just walked towards home. We began to enjoy life's small pleasures. We were getting back to reexperiencing life without fear. On the second day of our stroll a group of Rumanian soldiers stopped us and asked for documents. The Rumanians were very poorly fed and dressed. They didn't look very soldierly. They asked us to put down our meager belongings: a piece of soap, socks, blanket, almost nothing. They robbed us of part of our belongings. The Rumanian soldiers were not too threatening. It was almost like a stroke of bad luck rather than the terror of our previous experiences.

We continued walking. A half-day later, the same platoon of Rumanian soldiers stopped us again. They, or we, must have made a large circle. We went through the same routine. They asked for official papers, we were ordered to put down our belongings, and they started to take a piece of clothing here or another piece of soap there. The boys looked at me. We were upset and angry now. Enough was enough! We were free men now. I started to curse. All six of us were united in our anger and contempt. The soldiers aimed their rifles at us. I'm not sure if the rifles were loaded. Even though they didn't understand the words I used, they understood my fury. They showed us how little they had. They gave us back half of our own goods and walked away.

We stopped at a nearby farmhouse for food and water. We talked to the Hungarian-speaking farmer. He gave us food, and he was talkative. We listened for a bit. He told us about the Hungarian army's retreat. The retreating troops had stolen and robbed whatever they could put their hands on.

We also became talkative and told him our little adventure with the Rumanian patrol. The farmer started to laugh. He told us that the passengers on the daily train to Nagyvarad were robbed by Russian soldiers every day. The last train had arrived at Nagyvarad with two hundred passengers almost naked. We all laughed at this story, but inside I was seething. I remembered standing in the rain naked, humiliated by Hungarian soldiers. I remembered the shame I felt at being powerless. I remembered the humiliation. What did I care if a few passengers suffered just a fraction of what I had suffered?

We slept in his barn that night. When the farmer woke up, I am sure he was surprised at our early leaving and the absence of a basket of eggs and a whole ham which we took as souvenirs. Maybe my anger would stop his laughter!

After five days walking, we arrived at the first large city which had had a large Jewish population in the past. This was the city of Nagyvarad. Upon entering the city I could not help thinking about a very famous soccer player who had come to Budapest from this city. We argued about his name. I didn't remember his original name, but insisted then, as I do now, that his soccer name was Sarvari. We spent much of our days like this. We remembered and argued about the unimportant. Anything was fodder to talk over and to pass the time as we crept nearer and nearer home. I must have begun my healing process to be thinking of soccer instead of potatoes.

We found shelter in Nagyvarad with a single woman. She gave us shelter only because she feared us less than she feared the Russians. She had a two-room little house. We bunked down in the kitchen, and she went into the bedroom.

Around midnight two Russian soldiers came. They saw us lying on the kitchen floor. We pretended that we were asleep and didn't pay attention to what they were doing. They brought out the woman from the bedroom, and brought out the mattress and lay the mattress on top of us. One of them raped the woman on top of us while we were pretending to be asleep, while the other soldier kept a gun leveled on us. They then reversed roles.

We left in the morning. The woman's-sewing machine drawer was open and we stole her scissors. We weren't quite human then. We were filled with anger and hate. We had a complete unresponsiveness to her suffering. She was home alive. She had watched while our families and neighbors had been taken away. She had been a silent witness to our people's degradation and was impassive. Now we were a witness to her degradation, and the scissors was our souvenir of that. When we saw these atrocities, it felt like a reciprocation for whatever we feared had happened to our mothers and sisters. In some ways it helped give us back the power which we had lost in the labor battalion.

- *33* -

It was late November when we entered Rumania. Rumania had been a reluctant Nazi auxiliary. We had been told that the Jews had been left intact in their Rumanian cities. In 1944 the Rumanian army changed sides and joined the Allies in their effort to defeat the Nazis. Slowly walking towards the nearest city, Arad, the signs of war and destructiveness slowly vanished from sight.

The weather, with the icy rain and windy nights, slowed our progress. There was a dampening of our eagerness to progress as well as the strongest urge to get home. We were all sick, so moved slowly. When a beautiful sunny day occurred we rested and celebrated the sun.

Despite the leisurely pace and less dangerous aspect of the journey, the nights were terrible. For weeks I slept only a few hours. Others were having the same problems. We lay quietly, all pretending to be asleep. Our nightmares kept us awake. Lajos told me in a whisper one sleepless night that he was afraid to fall asleep again. Now he was afraid of dying. When we were in the camp, we had realized that the fear of dying was not too difficult to take. Death was more welcome there. Now, knowing that those who were close to us might have had a worst fate than ours subjected us to the worst pain. We were afraid of the night and afraid of the truth.

When we arrived in Arad, the first Rumanian city, we found the Jewish population untouched. The rumors had been true, and we were now full of hope. We arrived in a paradise. Well, almost paradise. On entering the city a Russian soldier so admired my shoes that he stole them at pistol point! I thought, "Easy come, easy go."

But it was cold. I could not give up my precious shoes that easily.

I followed the soldier barefoot for awhile. He went to a marketplace to sell my shoes. I found a Jewish Russian officer walking by and in mixed Yiddish and sign language, pointing to my feet, tried to explain my plight. He went after the soldier and ordered him to return my shoes. Then the officer told me to disappear, warning me that the soldier would retaliate if he found me again.

We walked to the railway station. On the platform was the Jewish committee waiting for a train of returning Jews to arrive. If we had known, we could have taken the train to the city instead of our two-week walk. Here, in this busy railway station, we presented ourselves to the Jewish committee.

The Jewish people in Rumania were kind. They had heard our story. They knew our history. It was theirs also. Rumania had been ruled by a dictator, General Antonescu. In the year 1941 thousands of Jews were deported to the eastern Rumanian territory of Transnistria. Thousands and thousands perished there, but many more survived than in the camps. Antonescu saw that the Germans would not win the war. In 1943 he told the Germans that Rumania would not tolerate this genocide. The Rumanians moved quickly to gain credit from the Western Allies by disbanding the camps. It was only after this that the Jewish population was left intact. This gave us hope for our families—that even after the disruption from home to ghetto in Kecskemét, things could be righted.

The welcoming committee asked us to wait until they could check the train for incoming Jews. People arrived, and the platform was in happy disorganization. We were given milk and cakes while we waited. This was the first cake I had tasted in years. We were put in horsedrawn buggies and driven to the Jewish temple. Jews showed up in twos and threes and took us into their homes. They cooked whatever we wanted! There was a shelter where extra clothes, shoes, shirts had been contributed for the returning Jews. We could take whatever we needed. We hardly took anything. We began to feel human again, with values and ethics. Our pride dictated that we were not beggars or hoarders. We needed to move on. We needed to go home and begin again.

We had a long walk ahead of us to get home Our group became restless. A few of us were eager to reach home rapidly. Others had different plans. We decided to follow our individual instincts about when to leave and in what direction. We said our goodbyes, and Gyurka and I were on our way.

We moved with the front, and the front moved slowly. We walked ten kilometers and had to wait a few days behind the reasonable safety of the Russian lines. Here the danger to us was to be picked up for their labor needs. It did not matter to them if one was a camp survivor. If they lost a prisoner, they had to have another to replace him. If they needed help for kitchen or cleaning work, they took whoever was there. Sometimes these unfortunates ended up somewhere in the Soviet Union in labor camps.

We were somewhat apprehensive during this time, but not fearful. When the Russians asked for our documents, we usually just kept walking. Our audacity and their fatigue saved us. Everyone was afraid of them. Somehow, we weren't. We had already faced our fears. That helped us. Bridges and railroad stations were the most dangerous points, since they were filled with people who could question us and even abduct us. Loitering there trying to catch a ride in order to cross the pontoon bridges was risky. Fortunately, by accident or chance, the Russian soldiers themselves always sneaked us through without any mishap.

We often camped with Russian soldiers. If a single Russian soldier agreed to take us across a bridge or let us enter a railroad station, that was good enough for all of them. No one questioned us as to who we were or why we were there. It was quite an experience to be eating their food and staying with the women and men soldiers. They had an easygoing lifestyle. They didn't have forced discipline in their army, and officer and soldier could playfully sport with one another. There was music and singing. As soon as an order came, the apparently haphazard group came together in an organized fashion.

We needed to get to the city of Szeged, the first large Hungarian city on the west side of the river Tisza. It was almost impossible to get near the pontoon bridge without Russian help. The crossing was very busy, with the troops marching forward towards Budapest. On the east side of Tisza, I heard the noise of a printing press from the bed of a truck. Inside we noticed a soldier operating a hand-fed antique printing press.

The soldier was pumping the press with his foot and feeding paper in with one hand and eating with the other. We explained in sign language that we knew about the press. He asked us to help. We did. To get over from the east side of the river to the west side took quite a few hours. The soldier printer put us right to work. Gyurka began to pump the ancient press. The middle-aged, friendly soldier, wearing a sergeant's black-and-gold bar on his tunic, put me in front of the type case with a manuscript for the press's next run. We began to communicate in broken German. From a few of the words he used we guessed that he was Jewish.

The truck was an old one. The familiar smell of the printer's ink gave a homey feel. On both sides of the truck were windows to let the light shine through. We hoped that our good fortune would continue, and we could work for our keep while the unit headed northwest towards Budapest, leaving us behind in our city of Kecskemét.

When his unit got the order to cross the river, he took us across with him. Now we were only eighty kilometers from home.

We stopped in a small village square. Not more than five yards from the left side of our truck was a group of eighty Hungarian prisoners. They were standing or sitting on the pavement. They were newly captured and on the way towards a prisoners' assembly point. They had not seen barbed wire yet.

I looked out of the truck's windows. The soldiers looked beaten, tired, unshaven, and dirty. Gyurka and the Soviet printer joined me in watching them. They were not soldiers anymore. They had become frightened tailors, blacksmiths, teachers, students, farmers, and clerks. Within a few days they would be indistinguishable from one another. They would wait in front of the cabbage-soup kettle while they dreamed about home, food, and family. While they daydreamed they would also scheme like I did: What order would be best to be in the food line? Would I get more in the front of the line or the back of the line? Perhaps the middle of the line is better. There is always enough food in the middle of the line.

Two Mongolian-looking soldiers with rifles on their shoulders were these prisoners' guards. They were talking to one another and not watching the prisoners. What were these former Hungarian soldiers waiting for? Why did these former heroes still sit there immobilized? They had not seen barbed wire yet, but they were already behind barbed wire in their hearts.

As I looked and observed these former soldiers, I realized that for the first time since the war began I felt pity for them. They were my Hungarian people. There were good people mixed in with the ruthless. I had come from these people. They were my countrymen. I looked at Gyurka. I looked at his bald head and his eyes deep in their sockets. He did not look like the twenty-year-old that he was. I felt pity no more.

What were they thinking about now? Did any of them think about their Jewish prisoners? Did any of them regret the looting and the murder? How many of them had raped and burned homes when they were the victorious and heroic Hungarian army. Perhaps a few of them were visualizing right now the rape of their own wives, mothers, or sisters by a Kalmuk or Uzbek soldier.

I wanted to get off the truck and talk with them. I needed explanations. I needed to know how their minds worked. The printer grabbed my arm forcefully and pushed me back into the truck. "Sit down and don't move. Are you *meshuge*? Do you want to die now?"

We all fell silent. I didn't want to die, but I needed explanations. Explanations never came, that day or any day.

From the other side of the square a Russian officer approached the prisoners. Beside him, dressed in a Russian uniform, was the Hungarian translator. We could understand all the Hungarian answers. The officer asked the prisoners questions about their names and regiments. As the officer and the translator moved on to the prisoners next to our truck, one of the prisoners asked the translator, "Are you Hungarian?'

"Yes"

"Why are you wearing the Russian uniform?"

Before the answer came, a neighboring prisoner retorted,

"Because he's a mother-fucking, cunt-sucking Jew!"

I turned to Gyurka and said sadly, "We're home."

We traveled with the printing truck out of the village. There were no more rivers or mountains, just the war between us and home. Our progress home depended on the speed of the Russian advance and the special orders for the printing and propaganda unit to either stay a few days or go forward.

The main roads leading north towards our home were jammed with Soviet fighting units surging forward. *"Berlin kaput"* and *"Hitler kaput"* were heard often. This was also the message of the printed material which was distributed by our truck and placed on the fences and electric poles.

During these days, traveling and working on the well-heated truck, we learned to differentiate the well-trained front-line units from the ones which had liberated my little group in Nagybegany. We saw the well-dressed and well-fed soldiers on their American-made trucks and tanks surging towards Germany. Our hearts were with them. We heard that the new democratic Hungarian army was looking for volunteers to fight the Nazis. Although we were too sick and weak to start soldiering, we talked about it and dreamed of joining the Soviet forces. We dreamed about revenge. We dreamed about righting the suffering and the humiliation we had endured. We dreamed of fighting along with these elite forces which now lined the roads.

- *34* -

*T*he Russian unit was ordered to take side roads through the small villages, and we progressed slowly on clogged secondary roads. Hungarians were on the road, confused, heading both north and south. The refugees were shaking from cold and fear and were forced off the road by the troops. The Russians had arrived on the Great Plain of Hungary from as far as Stalingrad and the Ural Mountains. They had seen the devastated villages and cities of their own country. They had seen burned-down houses and the carcasses of slaughtered animals and people. I knew that nothing would stop these soldiers until they reached Berlin. They would exact their revenge on anyone along the way. The Hungarians on the road, who had left their cities, would be the first of the victims. I felt that whoever the Russians took their anger out on was fine with me, since we had the same enemies. I knew what it was like being on the road afraid for one's safety and trying to stay out of harm's way. These people, not knowing what to do or whom to believe, would probably end up as I did—days later back in the same place after making a large circle. Any pain that these Hungarians felt was fine with me.

The Soviet advance slowed. We were forced to take a side road to Kistelek and wait a day or two. This small village with its fruit orchards and its gardens filled with snow reminded me of Kecskemét. This was the first time we left the safety of the truck. The two of us were billeted across the street from the Soviet printer. The printer put a Russian name tag on the house we were billeted in, along with name tags for the other officers.

In this village and in the surrounding hamlets the support units of the Soviet forces were stationed. Their wagons were filled with confiscated merchandise. A beautiful fur coat lay next to a sad goat. A sewing machine lay on top of a beautiful grandfather clock. On their way through the village, the victorious forces had taken horses and cows. Some of their own starved livestock had been left behind. As they rode through the village they discarded things that had looked good early on but had now been replaced by better objects. I noticed a gold chain on a Russian's neck with a Magen David it. I tried to approach him as he drank from the well. I noticed that he had another chain on his neck with a cross on it. He was just collecting. He was not someone to share my story with. I noticed a soldier handing out candy to a crying boy. On his arm were wristwatches up to his elbow. I saw soldiers go into a home and tell the old man to bring them some wine. When he did they told him to stay out a little bit longer. They told him they needed sleep. I noticed they kept the wife in the house. These units stayed in the village for a few hours and then moved to the next.

We observed. We witnessed. We had no feelings about this. The soldiers pillaged and raped, but they did not carry the old, the young, the sick, and the healthy into the gas chambers. This was the most important distinction to me. These men acted as unethical soldiers had acted for centuries. They had not begun a new regime of murderous behavior in which whole generations of people were the victims.

A Hungarian approached us and asked if he could have a Russian name tag like ours for his house. He explained that soldiers seeing the name in their language would not barge into his house to loot and plunder. He said this hesitantly, feeling us to be some sort of intermediaries.

The neighbor returned to our house a short time later with some wine which was the finest of the region and a friend of his. I said to him, "Where I just came from I was not given wine before or during or after our meal. In fact, I was rarely given a meal."

This opened up the conversation. He explained that he had been scheduled to retire from the electric utility company of this area. His wife and son took care of the orchards while he had continued to work past his date of retirement. He had to stay employed a year past the date of retirement since the gendarmes had taken away the owner of the company and his family.

"Why was the owner removed?"

"They were Jews. We are simple people in this village and were afraid to ask the village leaders about the fate of this family and the other Jews of the village."

"Where are the leaders of your village now?" we asked.

"When the Red Army got near the village, they ran, leaving us to face the music. My son left with them. He was afraid of the vengeance of the Yugoslav labor battalion."

This reply interested Gyurka and me for many reasons. First and foremost was our curiosity at the attitude Hungarians had toward work-camp inmates. Secondly we had heard of the various other labor battalions which were not Jewish. When Hungary was given parts of the old Austro-Hungarian Empire in gratitude for taking part in the occupation of Yugoslavia, some of the people in these regions were put into labor battalions. These labor battalions were for those not fit for military service for a variety of reasons. They were known to be regular labor battalions and not as murderous as the ones for the Jews.

"What sort of people were in the labor battalions? Were they young? Were they old? Did they have uniforms? How were they treated?"

The old neighbor answered. "We saw them daily. They were stationed in the school building. They were mixed ages and were without uniforms. They wore a red armband on their left sleeve. A few older Hungarians guarded them."

"How were they treated?" I asked.

"When they had to work in the fields helping with the harvest, they looked content and were treated fairly. Other times, in the road-building and railroad details, we heard about their mistreatment. A few spoke a little Hungarian. They were imprisoned because they were born in the northern part of Yugoslavia, which we retook from them with Hitler's help. I think that was their only crime. They were Christians like us. Not like the Jews. We heard from them that Hungarian soldiers had committed atrocities. Naturally we did not believe them."

"What stories?" Gyurka and I pressed on. "What sort of lies did the Yugoslavian labor battalion spread about the heroic Hungarian soldiers?"

"What they said could not be true. They said that our soldiers acted like barbarians, even against women and children.

We heard that Hungarian units had blown openings on the frozen Danube and chased naked people onto the ice, gunning them down. There were Serbs buried under the icy Danube, not just Jews!"

The neighbor and his friend kept pouring wine and warmed to the subject.

"These and other stories we heard over and over. People tend to exaggerate what they hear. It is hard to believe that soldiers of a Christian nation could commit such inhuman acts to other Christians. It was not just Jews that were killed on the ice!"

I could not take it any more. Nothing in his face or that of his friend showed any sign of feeling. I stood up and with the half-full wine glass in my hand shouted at him, "So you think that it is natural and humanly acceptable for them to be murdering Jews? Just Jews?"

By this time I had lost control of myself and threw the glass of wine in his face. We began cursing one another. He jumped up, facing us. Gyurka and the friend of the neighbor leaped up too. Threats and punches were exchanged between two enfeebled old men and two weak, half-starved younger ones who were unfit for attack or defense.

In the middle of our angry but almost grotesque melee, the kitchen door was flung open. Armed Soviet soldiers filled the room. Gyurka and I immediately offered wine to the soldiers. The soldiers ordered the old neighbor to fetch some more. The soldiers followed him. While we were waiting, the friend tried to pacify us with a few words now that he felt in jeopardy. He told us that this neighbor's son was the first Arrow Cross hoodlum in the village. He told this to us with the Hungarian's usual gusto on betraying his neighbor.

We heard a woman scream.

"That's Ilonka, his wife," his friend said, pointing at the neighbor's home. We heard gunshots. The neighbor returned, pale and shaky.

"They have my wife. Can you help?"

"We cannot. We will not."

Indeed that was exactly the situation. We could not help without risking our own lives, nor would we risk anything for these people. Shots exploded again. The neighbor explained that the soldiers were shooting holes in the wine barrel to get the wine out more quickly.

More soldiers in horse wagons entered the yard. They had also heard the gunshots The new arrivals began questioning us.

"Who's in the stable? Are you hiding Nazi soldiers?"

"No, No! Nobody is here."

At that moment two soldiers came out of the barn carrying a still-bleeding calf. They threw the animal onto the wagon. All the soldiers walked to the neighbor's cellar and filled their cups with wine by holding them to the bullet holes where the wine now gushed from.

In one of the wagons sat a young woman, crying. A beautiful fur coat was on her shoulders. She cried for her mother. She was answered by the soldiers, "Don't be silly, little comrade. You'll be a mother, too."

The soldiers in the wagon tried to console her. "Eat a little sausage. Have a big gulp of palinka."

Three soldiers disappeared with the young woman under the tarpaulin. All this did not move us. It only widened our apprehension about what had happened to our loved ones. If this was normal after a war, then what would be the unimaginable fate of the Jewish population of Kecskemét?

Our convoy began to move again. Next to the road was a train carrying coal. On top of the coal were people trying to get away. The soldiers chased the travelers off the cars. The soldiers demanded cigarettes. They asked for money. They took coats or fountain pens. The train left without the people. The soldiers rounded up the men for "*robot*."

"Just a little work."

Perhaps in a Siberian coal mine. Or perhaps just unloading a wagon and then they would be freed. They took the women as kitchen help.

"Just to peel potatoes."

Or to peel you out of your skirt.

We observed a victorious army as they took what they felt was due them many times along the way.

It was the day before Christmas when we arrived in the city of Kiskunfélegyháza. This was the city nearest to Kecskemét. The printing unit received orders to stay in the city and work from an abandoned print shop. We knew that print shop. It had been the shop of a Jew. The owner's son used to play soccer in the Jewish league against the boys from Kecskemét. Where was he now? Where were all of them now? We were too near home and too aware of missing people to stay. Without asking permission, Gyurka and I decided to walk the last few kilometers home.

Only twenty-eight kilometers left of our long journey towards home. We had walked all of Eastern Europe, and now had the longest part to go. Gyurka and I hardly talked to each other during the five-hour walk through the snow. Army trucks passed, but we didn't try to hitch a ride. We needed time apart from each other. We needed time to be alone with our thoughts. These five hours were the longest and shortest of my life. We were anxious and eager, hopeful and despairing at the same time. I would lose myself in dreams of home and family, and then wonder if I would be crushed with despair if I clung to hope. I would think the worst and frighten myself into tears. The most important questions would be answered soon: Did I still have a family? Did life have order? Had I survived for a reason?

We had walked hundreds and hundreds of kilometers through German-occupied cities and villages, seeing and experiencing the undescribable misfortunes of the Jews. Yet we still had moments of hope left in us. In the distance, a snow-covered sign, "Kecskemét 2 km.," came into sight. Under the sign was another one in Russian letters. We sat near the sign immersed in our private thoughts. We continued our slow walk with our heads down, throats constricted.

- 35 -

We arrived in Kecskemét. We reached the city's first house, which had a small garden. In front of the house was a shallow ditch which separated it from the road. The house looked vaguely familiar. At that moment a little girl opened the door and ran from the house. A woman came out and greeted us. She offered us bread. We did not take it. Then the little girl said, "Please wait!"

She returned with a basket of red apples. We looked at the mother and her nice little daughter. I remembered my eight-year-old niece running towards me long, long ago. I am sure Gyurka also saw, in his mind's eye, a familiar child in the girl's face. I thanked her, and without saying one more word we continued walking to find our homes and our families.

It was December 24, 1944, and we were finally home. With every step, with every crunch our shoes made on the snow, I wondered if arriving the day before Christmas was an omen of some sort. I wondered if seeing the little girl and the mother portended any kind of personal luck for me. I wondered if my suffering had some reason, an offering, so that my family would be there to greet me. I no longer worried that they might be sick or impoverished. I only needed them alive. I needed this crazy, brutal existence to make sense. I wanted a happy ending.

I stopped in front of the Pataki Wholesale Grocery Store, where, as a young boy, I used to buy flypaper on credit. I noted that Pataki, the name of the Jewish owner, had been painted over; just the words "Wholesale Grocer" remained. The new owner did not even feel the shame of the half-painted-over sign, the shame of having advantaged himself because of someone else's tragedy. The store was in a shambles and had been recently looted. Three people were inside trying to clean up the havoc. Someone noticed us and asked if he could help us. I asked him for flypaper. I watched his astonished look and walked out of the store.

Our arrival in Kecskemét and discovery that our families had first been carted off to the ghetto and finally to Auschwitz left us with unbelievable pain. Our worst moments were then, when we lost all hope. We became living sleepwalkers. We were without our loved ones. All had perished. All were gone. Our city, our families, our lives had not been spared from indescribable tragedy.

We stayed in the home of a friend's relatives. A strange woman cooked for us. We were like automatons. We ate and slept but were without vitality. Was it possible for us to start new lives here? Could I live among the same people who had turned against me and my family? Could I ever talk with those who had silently watched the fate of the Jews? Could I ever dance or show emotion again? I was suspicious of everyone and angry at everyone who lived in the city.

I wondered, as I looked around, who had profited from the Jews' disappearance. I wondered which of the city folk had protested or hid the Jews. Who had taken the Jews' businesses, homes, and factories? Who had thought only of their own greed and safety and allowed others to die? Who of my neighbors had killed? Who of my neighbors had betrayed my father? Who had joined the political parties of hate or the gendarmes with typical Hungarian enthusiasm? Who had hitched my father and other old Jews to plow their fields before dispatching them? Who wore the green Arrow Cross shirts so proudly? Who among these citizens followed the German example of needing power over the Jews? Who stole my early manhood years? Who is guilty here? The whole Hungarian nation is guilty. The whole world shares the shame.

Outside it was cold. Inside the room the air was stale. I opened the windows, but it did not help. I felt the stale odor of the rotten city of Kecskemét. Why had I rushed home? What home? I had no home.

- *36* -

We spent days wandering in the city. We tried to start living again. We visited former neighbors and former friends. We learned how to differentiate people and evaluate their various motives. Not everyone was guilty. Some offered help. More asked for our assistance with the authorities. Our special status during the war put us in a more trusted position to intervene with the Russians. A few more from former labor battalions arrived in the city. Among them was a friend's father. He moved in with us. Now the three of us lived together in a strange home with a strange woman cooking for us.

We needed to earn some money to restart our lives. I looked for Mr. Molnár, my *strohman*. He was gone. We reopened a print shop whose Jewish owner was gone. Life slowly and agonizingly began again.

Kecskemét was occupied by the Ukrainian army. They were different from the Russians, but it would take us time to understand this. One night two soldiers came to our house, one of them an officer. This concerned us. We were always friendly towards them, and during the more civilized daytime there was no problem, but at night we had to be careful. They might be out of control with liquor, and we could become their victims. We offered them a glass of vodka, hoping they would go in peace. It did not work. They wanted a woman, and somebody must have told them we had a *barishnya*, or woman, with us. We denied that we had a woman who cooked for us. By this time Gyurka was having an affair with her.

Before answering the door, we had hidden her at the foot of our bed and covered her with blankets. The Ukrainians started to threaten us after searching the house. Gyurka, in his foolishness, got up and with great pride and emotion pointed to his chest and said, "*Yevrei deportante.*"

At this early time we still assumed that all Soviets were our liberators, and that they understood that we were survivors of the Germans. We did not know the Ukrainians. They only understood *barishnya*.

The officer became hostile. He drew his gun and shot above Gyurka's head.

"*Ah, Yevrei.*"

He said this again and again, lowering his gun and training it on our bodies. He was drunk, which made the situation even more unpredictable. Hearing the gunshot, the woman got very scared. She came out from the under the layers of blankets folded over her at the edge of the bed. The pressure for us ended. Hers had only begun.

A soldier who had been very quiet during the whole incident was left to guard us, while the officer took the woman to a separate section of the house. After the officer went into the other room with the woman, the soldier departed. Without any hesitation, I ran out of the house to the commandatura. It was perilous being out after curfew, as soldiers tended to shoot first and ask questions later. It was not safe at night, but I arrived without incident. I explained what was happening in our home. The officer in charge got a patrol together, put me in the jeep, and came to our house. They ran in with machine guns ready to shoot. They found the officer, who was in a drunken stupor, tied his hands, threw him in the jeep, and drove away.

Far from relieved, we realized what a predicament we were now in. The officer would be sober in the morning. He would be released and furious. The commandatura would send him back to his unit. What would happen tomorrow? We were sure of his retaliation. We got a hand-pulled wagon, put all our belongings in it, and left for another abandoned home. This saved our lives.

The next morning, a group of Ukrainian soldiers led by the officer from the night before came to our former house. With machine guns they shot up the whole house. They asked the neighbors for our whereabouts, but no one knew where we were.

- *37* -

January 1945 was an unusually cold month. Kecskemét had been left without means of transportation. Houses were skeletons without windows or doors. There was no firewood or coal. Soldiers used the furniture in the houses where they were billeted for firewood. When the furniture was gone, the neighboring house was next. I watched these happenings without very much feeling.

The front-line soldiers, the fighting units of the occupying Soviet forces, were well disciplined and had left the populace in peace. The units which replaced them were sent into the city for rest and recuperation. Rapes and lootings were committed daily and indiscriminately by these units. I watched these happenings also in a detached manner.

The Soviet occupiers issued new money. Some people, believing the occupation to be temporary, used only the old money and would not take the new. Others, who felt the permanence of the occupation, used the new and would not take the old. The farmers were caught in the middle and sold food for barter only. Food shortages developed in this farming community. Barter became part of daily life. For a while salt became the basic unit of exchange.

There was very little of anything left, and very few small businesses. Everything was in disarray. My beautiful shoes got a hole in the sole. I could not find a cobbler to repair them.

Although we had been liberated and occupied, Budapest, which was only eighty-six kilometers from our city, was still under siege. There was continuous fighting between the Soviet and Hungarian-German forces in the capital. The Soviet ring around Budapest got tighter and tighter. Here in Kecskemét people noted sarcastically that the Germans would defend Budapest to its last dying Hungarian soldier. A few refugees from Budapest managed to get out and brought us news. They also tried to merge with us and assume our identity. We assumed that they were people who had been in power and were guilty of crimes and had used their power and influence to escape from the capital. They would be the ones summarily punished if caught. They attempted to hide their old identities as mass murderers or lackeys of the Nazi regime with new identities. They had the most to fear from the Russians.

We had heard about the murders and atrocities perpetrated on the Jews by the desperate fascists during the last days of the siege that had turned our Blue Danube red. We heard that there had been armed Jewish resistance in the ghetto and prayed that it was true. The idea that the war was over for us while eighty kilometers away Jews were still dying was appalling.

As news came that the German army was still resisting in Budapest, some people in Kecskemét rejoiced. Many of the citizens of Kecskemét still hoped that the old regime would return. To those who still hoped for Hungarian rule, reality was slow to set in. This steeled my heart as I saw that no one had learned anything from the atrocities of war.

The Russian occupying force in Kecskemét started to establish certain criteria as to who could now wear the mantle of power. Anyone in public office now had to verify his behavior during the past decade. People had to prove that they were not fascists. Everyone had to verify their democratic leanings by two reliable witnesses. Suddenly the people who had been the accomplices of the Nazis were humble, their former arrogance lost. Months and months before, freezing in the mountains, I had dreamed about this time. I remembered the forest men who wanted documents to testify that they had permission to beat us as I watched the former fascists asking us for documentation and witnesses to establish their democratic leanings during the fascistic years.

Being Jewish was documentation and witness enough. Everyone now claimed that he or she was the best friend of the Jews.

"My tailor was a Jew."

"My best friend in school was a Jew."

"I worked for the Merchant Bank. All my bosses were nice Jewish people."

"I was in love with a Jewish girl."

Everybody expressed his deep sorrow to us over betrayals of the Jews by others, now that we were valuable as witnesses. Everyone claimed to have helped one Jew or saved another. Everyone claimed to have had a Jewish friend. Others were to blame. Not them. Not them. We were suspicious because too often we were befriended for expediency only. We still ached from all the betrayals and treachery perpetrated on us. We were still grieving.

My former high school teacher asked me to be his witness. He was the only one I felt comfortable testifying for. Perhaps his intelligence and worldliness was the reason. Perhaps it was the way he inquired about his former Jewish students and my family. Perhaps it was that he spoke Russian.

After being his witness I got the idea of using my printing skills and his language skills to make a primer. We would call it *Learn Russian Fast: The Easy Way*. In less than a week this man prepared twenty-eight pages of Hungarian-to-Russian and Russian-to-Hungarian translations of easy-to-read phrases. I printed it.

I was back in the printing business! We hired a few enterprising fellows to sell the primers in the markets. We couldn't print enough of them. This was my first business venture in the new order. I made money even though the money was worthless. It turned out that the dictionary we printed was also worthless. The teacher had been a prisoner-of-war during World War One in Ukrainia. Although Kecskemét was occupied by the Ukrainian army, there were Russians, Tartars, Mongols, and other nationalities among them. These provincial soldiers did not understand the badly misspelled Russian dictionary that we concocted. It didn't matter. I was working again and thinking again of a future.

- *38* -

The rebuilding of Kecskemét became a major political aim of the new government. Everybody was supposed to take part in it. The city had not actually been damaged by warfare, but was war-torn, dirty, in disrepair, and had many abandoned houses. Everywhere was a ruined memory.

The Communists called a general meeting to proclaim the rebuilding of the city. During the meeting the speaker, a Hungarian Communist leader who had spent the last twenty years in Moscow, extorted the people in the audience to put aside their differences. He wanted us to unite and support the newly appointed mayor of our city and commence a new beginning.

The city hall was full. As soon as the Moscow-educated Hungarian Communist, Emanuel Shafranco, ended his speech, somebody three rows behind me stood up and started to make an antisemitic speech. He never used the word "Jew." He used such phrases as "former owners of fancy stores on the main street in their well-ironed pants." There were one thousand people in the meeting hall. It became deathly quiet because everybody knew what was happening. This was a challenge by a former fascist. This was a continuation of the old antisemitism which had tainted the population. Most of us had tried to believe that this part of our history was behind us now. His pronouncements confirmed that the war was not over yet.

Emanuel Shafranco returned to the podium and made an impassioned speech in rebuttal. By the time the speech ended the political police had arrived and took away the antisemitic agitator and a few other people. The fascists still had not admitted defeat. They were still hoping they would squash the Russians. We stood quietly subdued. We felt that no lessons had been learned yet.

Six months later there was a show at the theater which starred a beautiful and famous actress, Katalyn Karady. She was one of the best-known actresses in Hungary at that time. She had been jeered at and jailed during the last year of the war for supporting Jews and antifascist causes. Now was the time for people to celebrate her courage. The theater was full.

Unfortunately the theater was also filled with a group of her detractors. Despite the presence of the many who had come to thank her, the antisemitic jeering made it impossible for the show to continue. As the theater emptied, a large crowd gathered. No one knew what to expect. A riot was brewing. As minutes passed, more and more police and Soviet troops arrived. The near-riot was quelled, but our knowledge of imminent threat was not. With the need to rebuild and repair our spirits and our city came the realization of how much more pain we would need to constantly endure.

Slowly, the city tried to normalize. A former schoolmate of mine, a Gentile boy, Pali Fozo, remade my acquaintance. One day he warned me, "Mandel, the Germans are starting a heavy counter-attack from the Lake Balaton region to break the Russian ring around Budapest. You must get ready to run away."

I did not run. I would not go. His intentions were good, but I believed that the Germans were finished. A few of my acquaintances prepared fully packed rucksacks ready for the run east if the German offensive was successful. My running days were over.

Others who had survived labor battalions started talking about organizing an armed resistance to prepare for a German offensive. Lajos started to organize this underground group. I joined immediately. Twenty-four hours later the two of us were called to the local political police and were advised to stop. We were told that our action was understandable, but it might create undesirable false rumors about a need for such a resistance. I understood this. I also knew that I would fight before going passively into slavery again.

While horrified at the remaining fascist and antisemitic elements still evident, we noticed the decency and honesty of many families. There were some who had been innocent of any wrongdoing. They had been quiet during the turbulent times, helping Jews in modest but significant ways. They refused to be complicitous to evil events. These people still lived their lives with integrity. They did not try to extort the system or aggrandize themselves with the new government. Such a family was that of our former neighbors, the Gyorfis.

The Gyorfis were hardworking farmers. Their spacious home, with stables and a few acres of land, was across from our former home. My parents had given them a few objects of ours to hide just before they were taken away to the ghetto. Hiding Jewish property was a very dangerous matter, punishable by jail or ending up in a German concentration camp. In the February of my return, Mrs. Gyorfi handed me the money that my mother had left with her. With the money was a letter from my mother. The letter named a farmer, a trusted friend of our family, to whom my family had turned over everything for safekeeping that they were able.

This money from my mother was now almost worthless because of the inflation, but receiving it and holding the value-less banknotes in my hand represented a connection between myself and my dead and missing family. It also showed me that some neighbors could not help but be involved in goodness. The money also rekindled my thoughts about how much more valuable it would have been to me if they had spent it on shoes for my feet two years before.

The Gyorfis were not spared terrible times. Their farm equipment was gone. The soldiers had removed most of the farm animals, leaving a few pigs and one cow. They, who had endured the fascist regime with integrity, were named by the new Hungarian Communist state as the number-one Kulak family in our area. Those classified as Kulaks were well-to-do farmers regarded as enemies of the new socialist Hungarian state. Our neighbors were neither well-to-do nor enemies of the regime. They were simple, good farmers. They were the good that was Hungary, uncorrupted by marching boots and hate propaganda. They needed seeds to plant. They needed equipment and farm animals to start to work in the fields.

Old man Gyorfi asked me if I could help. I asked one of my friends, who worked as a high-ranking police officer, to aid me in helping my neighbors restart their life. My friend's answer was to stay out of this for my own good. There was nothing I or anyone else could do for these good people. It was very painful to me to return to them and advise patience. I wanted to return some the kindness they had so easily given my parents. I needed to silently do the right thing despite safety or expediency. Since I was an expert cowboy from my herding experience, I organized an expedition and appropriated a cow from a barely guarded herd and gave it to the Gyorfi family. A simple return of a favor!

- *39* -

It was February 1945 and very cold. I was still wearing the clothing I had brought back from Rumania. I had the oversized shoes with the hole in the sole. The year before I left for the labor camps, I had bought a custom-made long winter coat. I still remember the color and feel of the material of that coat. Whenever I walked in the street shivering that cold February, I appraised all passers-by in the hope that I would recognize my coat and identity the wearer as the thief who had robbed us of all our belongings. I never found my coat! Perhaps a Russian took it from the Hungarian thief and someone is still wearing it in Siberia. If that be the case, let him wear it with my mixed blessing.

During January and February all of us returnees tried to restart our lost lives. The daily activities which were mandatorily forced on us helped us to forget our anguish. We did not know the details about our loved ones, only that they had disappeared. Despite all the bad news I had heard, I still believed in miracles. Someone was always emerging who had been given up as dead. Someone who had supposedly been killed in a labor camp returned. Miracles did happen. So I waited for my miracles, knowing that there were none.

Finally Budapest was liberated. Hungry, suffering people came to our city for food. They were an additional burden on the limited resources of our city. Yet it meant that the end of the war was near.

During this time our print shop, which had begun with our language primers, started to flourish. If the city needed announcements or printed materials, it came to our print shop. At the bottom of every printed public announcement it was mandatory to state the name of the printer. Thus I printed: "The responsible publisher of this material is Odon Mandel." The significance of that advertisement would later help bring me a wife.

I was working in the print shop when two dubious-looking characters walked into my print shop and asked me if I wanted to buy a printing press and a few cases of type.

"The price is right," They told me with a wink.

I told them I was interested and to bring it in. They returned the next day with my dead brother-in-law's stolen equipment. They wanted me to buy the forfeited equipment of a Jew who had died in a labor battalion. I thought of my poor tortured brother-in-law. First, he was told that he couldn't have a license to work, then they took his life. Now these hoodlums were trying to sell me the machinery with which he had intended to carve out a meager livelihood for his family. I told them who I was, and with an axe in my hand ready to strike, I chased them out of my place.

These were dangerous, unstable times for everybody. One market day I was doing some shopping. I noticed that the shoppers were making a wide circle trying to avoid something. I got a little closer. A Russian soldier in his long army overcoat, long underwear, and no pants was terrorizing shop owners and shoppers with a pistol held high above his head. It was obvious that the soldier was a recuperating inmate of the hospital. He was drunk and had left the hospital without permission. A patrol came and could not persuade the man to leave with them. An NKVD officer was summoned and talked to the soldier. The soldier pulled out a grenade from his pocket. The officer wordlessly shot the soldier. These events were repeated by the scores.

I wondered what the soldier's family would be told. Would he be remembered as a hero of the Motherland or as shot while drunk? I wondered what had snapped his mind. I wondered at the transitoriness of life. Everyday I wondered at survival and death.

Russian soldiers were quartered in neighborhoods. We began to talk and share with these soldiers. We felt we had more in common with them than with some of our Hungarian neighbors. Among the soldiers was the printer who had transported us to our city and protected us during part of our homecoming. He had been transferred from Kiskunfélegyháza to Kecskemét and was searching for an abandoned shop to set up printing. He found us in our shop. We opened our hearts to him. We knew his loyalty. He was a friend.

Through the printer we met an officer from Kiev. His name was Shmelkin. He was a tall, middle-aged officer well liked by his soldiers. He told us that he was Jewish. We were asked not to mention this in front of the soldiers. All of us had such loneliness. All had friends and family who had died. We became very close and good friends.

In Shmelkin's billeting group was a political officer named Similkov. He was Shmelkin's commanding officer. We spent lots of evenings together. They brought over food, vodka, and bread. We had a wonderful time together. We relaxed, beginning to trust things like food, friendship, and a warm fire. Both of them spoke a broken German, so we did not have any problem in communication.

One day we had a big party and had invited Shmelkin, Similkov, and whoever they wanted to join us. Ten soldiers were in the room eating the food they had brought and the liquor I provided. The ever-present harmonica player and the singing soldiers made me feel good about the world. The sad melodies made the soldiers visibly homesick. We were all tipsy. The singing, music, and sounds of the party spilled over to the street. A group of other soldiers came in, and wanted to join us, but Shmelkin said, "No, we have no more food. Leave."

The intruders were drunk. They would not be refused. They got out their machine guns and started shooting above our heads indiscriminately. Our Soviet friends jumped up, looking for their pistols.

Gyurka was coming home and was right under the window when the shots rang out. He ran to the commandatura for help, fearing our imminent death. Five minutes later the patrol entered with weapons drawn, expecting to find us all dead according to Gyurka's account. By that time somebody had offered the gun-toting group a drink. Everyone was embracing each other as long-lost friends and their voices joined in song. The patrol started to drink also. The situation ended up in drunken chaos. Bullet-ridden ceilings enclosed the room of loud laughter and song. It was a remarkable, very Russian scene. It was a scene noted for closeness and peril, separated by seconds.

Shortly after this exciting afternoon shooting incident, Shmelkin came over alone. In short emotional sentences he informed us that his unit had received orders to take part in the offensive drive towards Berlin. This was the first time that this strong, stoic officer showed real emotion. He spoke at length about his family, his wife, and his son. They had all disappeared during the German occupation of Kiev. He cried for a few minutes. He then pulled out his revolver and handed it over to me. He said, "Just in case. Don't run. Fight and die, but don't be a slave again."

With these few words he turned and left. I looked after him with a feeling of emptiness.

- *40* -

On Sunday, April 1, the city hall arranged a dance for the young adults. This was the day of my twenty-third birthday. I still had the same jacket I had gotten from the Jewish shelter in the city of Arad. Not having a choice of clothes, I went to the dance in my best shirt, tie, jacket, and naturally in my only pair of clean, shiny oversized shoes. The soles were still not repaired. This was the day I met my future wife, Sara. She had come with another Jewish boy, a policeman. Centuries ago when we were young I had gone to the dance halls with him. He worked there as a drummer, and sometimes he let me play the drums.

I couldn't keep my eyes off Sara. I watched her as she danced. She wore a rust-colored skirt and a light-colored blouse with a light-blue design in it. I think her smile made me follow her. Finally I gathered my courage and asked her to dance. I had not danced for a long time.

My shoes were two sizes larger than I needed. As soon as we started to dance, she stepped on my shoes. She apologized without looking at me. At first I did not answer, but after the third "Pardon me," I stopped dancing. While I continued to hold her, I told her that my shoes were too long and that I enjoyed her stepping on my shoes. She finally raised her eyes and looked at me, and we continued to dance. I guess with that remark she really noticed me. A half-minute more or so and she stopped dancing, looked at me seriously, and asked my name. I introduced myself properly and so did she. Her name was Sara Yolan Paszty. We continued dancing. I started to feel proud of my dancing skills, a superficial pleasure that I had not had the luxury to feel in so many years.

She had light-brown hair combed in a pony tail. I liked that. I smelled the scent of fresh lavender soap, suggesting cleanliness and innocence. I liked that too. We sat down and I bought her lemonade. We talked some more. When she put her empty glass on the floor next to my chair, she inadvertently showed part of her breast. This I liked more than anything. She embarrassedly noticed what had happened and started to cry. I apologized. She smiled at me, and there was a slight flirtation in that smile. I liked that too. I asked if I could walk her home. First she had to talk it over with Laci Almasi, the policeman who was our mutual friend. He looked at me and answered in the affirmative.

On the way home I found out a few things about her and her family. She worked in the police department as a clerk. This was an important point. I knew that she wasn't Jewish, and I also knew that people who worked for the police had already been screened about their background. The police tended to hire former Jewish labor battalion returnees. During this time the police department tried to aid the new government in pursuing and bringing to justice some of the more notorious fascists.

The next day I inquired more about her. I had to know her and her family's activities during the war. Everyone at this time purported to have been a friend of the Jews. I had to know more. The fact that she was working for the police department was a tremendous relief to me. I learned from my police officer friend that her father had died a few years back. I found out that a well-known police detective was her stepfather. So it appeared that this was not an expedient friend of the Jews, but a long-term one. A choice made at some personal risk during the war years.

Learning these little things about Sara created an emotional sensation in me. Talking to her increased this feeling. I felt safe, finally safe. Our conversations were relaxed and honest. I wasn't hesitant to tell her I was Jewish. There was no need for pretence. In a few months I would know just how good this woman was.

I began to send letters with little presents to her. Meanwhile I found out from Laci that she had started to inquire about me. My friend showed her my name in one of the printed announcements and said, "That's him—your Odon Mandel."

I was also reputable because I was employed. Our first outing was to a theater. I had printed the show's advertisement and had been compensated for the printing with good seats. We sat in the third row until a group of Soviet soldiers came in from the hospital. Everybody was ordered to leave the first eight rows to make room for them. It was a very bad feeling to reexperience dislocation again. It was humiliating to feel safe one moment and ready to begin again with a normal or near-normal life, and in a second to be reminded of the dark time one is in. Yet I knew that being dislocated from choice seats in a theater was not the same as being put in a labor battalion and dislocated from life.

Sara had another young man who was dating her. Dr. Luszka was a young doctor in the city social services. While we tried to locate another seat in the theater, he was watching us from the best box. We both felt embarrassed. Every time I asked her for a date, she first had to wriggle out of a date with him. That night I demanded that she make a choice. That was the end of Dr. Luszka.

In April, when the days were short, I waited for her in front of the city hall to escort her home. It was dark when we arrived in front of her home. I wanted to kiss her. She moved her head, whether intentionally or not (we still have different stories!), and the kiss fell somewhere on her forehead.

"You really don't want me to kiss you? The time will come!"

"It is now," she said quietly. The next kisses were much better.

One day we were walking near my family's house. I realized then that I was in love with Sara because I had begun to talk about my parents, my youth, my life. I could talk from my heart. She asked if I wanted to marry her. I said, "Yes."

I immediately got frightened and wanted to take back what I had said. I fought with my doubts all night.

"We're too young . . . I'm Jewish . . . She's not . . . My family has been decimated. What would they think of my choice?"

All through the doubts, I knew in my heart of hearts that I would marry her. I had found the perfect person in this girl. I wanted to be with her forever.

We decided that we would invite a few friends to her mother's home for a Sunday lunch and announce our engagement. The date we set for our engagement was April 28. It was with mixed feelings that I planned for this important event in my life devoid of family. I was at home looking out the window when my old friend, Karcsi Harsanyi, came walking past my house. This was the diminutive former suitor of my sister whom I had admired with all my heart. He had survived! He had made it! I ran out of the house towards him. We hugged each other and tears of happiness streamed down our faces. He asked about my sister, Sara, his one true love. I told him I knew nothing. I told him about my Sara and invited him to our engagement party. He was the one special person that I invited. He was my entire family.

On April 26 I decided that I would rather be married than just be engaged. I wanted to be married quickly now. I took Sara to the city hall. We needed blood tests. Getting married so quickly was not as easy as it sounds. There was supposed to be a waiting period, blood tests, and announcements in the papers. All of a sudden the need to marry became urgent. The official who issued the license and would perform the ceremony was very strict and unpleasant. In questioning him about the procedure, I asked him what type of wine he preferred. I both pressured him with my insistence and offered sugar in the form of fermented spirits. I'm not sure which helped most or whether it was the combination of the two which made my wish a reality.

The marriage occurred on April 28, 1945, twenty-seven days after I first met Sara and four months after my return from hell. Two days later, when our few friends arrived to our engagement party, we were already married. Thinking back now I am amazed at how we found each other. I did not have a normal late adolescence or early adulthood. The war and the persecution must have left abiding scars, but it did not tamper with my capacity for loving or choosing the right friend and companion for life.

- *41* -

The total capitulation of the German army was just days away. Lajos, my former bunkmate in the labor battalion, and I were asked to carry the Red flag at the front of the May Day parade. We were honored. We were proud to carry the hammer and sickle. We owed so much to the Red Army. We were aware that the population was watching us from the curb. I assumed that some were making nasty remarks, but we didn't listen or care. Our hearts were in what we were doing. This May First celebration was the greatest show at that moment. It was a show of our personal freedom. It was a show of our allegiance to liberators rather than incarcerators. It was like entering our first Hungarian city singing, as survivors not victims. We were carrying the flag of our liberation.

When we got tired of listening to the speakers, we turned the flag over to others and walked towards the park next to the railway station. We met a group of policemen marching the opposite way. The group was led by a tall dark-skinned officer in a snow-white uniform. This dashing officer was our five-per-two group leader, Pali Kerekes. When Pali recognized us, he smartly saluted us as he led his detachment past. A few hours later we got together and talked and talked. This was our survivors' celebration! It announced a new world order of tolerance and life. This day celebrated at least three returnees from five-per-two who marched proudly as victors, rather than with hoes across our shoulders. We were now free men, able to move in the direction of our own choosing without the mark of a death warrant on our sleeves.

Our personal needs during this time were simple. Sara was sixteen, and I was twenty-three. We were in love and happy. During our short courtship I talked to Sara about my family and about my strong feelings about being Jewish. In spite of the persecution and in spite of the rebelliousness against my upbringing, I knew who I was. Sara's mother and father were Seventh-Day Adventists, a religion outlawed by the Nazis. We mutually decided that she would convert to Judaism. We both needed a base to build on. The structure had to start with us because each, in our own way, had no remaining family. It was not an issue of having to share the same beliefs as much as it was an issue of being together as one, as starting and building something out of the ashes which were my heritage.

I felt that now, being a married man, I had to be the head of the family. I had the address of the farmer that my mother had named in her letter, who had taken our belongings for safekeeping. I had the need and the obligation, as head of the family, to try to reclaim what remained of my family's possessions. I went to see this man.

"Yes," he said, "I took your family's clothing. I did it at a great risk to myself and my family. Unfortunately the Russian soldiers have taken all the goods."

I had already learned that most "good Samaritans" had similar answers when the Jews returned.

"Nothing is left. The Russians took it."

A few days later I met with my policeman friend, Laci, who had accompanied Sara to the dance. I mentioned to him my futile attempt to retrieve my belongings. He stated that returnees usually received the same response, but he wanted to look into it himself. The next day he returned with a police wagon and a uniformed policeman. He had checked on the farmer's background during the war and found it less than admirable. The three of us revisited the farmer. We were visible from the farm from a long distance before our final approach. We could see hurried activity near the stable area.

"He's hiding your stuff right now!" the uniformed policeman said.

It took another five minutes until we reached the house from the unpaved farm road. The first thing I noticed was that the farmer was wearing a blue vest. I recognized it immediately. It was the vest of my only holiday suit. The farmer had forgotten to hide it in the rush of his sighting us.

"Where did you hide my belongings?"

My voice became angry. The policeman reached for his gun. The farmer lowered his head and began to dig under the manure near the stable. There was a crate filled with my belongings but not my suit. Another crate with my suit in it had to be buried somewhere else.

"Where is the rest of it?" The policeman asked him.

I asked my friend to let it go. I had no stomach for this anymore. I visualized the farmer talking to my mother in our home. Maybe his intention had originally been good. Maybe the poverty and deprivation of the war had changed him. I wanted to believe that he'd at least had good intentions initially. With the part of the family's belongings I retrieved I started a new life.

In our everyday lives the Holocaust survivors pretended that they were not thinking about those who were dear to them whose fates were unknown. On the surface it looked that way. We listened to the radio. We read the papers. Now we knew about the gas chambers. We had seen the pictures from the extermination camps. By not talking about it we felt we could save ourselves the pain of thinking about it. How foolish we were!

I was married. I had good food. I was content. In spite of this the nightmares came. Sara woke me up many times when I was screaming, cursing, and crying in my sleep. In my dreams I saw my father defeated, being worked as a horse by the Nazis. I saw him in harness pulling the plow with three other exhausted old men. He was looking at me with his suffering eyes, begging for help. I tried to run towards him, but no matter how hard I tried, I could not move. At night in my dream world I was part of the human stampede, again and again. I was running barefoot in between my frightened brothers. At night I saw my brother József facing the gendarmes seconds before he was murdered. I wanted to yell at him, "Run, József, run," but no sound issued from my lips. In my dreams I was hiding a few yards behind him in the bushes, facing his executioners, trying to stretch out my arms to pull him to safety. In my dreams I came home early only to be captured and bayonetted. How many times Sara woke me, to hold me and comfort me! "You're home. I am with you."

She dried my tears, saying a comforting word. In the mornings after such nightmares, I felt calm and peaceful at finding Sara sleeping next to me. Because of Sara I was able, bit by bit, to live my life despite my nightmares. These nightmares lasted twelve years. Their cessation coincided with my arrival in the United States. It was only then that I felt truly free for the first time.

- *42* -

I was out of the city when the Jewish help organization from Budapest notified the Kecskemét Jewish committee of the homecoming of my two lost sisters. They had survived the death camp. I was not home when the message arrived. My sisters Sara and Iren arrived into the arms of strangers. The first sentence to my sisters by the Jewish committee as they alighted from the train was, "Your brother Odon is alive, but he married a Gentile girl."

My sisters came to our home shorn, burned by the sun, malnourished, terribly unhealthy, but very tough and embittered. Their features still showed the hardness and brutality they had endured in the death camp.

As soon as I heard that my sisters were home, I ran to them with an open heart. This was the first time I knew that anyone in my family was still alive. My most fervent prayers had been answered. Miracles did happen!

This miracle had an ice-cold core. They greeted me with cold stares and cruel questions. My marriage was an affront to them. It was more torture added on to what they had already endured. My wife Sara just stood there listening, not believing the cutting words she was hearing. She tried to show so much warmth towards them. She was wearing a dress which I had reclaimed from the farmer. My sister Iren's first words to her new sister-in-law were, "That's mine. Take it off."

They resented her. They despised me. I was hounded by countless questions. "How could you betray us? How could you marry a Gentile girl? Don't you know what the Christians did to us?"

Almost every evening during this difficult time, Sara cried in the privacy of our bedroom. I asked her to be patient and understanding of my sisters. Every morning she woke up smiling and ready for a new day. The trouble was that I lost my patience and my understanding for my sisters and expressed my annoyance. I had been persecuted by my fellow Hungarians. I had endured too much to now be persecuted by my own sisters. I knew that it would take time before the bitterness and harshness against the entire world abated, but I had served my own time and was unwilling and unable to endure its placement on me and my seventeen-year-old bride.

So it happened that within months, Sara's innate goodness triumphed over the ill will that my sisters had of her, and she became their long-lost sister. I was the strange, angry one. I remained somewhat estranged after this brutal homecoming and its aftermath.

Most of the time we were like brother and sisters. During the evenings my sister Sara would talk about the years when I was away in the labor battalion. Very seldom did either of my sisters talk about Auschwitz. I knew not to push. The subject of my father came up often. Who had reported him to the Gestapo? In what way was he a prominent Jew? We searched for an answer and dreamed about finding the guilty one. My wife's stepfather, who was a detective in the political department, discreetly told me that the person most likely to have been responsible was one of our neighbors, a veterinarian whose yard faced the back-wall section of our home.

One day I went over to the veterinarian's house, determined and full of hatred. A reckoning was to be made. Mrs. Szabó cried that her husband had left with the German forces in November. She was sobbing and did not know where he was. I left without saying a word. I was not like them. I could not harm a crying woman.

More people from the concentration camps came home. Among those who returned was Zsuzsa Schlessinger, the girlfriend of my childhood's best friend, Pista Virag. She visited us in our home. Pista and his girlfriend had been part of our bicycle circle. Both of them were passionate listeners to the Aush stories. By this time we had proof that Pista had perished in the copper mines of Bor. I cried with her about him and about her being alone in this lonely world. Her whole family had disappeared. I wanted to help her so much. But everyone returning needed help. Everyone had a tragic story, and almost everyone had their entire family wiped off the face of this sad, sad earth. I wondered why I still had some vestiges of family left and why some of my heritage had been salvaged.

I met some of my former soccer mates. They were all Gentile boys whose lives remained relatively unscathed. I tried to read in their eyes and body movements whether they were really glad to see me or whether I was one more Jew who had returned. Former teachers visited me and asked for my help in being witness to their character and their behavior during the prewar times. Sometimes I tried to ask questions to understand why these things had happened in our city. I wanted to comprehend what had happened, but answers were never forthcoming and always vague. Eyes were routinely cast downwards. I tried to adjust. I tried not to look at these neighbors and townspeople as possible murderers and torturers. Sometimes it was relatively easy, sometimes it was impossible. I tried to get on with my life. I tried to go forward. Sometimes, though, when wives came home without husbands and mothers came home without children, it became impossible.

It was time to start a new life with my wife and me as the nucleus. My sisters moved out of my friend's house and into another. Sara and I moved back to our old family home. We made minor repairs. We put back the fence. We refurnished our house in a very spartan manner. The Jewish self-help organization gathered enough furniture from abandoned Jewish homes whose owners would never return for those who had returned. It was summer when the new Mandel household at Mikes Street 4 began a new life. We knew then that we were expecting a baby. It would be the first Jewish baby born in the city. Sara was going daily to Rabbi Schindler to learn her new religion. She studied Hebrew daily. We were remarried according to Jewish law in Budapest in front of seven rabbis. Dr. Schindler was so proud of Sara as a student that he invited the entire rabbinical committee for the occasion.

- 43 -

I started to practice soccer again. I began slowly. I began with the idea of having some exercise and some fun. Naturally, I was far from the form which I had been before. Soccer, though, gave my life the continuity it needed. Soccer again became important. It was very difficult for me to regain the lost years. How envious I was when a former friend, who had been a reserve on the team with Koranyi when I was a starter, became the center forward of our team. I had to admit he deserved the honor. With time, I got better and began to play regularly. I still remembered all the potential the war had taken away.

We played a memorable game in the city of Szentes. Kecskemét was the sixth team out of fourteen. Szentes was among the last three. The two last teams would be removed from our division, so Szentes was desperate. They needed this win to stay in the division. The win would have no meaning to us in regard to standing. The Szentes team invited us to a dinner after the game, which clearly imparted a plea to let them tie or win. The game was coming to an end at zero-zero. I was near the eighteen-yard line moving towards their goal. I had no intention to try to shoot. The Szentes team would have been furious, and I wanted to give them the dignity of a tie. My teammates would have killed me, wanting that dinner invitation more than a win.

One of their players accidentally tripped me. I fell into the penalty box. The referee whistled and called for a penalty shot. Both sides protested. I told the referee that the foul was unintentional and outside the box. Three to four thousand fans rushed the referee from the stands. The two teams formed a circle to shield him. At first the situation was comical. The referee was short and bald. Fans tried to reach him with umbrellas but tried not to hit the players, who formed a taller wall around him. Within minutes the crowd's disposition changed. The fans became enraged. We felt that we were not able to fully protect this endangered little referee. He was pushed and hit with umbrellas until we reached our truck with him in tow. We kept going. Our team was chased from Szentes, stones hitting our truck. We missed our promised dinner. It took us a few days to retrieve our belongings from Szentes. The game was called a tie officially. The Szentes team was allowed to play one more year in our division.

During this time the Beretvas Coffee House was always busy with returnees trying to find a thread of normalcy in the comradery there. In the midst of conversation, music, and card playing there was an air of both desperation and unbounding courage. When I found time to go there after soccer practice, I watched the card games and listened to the conversations.

My little friend Karcsi was a regular at the coffee house. He was the best chess player in the group. I laughed at his side remarks and entertaining monologues. He was courting my sister Sara again. His whole life consisted of courting Sara.

The Beretvas Coffee House was a place of safety and comfort. For most of us who had only token families, it became a second home. It was more than a gathering place. It was a place where reaffirmation took place. People of different backgrounds and experiences could gather in that room, knowing that all of them were linked in a loss that was not spoken of. I liked to move around and observe. If I had a chance I would listen to the bawdy and gross stories of the Pacsirta bordello's owner. He was an ugly little fellow. The police were always after him for something. He never seemed to care. He was a hero to us since he, as a non-Jew, had saved one of us, Béla Schrieber, from the Jewish round-up by housing him in his whorehouse. His name was Somlo. He was vulgar, yet he was full of crass vitality. I loved to listen to his loud, fast stories comparing the sexual proclivities of the Hungarian, German, and Russian officers who had frequented his establishment. He had reverence for none of them.

There was in this coffee house group a braggart who used to boast of his sexual prowess. Karcsi bet him that he was just boasting and couldn't perform in front of the group. Six "volunteers" plus Somlo, who would be the judge, piled into carriages and drove to the Pacsirta bordello to observe his much-discussed powers. Days later the whole city was talking about this episode. Although they talked about how shamefully and immodestly we had all acted, they also talked in great detail about how the braggart had failed the public test.

Before World War II Kecskemét's distillery was very famous for producing apricot brandy. It was leased by an expert, a Jew named Izidor Fuhrer. He was in Budapest during the war. After the liberation of Budapest he came back to run the distillery. My sister Iren, who had worked there before the war, went back to work for him. Schnapps was in great demand among the Soviet officers. Iren had constant contact with the Soviet officials who purchased, demanded, and robbed them of alcoholic spirits.

One day a Russian general came into the distillery. He was very polite and ordered one hundred liters of apricot brandy, paid for it, and left. A few days later the general was back again. He stayed even longer this time. Iren and I sensed he was Jewish and that he wanted to talk to us. I told Iren that she should invite him for a Friday Sabbath candlelighting ceremony. The general agreed to come. When he entered our home he asked us to pull the curtains on the window so that no one would observe us during the religious ceremony.

He was very touched to be included in such an intimate ritual. He confided in us that he did not know the condition of his family. He was from Zhitomir, which was under German occupation for almost three years. We shared a common cord of sadness about dislocation and sundered family life. I had more in common with this Russian and his losses than with fellow Hungarians who had moved to more luxurious quarters when the Jews were removed from their homes and farms.

Onions and salt became unavailable and, therefore, in great demand. The lack of these commodities was caused, not so much by shortages, but because of problems with distribution and transportation. People became reluctant to take money. Barter was legal and flourishing. I offered a Russian officer a partnership if he let me have an army truck and a driver to go to the city of Makó, where onions were plentiful and schnapps in great demand. The deal was struck. With the help of a few bottles of schnapps, we managed to buy a full load of onions. On the way back, at a roadblock, Russian soldiers asked for our travel documents. For a leftover bottle of schnapps, we were waved through. We sold the onions for more schnapps. My partner, the Soviet officer, was now a profitable capitalist. He was eager to do it again. I thought it easier to split the profits and the partnership at this time because a night visit from the soldiers could wipe out my original investment and the profits.

Rumors went around that I had schnapps to sell. I now had another partner. My partner, a camp returnee, was one-quarter Jewish. Before the war he had not considered himself a Jew. All his friends were Gentiles. He was the boxing champion of the city. At the height of fascist power he learned that whether or not he considered himself a Jew, the state did. He was placed in a labor battalion.

He suggested that we barter the schnapps for linen, take the linen to the villages for lard, and then sell the lard in Budapest. We made the first exchange successfully. We then traveled from village to village with horse and wagon trying to barter the linen. Nobody wanted our linen. We decided to return home. On the way to Kecskemét he looked up to the sky and stopped the horse "The stars are up. It is the Sabbath. I cannot travel."

His camp experiences had turned him from a quasi-Christian into an observant religious Jew.

We spent the night next to the horses and the wagon, talking. His story was painful to hear. He had himself been antisemitic, calling others antisemitic epithets. He had thought Jews were subhuman. He had done this with no consideration that he too was a Jew. He told me this in tears. It was a striking confession. Tears ran down the face of this former boxing champion. Before he and the rest of his Jewish family were taken away, his eighteen-year-old sister had killed herself. This event and the tragedy of the entire experience had converted him.

The next day, as we thought about our plans to barter linen into wealth, soldiers came and robbed us of our linen, our horse, and our wagon. That was the end of my bartering experiences. But I will remember this observant Jew who became religious and felt most valued by God when he himself was considered worthless by the state and its countrymen.

A few weeks after this bartering experience a young man approached me. He said that he had some leftover pieces of colorful man-made leather of good quantity. If I found material for soles, we could try to manufacture women's shoes. Sara's older sister had worked during the war in a shoe factory. She was now unemployed with a baby. She checked out the material and said that it could be done. I found discarded rubber pieces for soles. I rented a few machines. We started to manufacture shoes. The shoes looked very good. They started to sell in the market. The trouble was, as soon as somebody stepped in the shoe, the sole broke in half. If they brought the shoe back, we would repair it.

During my shoe days, one of the owners of the print shop returned. I turned the print shop over to him. Now I was full-time in the shoe-manufacturing business. Eventually we sold out all the shoes and closed the shop. I then returned to my father's business, which was wholesale fruit and wine. I felt that the circle was closed. Here I was starting my new life and yet somehow repeating my past.

I stayed with the fruit and wine business for a year, doing small business deals. Money was worthless. It was impossible to keep ahead of the spiraling inflation. If I purchased wine on Monday, I resold it on Tuesday at double the price. On Wednesday, for the money I had received for a full load, I was able to purchase half a load of the same quality of wine.

Laci Kovacs was now the manager of the local bank. He, who saved so many lives as an army officer in charge of a labor battalion, was well respected by the citizens irrespective of their political views. He kept our small businesses going by opening his bank from early morning to late evening. Business people, with his help, could borrow money in the morning and return it that same evening. He was a wonderful person. He was full of integrity and embodied true heroics with a mild, self-effacing modesty.

In late September a circus came to our city. As I was standing in line to get a ticket, I noticed a Soviet officer scrutinizing me carefully. It was Shmelkin. On his gold epaulet was a shining new gold star. His unit had been returned to Kecskemét after having taken part in the final offensive for Berlin. I was so glad that he was alive and well. I invited him home. I introduced him to Sara, who was in her fifth month of pregnancy. Slowly, during his almost daily visits, he started to tell us about the final Soviet offensive to capture Berlin. His sergeant, who had been my friend originally and had introduced us, was the first casualty.

Shmelkin noticed, even with my sisters visiting often, the terrible void in my family. This emptiness allowed him to talk of his vacuum. He was able to talk about his family, who had disappeared from Kiev during the German occupation of the city. My sister Sara shared her grief about her vanished husband. A bond between them was created.

The cold weather approached fast. With my Sara expecting, an unheated house was unthinkable and yet firewood and coats were totally unavailable in the city. One evening about midnight there was a banging in the yard. A Soviet truck was parked in front of our house. Break-ins, burglaries, and rapes were common now. We were frightened and would not go to answer the door. Finally a soldier came to our bedroom window and began to bang on it, saying, "Shmelkin. Shmelkin!"

I opened the gate. The truck rolled into the yard. The soldiers silently began to unload a truck full of firewood. We were all silent and ashamed. We were ashamed of having feared them, and they were ashamed of doing things that engendered the fear. We invited them for tea and talked into morning, when Shmelkin came for them. Over breakfast we exchanged smiles but never words about the incident.

The water in our well became undrinkable. I had to bring water in from a well three blocks away. I was away on business and Shmelkin took over my job for pregnant Sara. He waited until it was dark to haul water in his uniform with gold stars on it. This officer who gave orders, this officer who marched heroically into battle, this officer could care about new friends. He became intertwined into the family.

Eventually, as we all had expected, my sister Sara and Shmelkin fell in love. They found solace and a little well-earned happiness in one another. He became part of our lost family and we became part of his. We were sad to eventually see him go. This time it would be for good. My letters to him remained unanswered. Was it his fate to die in one of Stalin's gulags or to return to the bosom of his family a hero?

- 44 -

*T*he years right after the war were both dangerous and exciting. Law and order was slowly established. Looting had stopped, but it was almost impossible to stop the Russians when they wanted a woman.

My sister Sara had been staying with us for a while. Late at night during that time, soldiers banged at our door. In great haste I pulled my two Saras into a back room and pushed a high chest in front of the door so that the entrance to the room was completely covered. I am not sure how I had the strength to accomplish this heavy task in seconds, but I did. I guess fear for the safety of my wife and sister gave me the extra impetus.

I opened the door and let the three soldiers in.

"*Barishnya, barishnya!*"

They repeated their desire for a woman over and over again. One of them looked around for a sign of women. I offered them a drink. This pacified them a little. One of them went out and came back with a petrol container filled with vodka.

Throughout the night we drank glassfuls of vodka and ate a bite of bread. A half-glass of vodka, which smelled a little of gasoline, and a bite of black bread with a toast.

"To your health,"

This was repeated again and again in German, Hungarian, and Russian. Once I toasted them in Yiddish, but they were too drunk to notice. The soldiers left at daybreak. Fear kept me sober. We treated the Russians like the liberators they were to us. At the same time we had to guard ourselves from their excesses.

We all wanted our pound of flesh. The Russians wanted revenge for the misery they had endured at the hands of the fascists. We, the survivors, wanted to restart our own lives. So we understood the Russians' brutality towards the Hungarians and hoped that we would not be caught in the crossfire.

The Jewish district attorney who was in charge of interrogations for suspected war crimes was a very handsome middle-aged man. His name was János Gerber. When he returned home from the labor camp, he had found his beautiful young wife and his two children gone. He thereafter lived a bohemian lifestyle for the world, but inside he was burning and suffering like the rest of us. János was a frequent visitor to the Berevtas Coffee House and told us stories about his interrogations. His stories told about his need to punish the guilty ones. We lapped the stories up as they gave us, the listeners, an avenue for our feelings to be vented.

One day János invited all of us to the hanging of a local boy, Komlosi who had been a childhood friend of mine. He had been found guilty of murdering Jews in Budapest. János now was highly placed in the local Communist party. We were proud of János as he stood ramrod straight and issued death orders against the murderer of innocents. His power represented our own power that now could be restored and reasserted.

His power, however, was short-lived. One day he just disappeared from Kecskemét.

In 1952, during the harshest part of the period of Stalinist rule in Hungary, I saw János step off a bus. He was pale, unshaved, and shabbily dressed. He did not answer any of my questions. He whispered something and disappeared into the crowd. In 1956 he escaped from Hungary to start a new life in West Germany. What had created this shadow man from the one with the power of life and death?

A wheeler-dealer came into town to sell an American-made Dodge truck. The vehicle was dark green with stainless-steel ornaments on the hood. I needed the truck for the fruit and wine business. I immediately became its proud owner. What a problem that truck was! All of the replacement parts were Hungarian-made and not the correct specifications. The radiator constantly leaked, and every ten kilometers we had to refill it. The tires would constantly develop flats. After repairing them, we had to used a hand pump to reinflate them. No one was prouder than I was to own a perfect American-made Dodge truck.

When the truck was ready, I hired a driver named Taller. He was short, good-humored, and no matter what happened he always handled it with aplomb. He wore the Communist pin on his jacket and talked about his various Communist meetings. I liked him and trusted him. Once we drove to the village of Uj-Kecske near the river Tisza to purchase a load of apricots. I was bargaining while Taller stayed with the truck. From the direction of the truck I heard someone yelling and cursing. I hurried back to see what was happening. I found a Jewish citizen assaulting my driver with a stick. Taller was sitting at the steering wheel waiting for the cursing and beating to stop.

"What did you do with my furniture, you crook? What did you do with my family's belongings?"

Taller eventually stepped out of the truck and ran away. When my driver returned I questioned him.

"Were you a member of the Arrow Cross, and did you take this man's belongings?"

"Yes."

"Did you believe the way the Nazis believed?"

"I believe in it the same way I believe what the Communists are teaching now. I believe in what I must in order to earn a living for myself and my family. I believe in what I am ordered to believe."

He asked me if I would fire him or report him. I told him I was thinking of doing just that, but that first I would talk to the person whose furniture he took. All the while I had other thoughts. I thought about my not having a driver's license. I thought about having to hire another driver. I knew Taller. I knew his secret. What would the new driver try to hide?

On the way home, he drove silently. I asked him his thoughts. They were simple.

"Mr. Mandel, the Communists will put you behind bars."

When I looked at him he explained further.

"You're a gentleman who is thankful to the Russians for saving your life. You have to acknowledge, though, that you have a capitalist soul. Do not make the mistake believing that the Communists do not know every step you take."

With this he indicated that he had to report everything about me to the authorities.

Taller had thus warned me about himself. I didn't fire him. We were both survivors in our own ways. He stayed with me until the government took away my livelihood "for the people."

He survived in a way I did not respect, which was to shift with the wind. But I also trusted his innate decency. I knew that there were lines of expediency he would not cross. I knew he would not betray me.

A short time after the liberation of Budapest, a highly regarded resident of our city arrived home. His name was Dr. Maxi Kertesz. He was the biggest wine merchant in our district. He needed a partner. Someone mentioned my name to him. He approached me with his offer. I agreed to it. It was a good opportunity for me to be a partner of such a well-known and well-respected person with real business experience. I would now be part-owner of a wine cellar with a holding capacity of two thousand hectoliters of wine. He was living in Budapest, so I ran the business in Kecskemét. We shipped wine to Budapest, Vienna, and Switzerland.

This was a heady time for a former Jewish prisoner. I had another car, an Opel Kadet. It was almost unheard of at that time in that city for somebody to have such a car. My situation was so good that even the tobacco shop's old lady started to be overly cooperative with me. Good cigarettes were worth gold. She always kept my brand for me. The price was very reasonable for me. The sports paper was put aside for me also. I had traveled a long distance from the time of her ignoring me.

It was in the spring of 1946 that I received the news from the Red Cross. My brother Sándor was in an army hospital in Debrecen. My sister Iren and I rushed to Debrecen in the Dodge with Taller driving. Sándor had been sent back from Soviet captivity with hundreds of other sick prisoners. It was another nightmare, looking for and finally finding him among the thousands of moaning, sick men in the makeshift infirmary.

As we were going from building to building, we saw psychiatric inmates dressed as soldiers in full uniform saluting us with a stiff-armed "Heil Hitler!" They were insane. There were "Hitlers" in all the rooms. Finally a tired, low voice whispered my name. We took Sándor to Budapest to the Jewish hospital. He never recovered. He was buried in Budapest. There is comfort, though, in having been able to say goodbye. This comfort was denied me in regard to my other relatives. I now knew everyone's fate in my family.

The compassionate "whore" Boske returned to the neighborhood. I was so happy to see her. She was in a terrible economic situation, and I offered her a job as a wine buyer in the outlying villages. She made a good life for herself in a couple of years. With all her sexual infidelities she had true loyalty to her friends and neighbors. Because of her emotional heart I knew what had become of my father. I will always carry with me the image of him fettered to the plow, alone. As horrible as that image may be, it is worse to have no image. The worst is to never know.

- 45 -

One day a security police officer unexpectedly walked into the winery. I wasn't worried about his surprise visit, but I was wary. These security police, who were originally a meld of Jewish returnees and people dedicated to the new regime, now tended to be doctrinaire and intimidating. There was only one right way of thinking, and they would decide what it was. True believers tended to forget human decency for absoluteness of dogma. As the state security police became more organized, the old nucleus of believers in the new democratic and Communist system were replaced by power-hungry people ready to serve any system.

The officer asked questions. As he was questioning me, I could not help but think about Taller's prediction. Had somebody reported me? What could I have done which was now suspect? Had I said something about the system? Was I too capitalistic for this government? I was sweating a bit. The meeting lasted about twenty minutes. He ordered me to be in front of his office at nine the next morning with my car. I did not know what to expect. I arrived as ordered and waited for an hour. He came out in his full-dress uniform. He continued to question me. This time, the issue of Palestine was foremost in his questions.

Most Jews had thought of emigrating to Palestine. He knew about my wife. He knew she had converted and learned Hebrew. He knew that the rabbi felt that she was a perfect example of the Jewish wife. He knew too much about me and Sara. Perhaps, I thought, he wanted to recruit me. Perhaps he wanted to find out if we planned to escape from the country to Palestine. I was very careful about what I said to him, but I wasn't afraid to say what I felt, although in a carefully guarded way.

I eventually found out the reason for our meeting. We arrived in the city of Kiskunfélegyháza. There my interrogator was fitted for boots with a famous bootmaker! I had a car, and he needed a chauffeur to take him to the fitting. He was using me because he had power and I did not. It had nothing to do with any interest in me or my family. It didn't even have to do with his official capacity. It was simply a blatant abuse of power. I hated this system. This country of mine seemed to continually abuse the power its government held. I knew from that minute that sooner or later I had to leave Hungary. The question was when.

The years between 1946 and 1948 were good years for my family. New money, the Hungarian forint, was issued. Commerce was conducted in a more normal way. The black market stopped. We prospered in the fruit and wine business. Our daughter was growing and filled our lives with happiness. How amazing it was to look at her face and see the face of generations in it. I saw my mother's smile and my father's chin. It gave me enjoyment and pleasure watching her milestones, her strength and vitality. Oh, if my father had only had a chance to help her with her first steps! Oh, if my mother could only have held her! I knew too clearly the fragility of life to ever take anything more for granted.

The years 1948 and 1949, despite the stability, were a time when quite a few Jews, older and braver than us, saw the handwriting on the wall and left the country. It was dangerous but not impossible for experienced survivors to cross the border. After 1948, the Communists got stronger and stronger. It became quite constricting to anyone who did not believe in their propaganda. They tightened the screws, and it became impossible to escape from the country. Travel to the West became impossible. The borders were surrounded by barbed wire and mine fields, and it became a faraway dream to leave. I had good friends in different departments of the city government, and they left me in peace. I was without many real problems, but time was running out.

The waves in our personal lives also quieted down. I was content. I had plans to build a house near a fruit orchard I had bought in 1948. The apples were much better than the ones my father had tried to store in the cellar. We had one hundred and fifty apple trees among other fruit trees. We had beautiful reisling grapes. I was satisfied with our life. I was young and did not foresee the future becoming black again.

In the spring of 1949, through a former five-per-two friend who was a border patrol officer, I had a chance to get out of the country. Foolishly and shortsightedly I decided against the venture. I decided to wait for one more harvest. I could make more money which would allow me more choices, or so I thought. That harvest was my undoing, because afterwards it was impossible to leave. Alas, another life-shaping choice. By the time the harvest ended I had made lots of money, but the money was meaningless.

After the 1949 harvest, on the first Monday in November, two Hungarian Communist Party functionaries, satisfaction written on their faces, came to my wine cellar and announced that in the name of the people, the government was taking over my business. It was not exactly unexpected, because by this time lots of other establishments had been nationalized and their owners jailed. How many times would my life and belongings be confiscated? First the Nazis and now the Communists! There was little wine in the cellar, but the value of the machinery and barrels was great. The whole confiscation process lasted not more than two minutes. I was ready to leave and tried to remove my coat from the coat tree. One of the comrades said, "There is nothing you can take from here. It is all nationalized. Walk out just the way you are."

My car was also taken away, so I arrived home early without it.

Without needing to explain to Sara, who realized what had happened the moment I walked in coatless in the middle of the day, we sat down in the yard and watched our daughter play. She was now almost three years old.

We decided that we had to leave the city immediately. The usual procedure was that after they nationalized a business, owners were asked to work for the nationalized company. As soon as the new people learned the ropes, the old capitalist was arrested and put in jail as an enemy of the people. I had gone that route before and had no desire to repeat the experience. So I felt I had to leave.

I took the first train that night to Budapest. I had to find a home for my family. This time it would be easier, I told myself in the dark train. I am an experienced restarter, I said to the wheels. We lost our home again. We would start again. We would live. My father's face materialized in my mind's eye in the train.

I remembered a saying my father had used often: "*Maul halten und weiter dienen.*" It meant literally to keep one's mouth shut and do your work. I kept saying the words over and over almost like a mantra. I improved on the translation. I felt it meant that I had to move on and continue the work of rebuilding. I did not have the power to protest these inequities. But neither would I ever apologize for my capitalistic heart or whatever I was. I would quell my anger. I would revise my view of my liberators. They would always be the ones who had helped free me, and yet now I knew the truth. I had freed myself, and the Soviets offered another kind of imprisonment. I would wait for another turn of the wheel for my time.

BOOK TWO

- 1 -

It was late 1949 when I arrived in Budapest to start fresh again. This was the second time I had to start from nothing. Communist oppression was now felt in every sphere of life. The Hungarian Workers' Party, the official name of the Communist Party, was in full control of the country. The other parties, including the Social Democrats, the Christian Democrats, the Smallholders, and the Farmers, all which had been in existence in 1945, had been forcibly disbanded. The leaders of those now illegal parties were in jail or serving their new masters in other roles. Hungary, as it was during the German occupation, was again a dictatorship. Any statement of views different from the official party line, which was dictated by Moscow, was dangerous. A joke about the Communist Party or its leaders was reason for being sentenced to jail for five years. What began for me as a liberation and a triumph of survival had become just another unity under one party with one form of thought. The color was different this time—red with a hammer and sickle in the middle, but the ideology was remarkably familiar.

Iron-tight rules were enforced by the Allamvédelmi Osztaly, or AVO, the state security police. This organization followed the format and the structure of the Soviet KGB. Without an exception every office, apartment building, sports organization, and factory had informers on the payroll of the AVO.

Politically correct thought and acts were monitored. The problem for most was to try and identify the informer and isolate him. This was a serious matter and one of some import, but it did not have the life-or-death weight of the Nazi regime. This was a situation under which we could live, though restrictively, but live nonetheless. Those who had survived the Holocaust viewed these restrictions as temporary, though there were rumbles of paranoia in all of us.

Apartment building doors were locked at eleven in the evening. The porters had the only keys to the building. If a person was frequently out later or had many visitors at late hours, he could expect a night visit from the AVO. The most likely result of such a visit was a sudden disappearance of the offender in a black car. To the question of where a neighbor had gone came a sarcastic answer, "On a long vacation with the Black Maria!"

Oh, those black AVO cars!

Just like those horrible Nazi years, we still had midnight visits, disappearances, and silent witnesses to these events. At the same time we survivors owed our very lives to the liberators. We had known worse times and worse atrocities, and we hoped for gradual improvement. Our hopefulness kept us alive, but also slightly blinded.

This was the political situation when I arrived in Budapest alone and needing to put down new roots after my business was nationalized. I needed to find an apartment and work before sending for my wife and child. According to the laws which were in force at that time, I had to report to the police department in the district where I planned to stay. As a young man, under the benign supervision of the police detective Virag, I had lived in the Seventh District. It was near beautiful Andrassy Street and Teraz Boulevard. I decided to return to that area.

As I walked on Andrassy Street towards the Seventh District's police station, I had to pass Andrassy Street 60, the notorious AVO Interrogation Center. In the three-square-block area of this detention center there were armed guards in full AVO uniform in front of every building. I turned off onto Iza-bella Street and noticed a blue sign noting the police station. There were no AVO guards in front of this building. I took this as a good sign.

I had heard of experiences with the uniformed AVO bullies and was well aware of their menace. I had also had two per-sonal experiences with the AVO. One was my drive with the officer who had questioned me the entire time but was merely using me as a means of transportation to his bootmaker, which made me adverse to their uniform and to the abuse of power it represented. The other was a more recent experience. I had run into a former five-per-two colleague on crowded Terez Boulevard who was now wearing the insignia of a cap-tain on his AVO uniform. I had heard that this AVO captain, this former Jewish slave under the Nazis, had not survived. Running into him was unexpected and astonishing. Without thinking I greeted him with open arms and a big smile. He looked at me very coldly and within seconds left me confused in the middle of the sidewalk. We had been good friends in the labor camp. He had been so decent. What had happened to him? Maybe he hated it when I cried out his Jewish name so loudly in my enthusiasm. Had he changed his name to a more Hungarian-sounding one? Maybe I should have addressed him with his title rather than informally as a friend. Had he already forgotten all the experiences which had bonded us together? These were not to be forgotten. This is why it was a relief and a good omen to see the police station not beset by AVO uniforms and their associations.

I filled out the required forms at the police station. I was instructed by the policeman to turn it over to an officer in the next room. The officer looked friendly, and I felt quite adept at judging a person intuitively. After checking my form he asked how long I planned to stay in Budapest. I told him that I planned to relocate permanently and find employment. After a few more friendly questions about Kecskemét, I told him that years ago as a youngster before World War II, I had stayed in Budapest and that a police detective had taken me under his wing. He showed interest so I continued in this vein about his being a manager of a soccer club.

A flicker of recognition passed over the officer's face and he responded, "You're talking about Sergeant Virag." Lowering his voice to a whisper, he told me that the soccer club had been outlawed and its leaders jailed.

He asked if I planned to play soccer again. My heart leaped as I thought about the possibility, "Yes!"

The "yes" came forth so spontaneously, and I knew that this "yes" was for everything I was and for everything I had to endure. For myself I would play. For my lost years I would play. For the jailed Sergeant Virag I would play. The police officer told me that the old team had been reorganized under a new name and new leadership. He also told me that he felt that Virag would be happy if he knew that I remembered him in such a kind way. He raised his hand, stamped my paper, and said, "Friends."

The first item on my agenda was to find an apartment. After that was settled I could bring up my family from Kecskemét. The police officer helped me in this matter also. I would be indebted to him twice. He informed me that in this three-block radius, the AVO had usurped every building except the police station and the building next to it, number sixty-three. The tenants of that building were worried that it would be the next to be taken over. Because of that fear Mr. Mann, who already had an exit visa, was having a problem selling his apartment.

I walked next door to visit Mr. Mann. He told me that he was legally leaving the country soon. He had sold all his furniture, but everyone was afraid to purchase the apartment, fearing its confiscation by the AVO. I told him I would take my chances. In two minutes the deal was done. I think one of the reasons that I moved so quickly was my concern about being away from my family. When I was away in the labor battalion, I had returned to emptiness. I felt I had to do everything possible to rush to get my family to my side.

Mr. Mann knew someone at the Housing and Development Department who would expedite matters for a bribe. Papers were signed. The civil servant took home several weeks of salary tax-free, and I became the owner of an apartment.

The apartment was on the third floor, facing the street. From the bedroom windows I could watch the AVO soldiers guarding the building across the street. It took me seven years and the Hungarian Revolution to finally know what kinds of things occurred behind the always-closed grated windows covered with white curtains.

- 2 -

My family joined me in Budapest, and we were moved into the apartment in the matter of days. We felt very fortunate. I had not been jailed in Kecskemét, and we were now in a nice apartment in the big city.

Sara enjoyed the city sounds. The streetcars, the metro, and the other wonders of city life enlivened her. Agi, our daughter, was wide-eyed at the move as well. After the nationalization of my business and after the move that followed, it seemed that fate had directed us to the right place to help us start a new life again.

Our new nextdoor neighbor, Mr. Oroszi, was a university professor. He lived with his quiet wife who was also a schoolteacher. Mr. Oroszi was a well-built, good-natured intellectual. He was friendly and always ready with advice or help if I asked for it. Mrs. Oroszi was a chubby, shy, motherly type. Both were very religious Catholics. In time we became good friends and neighbors.

After I found work and was receiving a salary, the Oroszis and the Mandels found a way to make ends meet. We received our salaries at different times. My salary was on the Monday of every second week. Theirs came on the first and fifteenth of every month. The day I received my salary, the Oroszis routinely walked over to borrow a few forints until their paycheck arrived a few days later. Years later, when our reserves were gone, the forints went the other way.

Next to the Oroszis' apartment were a young couple who were ardent believers in the Communist dogma. The husband was a small, pleasant physician. Everybody on the third floor warned us that he was a highly placed member of the Communist Party.

"Be careful of what you say around him," I was warned.

It took me years to learn that he was a member of the progressive side of the Communist Party and in and out of political trouble most of the time for that affiliation. I was pleasantly surprised when I found out that he was a founding member of the progressive Petőfi Club. This club was made up of intellectuals who had lost their good standing with the party's leaders. Even so, they could meet with the tacit approval of the party apparatus. Their belief was in the humanistic socialist concept without their tolerating the totalitarian excesses.

I had to find a job. I went to the printers' union. The real unions, which represented the interests of the different trades, had been closed one by one by the Communist regime. The remaining unions were tools of the regime. They were unions in name only. We had been told that the workers did not need protection from the capitalist managers since there were no more capitalists in Hungary. The Communist Party would now take care of all the needs of the workers. The workers had lost their voice. Their voice was now the uniform voice of the party.

The AVO had a file on everybody. Sometimes there were just little notes about a shady business deal or about someone's past history. An affair with one's secretary was recorded the same way as one's wife's infidelity was recorded. I remember talking with Taller, my former truck driver, who warned me of such things. I was sure that he himself was made to inform due to something written in his file about his former Arrow Cross activities. When information was needed, the AVO could enlist those with some cloud on their files to inform or ferret out information on another person. This new person, who now had a besmirched record, would be called upon later.

I went to the personnel director at the union office and told him my work history. This man advised me to prepare my answers carefully. He told be to avoid mentioning any capitalist endeavor of mine in interviews at any prospective workplace. He sent me to the Capital City Printing Company. After thorough questioning and my intricately prepared answers, I was sent to the typesetting department and began work there. Two hours later I was called back to the personnel department and fired without explanation.

I returned to the union wondering whether the interviewer, who had heard the entirety of my history, had warned the printing company about my background. I wondered about my AVO file. This was the only way I could understand my immediate firing.

The personnel director of the union looked at me for a few seconds and then told me that the army needed a typesetter it could trust. I gathered that my being a Jew gave me a favored position of trust in the new Communist regime. I was sent to a three-story building near the Eastern Railroad Station and presented my papers.

Sitting behind the desk was a young, good-looking lieutenant with an intelligent face. He offered me a chair. I felt more relaxed. While he looked over my documents, I tried to find his name-plate on the desk. I needed to feel some connection with him. He asked about my childhood, my whereabouts during the war, and what I had done after the war. I spoke mainly about my five-per-two years. He appeared knowledgeable and understanding. I asked his name.

"I am a lieutenant in the army. I am here only to ascertain whether you will be a good worker for the state. You will answer my questions. I do not have to answer yours."

That was his cold answer. It didn't matter what his name-plate said because there was nothing warm or human about his response. I had to learn that my feelings for the liberators needed constant retooling. I might have felt a brotherhood towards them, but they felt little kinship towards me. They had their own agenda.

Behind him on the wall were large colored prints of Stalin, Lenin, and Rákosi. The latter was the most hated Soviet-educated Jewish Hungarian leader. He was despised by everyone—Jews, Christians, party members, and nonparty members. I started to feel concerned about my situation, surrounded as I was with stern Communist faces. I stopped feeling relaxed. I realized that I was being interrogated and not interviewed for a job by this officer.

After more questions he stated, "Comrade Mandel, everything looks in order. Read this statement about yourself and sign it."

When I read his summary I began to realize my predicament. The statement began with the "fact" that my father had been a landowner and speculator. My poor father, who couldn't make any investment or business venture work, was now a capitalist! It went on to state that I had been in black market activities after the war. The next paragraph stated that my friends were all intellectual reactionaries who disliked everything Hungarian and democratic. Furthermore, by signing the paper, I was pledging to change my thinking and become a true patriot fighter for the new socialist Hungary.

My fear disappeared as my temper flared. I realized that in order to hire me, the lieutenant needed to protect himself from my political views. This paper, while protecting him, could be my arrest warrant. This confession would put me in the position of being blackmailed into becoming his informer in return for a job.

I took a deep breath, raised my head, looked straight into his eyes, and told him that there were two statements that were accurate in the entire document: my name and my birthdate. He looked at me and forced a smile.

"Think it over."

I tried to appeal to his decency. I told him that I had not been in the black market, but was a merchant along with hundreds of thousands of other honest Hungarians. I told him that I had paid all my taxes. All I wanted was to be left in peace with my family and be able to work. I whispered a last plea almost to myself.

"I deserve this. I have earned it."

He didn't answer. He closed his eyes for a second and said, "Go in peace."

Naturally I did not get the job, but I had not sold myself out and had not been sold out.

I left the building shaking, my body weak. The shirt on my back was wet. Life was so dangerous. I walked into a coffee house to pull myself together before returning home. I ordered a double espresso with a double shot of rum. I needed two more before the abject fear left me. I kept wondering about how harrowing life was for me. I had survived one dehumanizing experience to end up fearful again. I was somewhat drunk. I knew that good or bad I had to face what life had to offer. This time, though, I would face it with my family.

- 3 -

*T*he next day, I returned for the third time to the old fellow at the union. He looked at me, surprised to see that I had returned and perplexed as to what to do with me. He looked in his files, and sent me to a printing establishment on Aradi Street, the Globus Printing Company. This place was a two-minute walk from my newly acquired home. I knew that it was probably the last job I would be offered. I knew I had to make this interview work for me.

I presented my papers to a lady comrade. I knew that the only possible way to present myself was to be truthful and as forthright as I could, since information had probably preceded me. I told her I was from Kecskemét. I told her that I was a former merchant whose business had recently been national-ized. I told her that I had been fired the day before yesterday by Capital City Printing Company after two hours' work because my business had been nationalized. On top of this I was not hired by the army's print shop after a lengthy inter-view.

"Consider all this as you inquire about my past. Also know that I will be an excellent worker."

I did not know that as I was making my little speech, some-one was behind me, leaning on the doorframe and nodding his approval of me to this woman. I was hired due to a sign from this hidden person. I was told to report to the company's technical director. The nameplate on his door proclaimed his name, Ferenc Nagy! I got a warm handshake from the man who had cleaned my bloody nose after a soccer game a long time ago. He had urged me then to hit harder and land the first blow. He had been the person leaning on the doorjamb giving me an okay which only the personnel director at Globus could see. Perhaps he felt that my speech to the personnel director followed his earlier suggestion of direct punching. After a few minutes of friendly talk and a few questions about the war, the family, and mostly soccer, Ferenc told me to be at work early the next morning and at soccer practice at two the next afternoon.

I had a job. I had a new home. I had a sports team that was anxious to have me. I had my family. How lucky could one person be!

Globus, one of the largest printing establishments in Hungary, occupied two buildings and employed eight hundred people. The company had its own soccer team. Most of the team members were employees of Globus, but a few were recruited from the outside. Béla Nagy, a former Hungarian all-star, was a player on our team.

Another member of our team was someone we nicknamed Rozoga, or "Weakling." He told me that he was from Szolnok. I told him about my championship game in that city and the offer I had received to play semiprofessionally by changing my name. From that moment on, Rozoga attached himself to me. Every moment of free time, he sought me out and told me fantastic stories about his life. He told me he had been a spy for the Soviets during the war and other unbelievable stories. Sometimes, listening to him, I felt that he had read Baron Munchausen's tall tales and had adapted them to his own needs. I felt that he needed to impress me with his lies. He always looked unkept and in need of a shave or a haircut, and sometimes both. On the field, although feeble-looking, he could maintain his position. In time I got used to him and my dislike changed to amusement.

When the other teammates started to know and trust me, I was warned by them that Rozoga was a suspected informer. Somehow I felt that I had nothing to fear. I felt sorry for him, knowing from my personal experience with Taller and with the army's interview of me for the print shop that it was easy to be blackmailed into doing what was required. I also knew that once designated an informer by others, rightly or wrongly, that became one's station. No amount of protestation and no amount of good deeds could turn the epithet around. One was thought either to be protesting too much or to be too wily. It made whoever carried the title a pariah and an outsider. I could tell that Rozoga was hungry for approval and would never say anything harmful to his AVO superiors about me.

To again belong to a sports team gave me great advantages. I was a part of a group. I had others to defend me. I had friends. Twice a week we had a half-day off for practice. After a winning game, we earned a small bonus. Months passed by in this easy way. I became close friends with two Jewish men. Their last names also began with the letter *M*. We had all been born in 1922. We had all shared similar experiences during the war years. There were so many similarities that made us close. They loved soccer and came out to watch the games and even the practices. We were called the Three M's. We called ourselves the Three Musketeers.

Sanyi M. was tall and good-looking. He was a firm believer in the Communist system. Béla M. was a skinny, excitable fellow who also believed full-heartedly in the Communist Party. At the beginning of our friendship they housed their comments in Communist generalizations. Both of them had high positions in the company, partly because of their party affiliations. As we grew in friendship we could be more candid and honest about our beliefs. They could share more of their individual feelings and not just the party line, and I felt free to deviate my own individual way.

In the print shop I also made other friends. I heard stories from fellow workers who were former soldiers. They had been in the same place at the same time as I during the war. We had been on different sides, however. Many of them might have been fascists and had now covered their pasts. I had no expertise about how to evaluate these people except by my intuitive sense. I made friends with many of them, and they thought of me as one of them. It was interesting to hear their war stories and to compare their versions with mine.

Friendships developed in the workplace almost by accident. My friendship with Faludy was due to the fact that I was assigned to a workbench next to his. In the beginning I did not like him at all. I considered him a bumpkin, a village boy. He was a former soldier and proud of it. Faludy was popular and well-liked by others.

I began to notice him during the fifteen-minute propaganda meetings. A few times he raised his hand to indicate he wanted the floor. Faludy never openly opposed the speaker. That would have been suicidal and futile. The tone of his voice was always friendly and sounded supportive. He played dumb with the speaker's remarks in order to mock the speaker. He asked questions which sounded curious, but really showed the sparsity of logic in the propaganda. This country bumpkin was as shrewd as they came.

Once, after a propaganda meeting about the Brigade Movement, which was an attempt to have the workers form brigades to enhance productivity, Faludy asked me to form a brigade with him. We became the FA-MA brigade after the first two letters of our last names. The purpose of competitive workers increasing their quotas was swept aside by us. We always managed to achieve a 150 percent or more quota with little work, a friendly wink to a supervisor, or a bit of homemade sausage to the foreman. Faludy knew how to work the system well. I had learned how to do this in the labor battalion. I wondered where Faludy had learned.

After a few beers we would talk about the war years. At first I would tell him about the labor battalion, although I emphasized the good Hungarians such as Szonyi and Bimbo. I emphasized the barbarous Germans. He told me about a soldier in his unit who killed his captain for taunting him with allegations that his mother had syphilis. After the killing the soldier escaped with Faludy. The solider then joined the partisans. In his telling of the story, it was clear that Faludy could have killed or betrayed him on several occasions but did not. This emboldened me to speak more about my experiences. Faludy had been at the Prut crossings when I was there. I asked him if he had any special recall of the Jewish prisoners; he said he did not.

"How could that be?" I asked

"We had our job and our sufferings. You had yours."

He did not realize that he had made my sufferings. I continued talking about turning over supply wagons in order to steal food. I noticed his light-blue eyes become steely like those of pitiless Darazs and Randovitch. I decided that I had said quite enough. His eyes were telling me that I had gone past a line with him. From then on Faludy was still friendly but not about "those years." If talk was unavoidable, my standard statement became, "When you and your friends were in terror over a partisan attack, I was eager to shake their hands and join their ranks."

How could I explain to him the difference between his sufferings and mine? How could I tell him the difference between having a weapon in one's hand and fighting or even dying for one's country and the worlds-apart experience of being a human mine detector for your countrymen with someone's gun trained on you? No, I could not explain the difference to Faludy. The gap between his understanding and mine had caused the subjugation of my people to begin with.

My earnings as a typesetter were very little. I had some reserves from savings during my Kecskemét days. I wondered how others without reserves were able to manage a minimal living standard. One would have to work more than a week for a pair of shoes. One would have to work three days for a shirt. Doctors, hospitals, and medications were, mercifully, free.

Rent, theater, opera, tickets to sporting events, and transportation were almost nothing. So somehow, by being frugal, people were able to manage.

Fifteen minutes before each shift we had a mandatory meeting for political indoctrination. This was political reeducation in the Communist tradition. The purpose of this universally hated fifteen minutes was to read the Communist version of world news. Everybody knew that it was pure propaganda and a distortion of the truth. It was something one bore silently. Sometimes there were sarcastic remarks whispered as an aside, but that was dangerous, as one's job and freedom depended on one's anonymity.

Someone was always selected before the meeting to speak on behalf of the Communist Party and support the just-read article and the party line. He was told what the content of his remarks should be.

The object of these meetings was to reeducate the thinking of the masses. Newspapers, radio, books, theaters, movies all had to follow the same thinking that was prescribed by the leaders in Moscow. In every factory and in every office this type of Communist education of the Hungarian populace was taking place. Under the guise of unlearning fascist or capitalist propaganda, we were given a dose of another brand of same thinking. I had already seen what mindless following of orders could do and had no desire to be part of it again. Yet the meetings were mandatory, and I was a worker who needed his job.

Someone who was more learned and more informed was making the decisions for us, and they knew best. Someone more sophisticated and worldly was deciphering the news. Someone higher in the Communist Party knew better and would handle things for the simple workers. The workers were supposed to be fortunate, for this type of government could and would think for them. There was not to be any questioning of pronouncements, since all was being done on the workers' behalf.

We workers were all to be the same. The old economic order was over. Intellectuals earned less than workers. Doctors earned the same as machine operators. Very few people had the initiative or the will to work harder or to produce more than the bare minimum, since it went unrewarded and unrecognized except for propaganda purposes. Being an individual and becoming visible was dangerous.

As workers we were supposed to gratefully embrace these decisions and work accordingly. I was neither grateful nor willing to forgo my thinking for the thinking of another. At these meetings I was there, with millions of others, as a unwilling participant in the mass reeducation program.

Religion was denounced by party propaganda. The churches and synagogues were not closed, but were excluded from any social activities. In every form of public life the Soviet model was slowly enforced. As stifling as it was, I still regarded the regime, with all its faults and its oppressiveness, as infinitely more humane and nongenocidal than the one I had lived through previously. There would always be a part of me that felt this large difference when I or someone else compared the two systems.

Intellectual and religious freedoms were suppressed. Those few freethinkers who dared to express their own thoughts were put behind bars. The party's goal was to create a new intelligentsia, hoping that the new intellectual elite of working-class origin would be the new loyal leaders of Hungary. The results must have gravely disappointed the rulers when, in October 1956, this group of newly educated and indoctrinated university students were the torch carriers of the Revolution.

- 4 -

*T*he winter and spring months flew by. There was so much to adjust to, and yet there was a routine momentum. The foreman of the typesetters was a decent old man and a former Social Democrat. One day he did not show up at the shop. Rumors flew that the Black Maria had visited his apartment the previous night. I was named temporary foreman in his absence. I think that my "M" friends had put in some good words about me to the director, who had also spoken to Ferenc Nagy.

As foreman, besides the daily reeducation meetings, I had to attend the weekly production meetings in the director's office. The foreman of each section had to make his weekly report to the rest of the group, which was chaired by the director of our company. Naturally the Communist Party secretary was always present. Everyone talked in platitudes about progress, but no one spoke of the actual problems the workers had in trying to realize the production schedule, which had been set according to a political agenda and had no relationship to them or their factory.

The director of the factory was a Jewish Communist. The party secretary was not. A few months after I was named typesetting foreman, the radio and papers were filled with the arrest of the Kremlin physicians, most of them Jews. The charges were that the doctors had plotted against the lives of the Soviet leaders. The papers were full of anti-Zionist propaganda. This had the same smell as the Nazi propaganda before the war. We were sure that the bulk of the weekly meeting would be filled with the Communist Party secretary's comments about the evil Zionist enemy. A very humiliating hour or so waited for us.

It was worse than we had imagined. We all listened with great shock as the reader in a quiet voice told of the arrests of leading Kremlin physicians, most of them Jews. Their Jewishness was the point of the story. The Jewish doctors were charged with plotting against the lives of Stalin and other Soviet leaders. We were compelled to listen to an inflammatory anti-Zionist tirade too reminiscent not to sear. It appeared that Stalin was searching for a new scapegoat for his failed economy. He found the Jews. This meeting became a turning point for me, as I recognized that the regime was now becoming more dangerous for me. It had all the earmarks of the Nazi anti-Jewish propaganda. The familiarity scared me deeply.

We all sat quietly, not daring to say a word during the racist harangue. Labor camps provided good schooling in this type of anonymous, impassive group behavior, and I had learned my lessons well. I sat in the second row and clenched the chair in front of me as the propaganda continued. To be held hostage again and not to dare speak up, not to dare ask questions, was a torture. How could I sit quietly and not protest? How could my Jewish friends look so impassive? Were we becoming slaves again? I thought back to the antisemitism of World War II and could not believe that we were listening again to antisemitic and anti-Israel verbiage. Were we giving our silent approval to this outrage? Were we being survivors, or were we burying our heads in the sand?

I looked at the Jewish director, hoping for a sign of recognition of our mutually shared ordeal, or a sign that I should speak up. I needed some sign that there was remembering going on. There was neutrality in his face. We all wore the mask of neutrality. Neutrality would get us by. I couldn't stand it, but the individual helplessness was immense. This system had saved my life, but it was a cruel salvation. One that would spare one's life and family, but at the immense cost of integrity and personal honesty.

As I listened to the propaganda, I did not fail to think that at this moment, in thousands of offices in thousands of factories, millions of people were listening to the same speech, the same garbage. To me, a Jew, this fallacious and dangerously misleading propaganda was doubly painful. During this time the fascist elements in Hungary were using the same propaganda to spread their own brand of antisemitic doctrine. They felt that Jewish Communists were to be blamed for all the hardships in Hungary. We were hearing anti-Jewish sentiment from both sides now. I was caught in the middle. Who would stand up for the Jews now? Who ever stood up for the Jews?

Next to me at the meeting sat a gentleman who had just been named the bindery foreman. He was convinced that no one knew that he was Jewish and that his Aryan-sounding name, though recent, was accepted. He sat nervously chain-smoking and finally raised his arm to speak. I was sure that he was one of the three dedicated party people who had been designated to say a few words at the close of the set speech. Actually the raising of his arm was more a nervous gesture due to fear that by not promoting the party line he would get in serious trouble with the party. Despite his fear of being discovered a less ardent Communist, a more decent quality prevailed. He kept quiet, lowering his arm. He would not and could not protest, but he would also not assist.

The least-educated and the wildest demagogue amongst us raised his hand and looked around before he said a few words. As he began to speak his preapproved comments, he looked at the faces of pain and displeasure on his Jewish colleagues' faces. He veered from the strict party line and seemed to apologize for what he had been made to say. His sentences remained incomplete, and after a moment of deadly silence, the director, with the party secretary's approval, closed the meeting. We all walked out of the meeting, shamefaced and subdued.

I prayed that everyone at the meeting, Jew or non-Jew, knew that everything that had been spoken was a lie. As the elevator doors closed behind us on the way down to the street level, a barely audible whisper came from the back of the elevator,

"These lies are horrifying."

Remarks such as these left me with the hope that some people were thinking for themselves and not just exchanging one form of propaganda for another. But we had to let it go, for our safety as well as our family's, just as we always had, hoping that lies and distortions would disappear with time.

Our special Jewish tragedy was the tyrant Rákosi. He was a Jew and did not fear the reawakening of Hungary's antisemitism with this violent anti-Zionist campaign. Amazingly, the Stalinist Rákosi regime was hated by the majority of Hungarians because of their hatred for a foreign victor. Hungarians might have embraced the antisemitism as Hungarians, but not when it came from Moscow. During this anti-Zionist campaign, most Hungarians, probably for the first time in their history, sided with the Jews and were on the side of Israel. Hungarians were one hundred and eighty degrees from adherence to Soviet propaganda. These views were obviously held privately. Publicly everyone toed the party line.

At the factory meetings it was customary that when Stalin's or Rákosi's name was mentioned we would stand en masse applauding. It was dangerous not to join in the clapping, and no one wanted to be the one who stopped too soon. Glances were exchanged wondering when we could stop this charade. This was the system. You obeyed, or one evening the AVO would come for you. This was a charade that would continue because one's freedom, one's chance to get a better-paying job, or one's being left alone depended on it. No one would stop clapping first. No one would be the first to risk a challenge to a Communist lie. Blending was a way to survive. Being a martyr was a way to be dead.

- *5* -

In the last week of April 1950 the maintenance people, the carpenters, and the sign painters were busy preparing for the upcoming May First celebration. This was a mandatory orchestrated rally, not unlike our education meetings only far vaster in scope. As the dreaded day approached I couldn't help but compare my feelings with that of my first May Day celebration in 1945.

At that May Day, newly liberated, I was so enthusiastic about carrying the Red Flag. Then it was the banner of liberation and emancipation. Now the celebration was the symbol of another imprisonment. Before the hopefulness had been contagious, now the contagion was hopeless. In the intervening five years I had watched and I had grown. I had exercised some sound independent judgments about practical and political matters. No longer did I see things as simply as before. No longer were the Soviets the saviors and their limitations overlooked.

Yes, they had liberated me. For that I would always be thankful, but theirs was also a regime which strangled those whose spirits wanted to soar. The world and its events had become more complex and convoluted than the simple delineating I had once used. I felt that I could rely only on my judgment and thought processes, and certainly not on a beneficent government. Grateful as I was and would forever be at the liberation of the Jewish labor battalion by the Soviets, I could not help but recognize the familiar clang of chains.

When May First arrived, we obligatorily lined up in front of the Globus. Prefabricated signs were issued. This time I again used my old survival technique of staying in the middle of the march among the other typesetters, trying to be as invisible as possible among my colleagues. Unfortunately, I was not honored by anonymity. I was asked to carry the picture of Comrade Gerö, the most hated Hungarian leader after Rákosi. The march slowly proceeded towards Heroes Square. It took us two agonizing hours of stop-and-go marching to finally end up at the stage in front of the huge statue of Stalin.

From the stage overshadowed by Stalin's likeness we were supposed to return by a side road to our starting point and turn in our signs. I remembered the pride and enthusiasm I had on my first such parade. Holding the flag then was a sign of being alive and free. This day it was an ordered, prefabricated, feelingless charade—a mockery. Instead of banners of freedom there was the picture of the tyrant Gerö.

All of us had had enough by this time. Enough of false celebration and enforced brotherhood. Enough of hypocrisy and forced comradeship. We spontaneously got rid of the signs in a side street. Hoping to avoid attention we turned in to the city's largest park. I got separated from my friends and sat on the grass to rest my feet for a few minutes. Stepping on the grass was forbidden, but due to the enforced air of celebration on this workers' holiday, it was overlooked.

Within minutes I was joined by three men from my soccer team who had noticed me resting on the grass. Rozoga was one of them. I told them that I had never seen so many people gathered at one time. My statement seemed innocent. I was thinking that this group seemed the same as the fascistic Hungarians. At the same time, the distinctions were essential and profound. Their leaders were better, not much, but better. I had no love for either group, but lasting gratitude to one.

My noncontroversial statement about the number of people gathered this day was how everyone now talked to one another, in riddles. Only to one's closest friends could one be direct. One always had to worry about informers and lists held by the AVO. Yet in asking these indirect questions one might find another soulmate. I had to know if my soccer teammates knew the difference between the two regimes. I could only address my negative feelings about the present regime if the atrocities of the former were acknowledged.

Rozoga was quick to speak. "I was at the same location in 1944 when Szálasi was named head of state. The crowd was huge at that time too. At least this large."

I hesitantly added, watching his face for expression, "But this is different."

"No," Rozoga said, "These are the same people. Only the salute is different."

I didn't know what his response meant. Was it a truthful one which was identical to my feelings? Was it a trap, enticing me to compromise myself? Would it be reported to the AVO? This May First celebration celebrated nothing but defeat.

We got rid of Rozoga somehow. The three of us, now thirsty, went to a large open-air beer hall. I was subdued after a few beers. The others, especially the goalie of our team, began to talk. The talk slowly turned to politics. The goalie expressed his wish to join the Communist Party. I wished him luck, liking him personally and not wanting to continue this conversation, since it would lead nowhere. I was a bit tipsy from the beer, and I felt I had to exert caution with every word, every utterance. Anything could be misunderstood.

The other teammates questioned him as to why he would want to do such a thing.

"Because they have the money!"

His statement had some merit. A party member in good standing had a better chance for promotion and for a better-paying, easier job. My friend the goalie was a realist and honest enough to make such a statement. When he realized how honest a disclosure he had made, he turned on his charm and said, "One cannot urinate against the wind!"

He was going to play the system for all it was worth. He started to laugh and ordered another round of lukewarm beer.

As soon as I stepped out of the beer hall, Rozoga caught up with me again. It was obvious that he had been waiting for me. We walked a few moments without saying anything special. He stopped and faced me.

"Odon, you are a friend of mine and a decent person. You are the only one who never singled me out as the butt of a cruel joke or something worse. Nobody trusts me. I want you to know that when I compared the 1944 fascist crowd to this day's gathering, I said the truth. These people are not yet true Communists. Some people have zealous beliefs in God. My belief is the party."

I continued walking and tried to avoid looking at his pleading eyes. I think he was trying to tell me that he understood how cruelly I had been treated by the fascist regime. I think he was also telling me the truth and pleading with me to believe him and trust him. I think he wanted me to believe, as he did, that things would get better when true party teachings were in place. Then he stopped and grasping my arms said, "What can I do for you?"

I tried to change the subject. I told him what I had learned during my self-education classes during the period of the anti-Jewish laws. I had learned that the opposition to fascism is not necessarily Communism. I told him that all I wanted and needed was a red-white-and blue visa for my family and myself. I was a bit careless and drunk at the time, but either he didn't get my meaning or he chose to ignore it.

That night nightmares plagued me. Had I endangered anyone in talking to Rozoga? All I had wanted was to unburden myself for a moment. Would I regret one moment of relaxed, uncensored conversation for the rest of my life? Had I taken the wrong path? Had I endangered my family with my careless sentence about an American visa? I wondered if Rozoga would bring me down.

I ran to Agi's bedroom and brought her to our bed, listening to her breathing as she slept. The innocent sleep of a child reminded me of what was due me and any other human being.

- 6 -

*T*ime passed quickly, and it was already midsummer. As I became close friends with the other employees of the company, I was more able to feel comfortable talking to them. Party membership was not of consequence, but the person's inner thoughts and beliefs were. In private among friends, I was not afraid to express my deepest thoughts. In private among friends, differences were well tolerated. One day Sanyi M. asked me if he could ask a very personal question and hoped I would answer truthfully.

"Why have you stayed in Hungary?"

"Because the border is guarded by men with weapons and guard dogs."

"Yes, but why didn't you go earlier when the border was open?"

I was quiet and pondered my friend's question. I didn't have a ready answer for him. I wondered why I had missed my chance. I had missed the writing on the wall when the Nazis were gaining power. Had I missed the writing again? Had I again stayed too long, hoping that the winds of change would improve the situation when all they did was blow further havoc?

It was in this midsummer that Karcsi, my small but large-hearted friend, visited us. He told us that the expected had happened to him, too. His clothing-material store had been nationalized. He asked me to try to get him a job. A job! I owed him so much more. I owed him whatever self-esteem I had managed to garner in my youth.

I asked my friends for help and received the same negative answer. The Globus could not absorb another capitalist who had been nationalized without facing dangerous consequences from the ministry.

I could not let Karcsi down. A few days after I received the negative answers, there was an open chess tournament organized by the company's chess team. I brought Karcsi and introduced him. I arranged a few unofficial games between him and the other fine players. I had an ulterior motive. By the end of the evening, everyone had surrounded Karcsi and his opponent. Everyone was laughing and smiling at his jokes, his side remarks, and the largeness of his abundant personality. The next day he was hired as an assistant laborer, loading and unloading trucks. I assured Karcsi that this was just tempo-rary and that he would be moved soon to an office. I could say this to him, not because of any influence I could exert, but because I knew his character, smartness, and the hard-work-ing aspect of this great man. A few weeks later he became the buyer for the company.

- 7 -

In the years 1951 and 1952 the targets of the first Hungarian Five Year Plan were greatly increased due to the burden of the Korean War. The socialist countries were pressured by the Soviet government to help financially in the North Korean war effort. The burden was born by the workers. People suffered great hardships of long hours and ruthless pressure for higher output per worker. On top of this, the low wages and declining purchasing power resulted in the further decline of the already low living standards.

The Communists found inventive ways to further deprive the workers of wages. One way was the system of "peace loans." This loan to the government from the people was supposed to be voluntary. Actually every form of persuasion and pressure was used to extort as much as 15 percent of the workers' gross earnings. Those who refused to sign up were subjected to public ridicule and faced arrests on trumped-up charges.

Another manner of wage deprivation was the "voluntary" shifts. These shifts were days that we honored someone or something by working without pay. We would honor the liberation of Hungary, May Day, Stalin's birthday, the Korean people, and anything else someone could think of.

On paper we looked like the most dedicated and idealistic of people, who gave of our time and energy "according to our

253

means." In actually we were becoming a harassed and bitter people bludgeoned into poverty and pessimism.

The mandatory political work of spreading the doctrine to the outlying villages gave excuses to the thousands and thousands of "in name only" party members to spend hours away from home. Boys and girls, husbands and wives were tired of pretending. They were tired of Youth Days, Women's Days, Sports Days, and Health Days. They were tired of the monthly Soviet-Hungarian Friendship Days. This tired and oppressed people used whatever time and freedom they had on the days dedicated to spreading the doctrine to drink or to search for sexual solace. It was only in these ways that expressions of individuality and vitality existed. Both of these exercises had a type of desperate frenzy to them. The drinking and libertine sexuality were overlooked by the party bosses with little winks of understanding. In the meantime the authorities diligently marked down these affairs in a person's file. If and when the time arrived, they could be used for blackmail.

We had to attend weekly political seminars. We listened to a speaker who himself did not believe in the drivel he had to say. There were plenty of negative aspects of this system which drove one's spirit deeper and deeper into despair. There were also things that allowed one's life some softness.

The positive parts of the system had to do with the free medical care, and the nominally free opera, theater, and sporting event tickets. The resort areas of Lake Balaton and the mountain resorts and castles were turned over as company rest areas. Workers could spend a free week or two each year at one of these beautiful places, originally visited only by the rich. Boys and girls who were born to working-class parents had a good chance to get an education free of charge.

Life was bearable because we all had the same low wages. We shared the same lunch of bread with a little chicken fat. Life was hard but shared.

There were constant political trials and purges. There were sudden disappearances of prominent intellectuals, artists, and other thinkers which were reported only in the Western European press.

Everyone tried to find a dependable news source to sort out what was happening. People listened to the BBC from London and Radio Free Europe. The channels and times of the Hungarian-language news programs on those stations were known to all of us.

When Radio Free Europe transmitted the news, the streets were empty. People hid behind closed doors and windows so that the sound would not betray the listeners. A typical self-mocking story went around that there were three types of Hungarians: those in jail, those leaving jail, and those about to go to jail. This little joke explains the political situation in the early fifties.

- *8* -

The typesetters' union used to have strong national ties to the West. This communication was still guardedly left open with socialist-oriented Western countries. The Hungarian government, trying to improve its reputation in the West, invited labor leaders from different industries to visit the country. Obviously the visiting delegation was shown only model working situations.

An Italian printers' group was assigned by the ministry to visit our factory. Three days before their arrival I was called to the director's office. The party secretary and three strangers were present. I was introduced only to one of the strangers. I knew that the unintroduced men were AVO agents, as one can easily discern such things. I was told by the director that the stranger he had introduced was a new typesetter and to put him to work immediately. I was told which workbench to assign him. The new typesetter was average in appearance in every way, and he radiated friendliness and self-confidence. He was dressed simply and looked like a typical printer.

The Italian visit was the first one by foreigners to our factory. Everyone watched with great interest as the Italians began their tour. When the Italians reached a bench, the workers would stop their work to appraise the Westerners. When the visitors reached the new typesetter's table, he did not look up but continued working. The translator stopped in front of his work area with his back towards the worker. The visitors were, therefore, forced to face this very self-contained worker as the translation went on.

Noticing where the eyes of the Italians were focused, although it was orchestrated to be such, the translator turned towards the new worker as if discovering him for the first time. It was so simple. A perfect set-up! I think I might have been the only one in the room who noticed how smoothly it was done. The Italians started questioning him.

"How many hours do you work a week?"

"Forty."

We worked forty-eight hours.

"How much do you earn?"

"Three thousand forints."

We earned half that amount. The Italians smiled and asked about his family. He had a wife who was expecting momentarily, and she had a paid two years' maternity leave. The translator explained that this was mandatory in Hungary. This was new to me.

"Where do you live?"

"I have my own home in the outskirts of Budapest."

"What sort of transportation do you use to get to work?"

The worker went to the window and showed them the parked new German Puch motorcycle. One of the Italians turned to me and explained via the translator that we were very fortunate, since he did not have the job security nor the accouterments which we were able to afford. The delegation left to spread the word of how wonderfully the Hungarians were prospering under the utopian Communist regime.

An hour later the new worker looked at me and, with a wink and a small wave, left. I did not wave back. I had participated in being a tool for this deception.

This charade reminded me of how in 1944 a Swiss Red Cross delegation had visited Theresienstadt, a large Jewish ghetto in Czechoslovakia. The Germans showed the delegation the good life the Jews had, surrounded by their own people and culture. They showed them the good food, schools, theaters, and hospitals which had been hastily prearranged. The Red Cross was appeased and impressed also. This was not very different.

In the following days I told the workers around me about the whole episode. My fellow workers were not oblivious to what had happened. They were also gratified that I had enough confidence in them to tell them my observations. It sort of bonded us as a group to trust one another more than perhaps we had done previously. They trusted me. I trusted them. We all felt free to express our feelings to one another without fear. As I had previously escaped the labor camp because of a toothache, I had now made another "brave," and perhaps foolish, step towards individual freedom because of anger at a system. I would let there be less schism between my public and private thoughts.

A few days later the director sent for me. He asked me my opinion of the Italian tour of our factory. I was hesitant to answer him, since I did not know what his intention was in questioning me. One always tried to ascertain the other's intention before answering. It was critical and helped one phrase the appropriate answer. Truthfulness was seldom asked for. Was he trying to intimidate me because I had witnessed the deception? Was he trying to communicate a bond with me because we were both silently coerced partners in the episode? I wanted to be truthful yet not foolish.

"It was a charade. It is not a question of believing or not believing in a particular political system. This was a question of being truthful or false. This was a question of doing things honorably or dishonorably. This was a question of right or wrong. If we are forced to lie, let us do it less enthusiastically next time."

To my great surprise he did not stop me mid-sentence. His eyes shined with friendliness and understanding as to my stand. I was grateful at the opportunity of speaking my mind. It was allowed so seldom, and always with a risk.

- 9 -

Our economic situation worsened. The time now came when Sara had to work in order for the family to be able to manage.

Our company gave bindery work to a cooperative. In time I became a good friend of the leader of the co-op. Sara was given a job doing piecework at home. She was a worker in name only, since the leader of the co-op sent already finished work to her. She would get paid for it even if already finished by another. Naturally the director of the cooperative got a kickback from us for his largess. Sometimes working the system was the only way to survive. Being an opportunist was essential. It was also essential that one not lose all of one's standards and ethics in the struggle to stay alive. Somehow we believed that helping other workers in this large, impersonal system and getting something back oneself was fair.

This is how one got along. We worked hard and yet could never do the work required by governmental decree. The pay was so low that soon working hard felt like depleting oneself. It became easier to try to work around the system. We learned to cheat the system as much as we could get away with in order to have some profit in life. It was part of everyone's life. One took advantage of the system whenever one could. It certainly took advantage of us. One was honest with one's closest friends. One spoke up against injustice if there were ears that could hear and could understand. One never informed. One always protected one's friends. This was the honor code of the oppressed.

Sanyi M. and Béla M. were very close friends with the director of the company. Béla M. had served one year with him in the labor battalion. I told the two M's to come with me to temple for the upcoming High Holy Days. They mentioned this to the Jewish director, who absolutely forbade us to go. It was 1952, and the atheistic doctrine of Marxism was in full swing. The party had set itself the task of creating a new working-class intelligentsia who had no religious beliefs. It would have greatly embarrassed the director if three of his mid-managers went to temple. It would be a black spot on his record.

On the morning of the High Holy Day we all reported to work as ordered. Our yarmulkes were tucked into our jacket pockets. At ten o'clock three brave and foolish souls disappeared from our workplace, left the factory, and went to a nearby temple secretly. We only stayed about an hour, but somehow we felt good about being true to ourselves. None of us was religious, but it was our personal protest, our way to remain individuals. It was the day to remember our families. Staying an individual by avowing religion was as important to me now as it had been when I was a boy playing truant from religion.

Soccer continued to be an important part of my life. It was one of the constant melodic strains which weaved its way into whatever symphony my life was. I was still young enough to play a competitive game—thirty years old—although the eighteen-year-old players would tease me when I missed the ball. I needed the extra money like everyone else. At the urging of Nagy, I signed up to be an assistant coach to a third-division team where he was the head coach. Their game was played on Sundays. No player was allowed to be signed up on two teams. In 1939 my coach had changed my sports name to Angyal to cover up my Jewish-sounding name. So at this time Nagy secured me a player's license under the same name. The little extra money helped maintain our budget.

Friendship was an important and necessary part of my life, and being under Ferenc Nagy's wing made life a bit easier. Work, family, soccer, friends—once in a while a theater or opera ticket, sometimes a movie—this was my life.

We sometimes saw pre–World War II American films. There was always a line in front of the theaters which showed these oldies. The new, heavily promoted Soviet films in the main movie houses ran without public interest. Western films rarely came to Hungary, and when they did they were very old but always well attended. The subject matter was always preselected, censored, and appropriate to Russian sentiments. We heard via the BBC and Radio Free Europe of the great success of *Gone with the Wind.* We all longed to see this movie.

Hungarians are lovers of reading. Even our printing company had its own library. In order to save time the librarian pushed a cart filled with books down the aisles to the workers. The books were mostly old classics or Soviet writings. The new Hungarian books were written to confirm and strengthen the political reeducation of the people. Everything was preselected and predigested for us. We were force-fed formulaic information. Individual thought was never nurtured.

Christmas 1952 came and went. We spent a memorable New Year's Eve with my five-per-two leader, Páli Kerekes, and his family in a restaurant in Buda, the famous Sipos. All of us got a little drunk. We all had busy lives, struggling for work and wages and some of the niceties. We all tried to merge and be invisible in public, as we had done in my labor battalion times. In private we could be real, authentic, and genuine. It was a schizophrenic lifestyle, but it allowed us to be true to ourselves under carefully controlled situations.

In the early part of 1952 I was promoted again. I became head of the production-planning department. This was an easier and more pleasant job. I wasn't as constantly watched in this new position. My new job was a desk job in a separate office. I could be more myself.

Before I became head of the production-planning department, I had a problem with one of the quality supervisors, Pataki. I knew that he had been an officer in the Hungarian army, and although I did not know anything more personal than that, I knew that some army officers had been fascists and antisemites. The only other fact that I knew about him was that he had been captured during the 1944 Soviet offensive and released shortly after the Soviet occupation of Hungary. This indicated that he had been reeducated and found to be reliable to the Communists. Neither of these two bits of knowledge made me yearn to be near him. Through the grapevine we learned that he had spent time in jail in 1949. Naturally we all suspected that he had exchanged his freedom for an informant position and now could compromise us.

All these bits of information were enough to make anyone suspicious and cautious whenever in his presence. I did not fail to notice how he was always on the outside and wished to be part of the typesetters' tight-knit group. His constant fault-finding and criticism of us, and of me in particular, might have been his reaction to the wooden encounters he had with us. He was someone to be kept at arm's length.

Now that I was part of the production-planning department, our relationship slowly changed. Pataki came quite often to my office and pretended to work at one of the unoccupied desks in my office. I couldn't figure out what he was doing. I started to feel sorry for him. He was trapped between his wish for relationships and his coerced loyalty to the political structure. The coldness that was between us earlier started to melt.

During a company interdepartmental soccer game, my ankle was sprained. Pataki, a spectator, was asked to accompany me to the first aid station. On the return from the first aid station, Pataki asked me to have coffee with him. Drinking and talking, we began to find out more about one another. He was a former officer in the Hungarian army, as I had already discerned. He talked about his time in Soviet captivity. He was anxious, eager, and hungry to tell his story. He did not want to be alone.

He told me that among his fellow prisoners were Germans, Hungarians, and Jews from the labor battalions. The Soviet officers in charge of the camp did not differentiate among the prisoners. They thought all of them were the same—all the enemy, all prisoners. Their lot was not a happy one. Work, hunger, and constant interrogations were their daily routine. Among the prisoners was someone who became a member of the new Hungarian government in 1945. Pataki guarded his name in telling the story.

In the third month of Soviet imprisonment Pataki and thirty others were told to get ready for relocation. They were put in a truck and traveled east for two days. Hungarian-speaking Communists began the reeducation process. They were being groomed to be the new political leaders of Hungary. Among the teachers was Zoltán Vas, who was the only political leader trusted by his fellow Hungarians; Gerö, whose hated picture I had carried during my second May Day celebration; and the most hated among the disliked, Rákosi.

When the Soviet army defeated the fascist army in Hungary, the old administration in power during the German occupation ceased to function. Compromised civil officials fled to German territory. A nominal Hungarian government led by General Béla Miklós surrendered to the Russians. At this early time of the occupation the Soviet leaders did not set up a Communist regime. They brought with them a number of Hungarian Communists who had been in exile in Russia, among them the above-mentioned Rákosi and Gerö and some other reeducated former prisoners considered reliable enough to serve Moscow's interests.

This small group, which included Pataki, now rapidly enlisted opportunists among the former fascist officials to establish a popular front in internal politics. It took a few years for this Moscow-educated group, with the help of the Soviet army, to take full control of Hungary.

In 1945 Pataki was sent home and assigned to a managerial job in the Department of Light Industry. Naturally he was a party member and very well placed. His future looked bright and promising. For years he did his job with great enthusiasm. As time passed he began to see the truth inside the illusion. He saw how the system used the masses instead of truly benefitting them.

From here his story became tragicomic. While he was preaching the prescribed political views, he constantly became aware that every word was a lie. At an official dinner at the ministry, during the continuous toasting, he became drunk and careless. When his turn came, he stood up with a glass of wine in his hand and waited for silence to fall on the gathering.

"Comrades, is this already socialism, or does it get worse with time?"

One short sentence! He had intended this as a mild joke. The next day Pataki was picked up by the AVO. He received a ten-year jail sentence.

Somehow through a jail visitor he sent a message to the unnamed member of the government with whom he had been in prison camp. He was released after serving a year in jail. The former Soviet prison camp colleague, who now was a high official in the government, got him the job in our print shop without ever giving him an audience. Pataki refused to name the highly placed leader in order to screen his protector from possible accusations of favoritism.

"Now everyone looks at me with a little mistrust and coolness. No, I am not an informer, never was, and never will be."

I asked him what his future plans were as we walked home like two good friends.

"I will go back to night school. I plan to be a printing engineer."

Before I escaped from Hungary, Pataki received his engineering diploma. He was named the head of a large printing concern. I was happy for him. Did he become a member of the party again? I don't know. We moved in opposite directions and I did not hear from him or see him again.

- *10* -

*T*he economic situation became worse and worse. Prices kept climbing. Shortages of food and other necessary items developed. If the government announced that sugar prices would rise, people hoarded sugar at the old price. This, of course, created more shortages.

There was then an official crackdown on those who had hoarded sugar. The government papers reported arrests of individuals who had more than a week's supply of sugar in their homes. Panic developed. How much constituted more than a week's supply—two kilograms? Less? But for how many people? Two kilograms for two persons? For four persons? These were not idle questions. These were questions whose answers meant freedom or imprisonment. Rumors flew. The tales about those arrested were so terrible that thousands and thousands of kilograms of hoarded sugar were flushed down toilets across the country. This naturally created more shortages.

Learning from this mistake, the government did not announce price increases again. The public always knew. Panic always ensued. If the government was going to increase the price of shoes, by the time the secret was publicized, the news had filtered down and shoes, shirts, and linens were already being hoarded. Arrests followed. Hanging for black-marketing and imprisonment for hoarding were the punish-

265

ments. Everyone knew of innocent people who disappeared amidst accusations of hoarding.

My extra earnings from soccer did not help my economic situation much. Top players, all-stars, world and Olympic champions got good-paying jobs without ever having to report to work. Jobs in name only in the government, the army, or the police department were their compensation. Players like myself got a little extra money. Sometimes I earned nothing, sometimes a winner's bonus. It helped, no matter how small the extra amount was.

Sara, like other middle-class people, started to barter our household items for food and other necessities. In our entry hall we had two antique upholstered armchairs. In better times, when I had owned the Kecskemét winery, I had paid a fortune for them. For days I felt strange upon entering my home. I felt something was amiss! Finally Sara told me that for eight weeks in a row we'd had "armchairs" for dinner. The chairs were gone. She had bartered our furniture for food.

During winter, I complained that our heavy comforter was not as warm, and our pillows felt thinner.

"Maybe you're getting older or the outside temperature is unusually low," was my dear wife's answer.

When we were established in the United States I brought up the fact that I wanted a comforter like the one we had in Hungary. Sara asked me whether I meant the thick warm one or the smaller thin one. She told me smilingly that she had a gypsy woman who came and exchanged some of the goose feathers for food.

"Never fully trust a wife!" was my answer, knowing that she too had shivered in the cold and had kept silent so I could keep my pride.

We were so needy of money that luxuries, even penny luxuries, were unaffordable. One summer evening I was taking a walk with my daughter. We passed a pastry shop, and people were exiting with ice cream cones. I had no pennies to spare. I saw in my daughter's eyes her wish for an ice cream cone. I was holding her hand, and I rushed her past the shop. She did not cry. I myself was ready to cry. Why can't I afford an ice cream cone for my daughter? For two days I did not smoke to make up the pennies I needed to buy her an ice cream. That ice cream was a worthwhile investment.

My chance to get higher-paying job in the company was nil. I was not a member of the party. Without this affiliation I had as an important a job as I could possibly get. Compensation for the job was very low, but I was considered lucky.

- *11* -

Companies, shops, and factories—both large and small—had to complete the yearly production plans mandated by that branch of government to which their industry belonged. These production plans were centrally designed and had nothing to do with the reality of the situation of the workers in the individual factories. They were idealized plans created by bureaucrats. The problem was complicated in that each industry was dependent on others for its raw materials, shipping, machine repair, and delivery. The other industries would be dictated to by another branch of the government.

Our company's plan was directed by the subsection of Light Industry. To plan and administer the yearly production plans was a bureaucratic nightmare administered by hundreds of thousands of people without any education or knowledge of the company's business. A reasonable plan was impossible under these conditions.

The yearly plan was broken down into quarters. Overproduction was rewarded by quarterly bonuses. Sometimes these bonuses were larger than the salary for the entire quarter. Overproduction of 110 percent or 120 percent was a good company performance and promised a good bonus for everybody.

Bonuses were awarded to the administrators and the technical people. I, as a foreman, was entitled to a bonus based on my monthly salary. Workers, on the other hand, were given bonuses far less.

Despite the idealism of Communism, the workers who worked piecemeal at their workbenches were forced to produce more and more for their small wages. It all fell on the workers' shoulders—the unrealistic plan, the burdensome work, and less than adequate bonuses. There were constant organized competitions at the factories to increase production. The winners of the competitions were favored, and they received medals and financial awards amidst great fanfare. Often the award winners were promoted to nonproductive managerial jobs. After the monthly competitions, brutal increases in the norms of all the workers in the unit followed. Reaching the norms without inflating the actual results was very difficult. We were all overworked and paid so minimally that we joked that the government pretended to pay us while we pretended to work. The requirements of the plan kept on expanding.

"New" machines, which was the name they gave to outdated and reconditioned machinery, were brought in to increase productivity. The workers were given no time to readjust to these machines or to learn how to use them. There was usually a reduced workload at the beginning of the month due to raw materials shortages. This was followed by a crushing overload on the workers to make up for the lost production.

To administer this system required more and more administrative employees. Soon the ratio of productive and administrative workers approached unity. Now there was no way the system could work. Stealing from the company was almost expected. Cheating on production quotas was natural. Getting caught was a terrible problem unless one had powerful connections.

As typesetting foreman I helped workers who cheated on their quotas. This put a few extra cents into their earnings. I put on paper that there was an improved productivity level in my department. This was only on paper. In reality we were down-spiraling. This was happening in every section of every factory. On paper the system looked economically sound. Reality was much bleaker as we approached the lowest common denominator. The gap between what was and what seemed to be grew more and more disparate. No one seemed to notice that the Emperor wore no clothes.

When an administrator was called up for army service, hospitalized, or on vacation, I was usually called in as a substitute. I learned a lot during these temporary job assignments about how the system worked. For example, I might be told, as I left to go to another department, "Take care of so-and-so," one of the girls who worked there. Not much more needed to be said. I knew that theirs was a special relationship, and I would keep their secret.

Or "My wife works in the bindery. Make sure she gets off a day or two at the end of the week. Naturally with wages coming. So-and-so in the bindery takes care of that usually. You must not notice it."

Yes, I would close my eyes.

"Odon, I'll be back on Monday but will not report to work until Wednesday. That way I'll have a few extra days with my secretary."

Yes, my eyes remained closed. Closed as far as the system, the anonymous government, was concerned, but not closed to the plight and daily life of my friends and acquaintances.

When Béla M. was called into the army for six weeks, I was asked to substitute for him. It was easy to walk around and pretend to take over something I barely understood. Béla's job was to coordinate production with shipping and invoicing. Just as I had begun to grasp the job, the quarter ended. The chief financial advisor and a highly placed party member visited me.

"Mr. Mandel, it looks as if we will be short of making the plan. It is essential that we make the bonus."

I knew the rest of the message, although it was delivered wordlessly. I was to do whatever necessary for it to appear as if the plan had been completed. Bonuses were needed. Families were running out of furniture to eat. If I managed it somehow, I would be a hero for two days. If caught, I would be in jail for a few years.

At that time we manufactured all the calendars for the entire country. They were all distributed by one outlet. As the head of the production-planning department I met with the assistant director of the outlet quite often, as he often checked the size and specifications of the calendars. I told him that we had to ship the leatherbound pocket calendars before the week was over, otherwise we could not meet our quarterly plan. He became a little pale. Their own plan and their bonuses hinged on our reaching our production quota. If we were short, his plan could not be met either. I told him I would begin shipping immediately. I told him not to check the shipments until the third of the month.

Truckloads of cartons festooned with an example of the calendars inside were shipped. Loading and unloading dockets were signed. We got so ahead of ourselves that the chief accountant begged me to slow down the shipments. We had far exceeded the quota. We were safe. We would all be given bonuses, including my friend's company.

The first week of the new month, all the cartons were retrieved. The calendars had yet to be finished. Only the covers had been done. After being finished, they were redelivered. Since this was early in the new quarter, the calendars now appeared in the new quota, and we were off to a good beginning. Although this deception was punishable with years in jail for falsifying or doctoring production plans, somebody was always doing it. This time it was me. All of us needed our bonuses for necessities of life. No one involved in our calendar charade cared about the deception. It was all for us anyhow! Anyway, that was what the propaganda told us daily.

After Stalin's death in 1953, we saw the gaping holes in the way Communism worked. I tried to separate the real gains under the Communist presence with the ones we were constantly told about. All the speeches, radio reports, and newspaper articles painted a fatherly picture of Stalin. It was amazing to try to separate that picture of him from the slowly emerging one of a tyrant that followed.

I remember vividly the extremely hot and humid July 1953 day when we were ordered away from our work to the meeting where his death was announced. I remember the speakers, but not their speeches. No one cared or believed anymore in the speeches of the puppets. In fact, we all just turned every pronouncement around one hundred and eighty degrees. I remember the faces, glances, and whispered words amongst us. There was hope and faith that better times would now come. There was fear in the eyes of others. In the past any change had usually been for the worse. Rightly so that most people were pessimistic.

The mood after Stalin's demise was strongly for change. There was a strong desire for a little freedom to say things that were not dictated by Moscow. This desire began to emerge from the thin cracks made possible by Stalin's death. Through these cracks there emerged an unstoppable force. Rákosi gave up the premiership to Imre Nagy, but remained the first secretary of the party. Through this job he maintained his firm grip through the AVO. This security organization was the only one in Hungary over which the party had full control.

The Writers' Association had a monthly publication. This publication had previously served the system. Now a few brave intellectuals began to deviate and express independent thoughts. In the beginning they did so guardedly, but then more and more freely their expressions emerged. These writings were not against the Soviets, not yet. They were not against Communist dogma, not yet. Slowly, though, among this group a circle of dissenters was formed.

During the following three years their monthly publications disappeared from the newsstands within hours of distribution. Some of these publications never reached the newsstands. If an edition had inflammatory articles, it was confiscated by the authorities. From these confiscated editions, through the printers and the writers, copies of certain articles were secreted and then redistributed. This was dangerous. It was sedition. Many of the writers and their followers received long jail sentences. More daring writers replaced them. Some of the copies which passed the censor were picked up by the ravenous citizenry, who were hungry for new voices.

Inside the small circle of intellectuals, leaders emerged. Some were free-spirited, questioning sorts. Others were adventurers tied up with the fascist inspiration which was so much a part of Hungary's past. The young Communist doctor who was my neighbor belonged to the former group of thinkers and dissenters. He showed me copies of these articles. I forwarded them to my trusted friends. An underground network of ideas and communication had now begun in earnest.

- *12* -

It was barely a decade after the war years, and my friends and I were cautiously optimistic and yet very anxious. Part of our optimism was the hope of liberalization of thought and expression which we felt was sure to follow Stalin's death. We were pessimistic because we also feared the new anti-Soviet thinking. We were concerned that once free of the fist of Moscow the reactionary spirit of fascism would flare up to be spoken again.

Antisemitism was not rampant, but remarks were again being made. Graffiti appeared on the walls. Sarcastic gestures and remarks indicated which of the political leaders were Jews. Many of the leaders were Jewish because the Soviets had trusted the Jews after the war more than the fascists. The Jews looked on the Soviets as liberators and worked with them and were elevated to leadership roles. As more and more hatred surfaced against the Communist leaders, it fanned the hatred of Jews, who were hated for being Jewish and also for being part of the Communist regime. Hungarians had an uncanny ability to ferret out Jewish or part-Jewish leaders. Being Jewish gave the people extra reason to curse and hate. Being Jewish and Communist united people's hatred.

My daughter was hospitalized during this time. She was seven years old. Sara had made her a nightgown from an old dress with flowers that someone had received from an Ameri-

273

can relative. It was a different fabric and pattern than those the other children wore. The other children teased her because it was different, saying she would have a different gown because she was different, a Jew. How did they know that? They were all children. Agi had blond hair and blue eyes. Her mother was not born Jewish. But they knew. The bigots always know. If this was from children, one could only imagine the hatred that their parents felt.

Through a friend, I attended a Petőfi Club meeting. At that meeting I heard Zoltán Kodaly demand from the Musicians' Association an improvement in the quality of Hungarian musical life. He wanted a wider selection of music offered. To me this was quite revolutionary, this mild protestation. From the beginning I thought that the Petőfi Club meetings were a minor revolution, a place for expressions of dissent, a minor miracle.The conditions of the 1956 Hungarian Revolution had been created within the party itself, by reform-minded writers and the intellectual leaders of the Petőfi Club.

By the fall of 1956, I was thirty-three. My soccer-playing time, although I couldn't admit it then to myself, was over. My reflexes had slowed. I missed easily convertible balls. I had a good season followed by a very mediocre one. I was reliable, had willpower and would not give up. But I grew afraid that now I was an example of a middle-aged player. It became more and more difficult to get up enough strength to start a new fight, a new game, another practice, another day away from my family, to play somewhere among a group of younger men. I was more of an example than a player.

My dream of becoming the best on the soccer field became a fanciful idea of youth. In the evenings just before I fell asleep I gave my imagination full rein. In my secret thoughts and dreams no illusion had to be relegated to realistic evaluation. In my dreams I could regain those lost years. Instead of toiling under the yoke of Jewish slavery, I could replay those years as ones of success in athletic prowess. I knew I owed my survival to physical and mental stamina, but I had wanted more from my youth than survival. I had wanted to be a hero.

During the summer of 1956 the Writers' Association published demands. I asked my doctor neighbor in the Petöfi Circle about the demands. He told me that the demands were an attempt to negotiate a higher standard of living. They wanted to give back to the unions their true functions without endangering a Soviet response. There was never a word about a revolt or uprising. By the fall Moscow's response was to allow freer speech and writing, which, ironically, made the ground ripe for a revolt. We were now in a never-ending spiral of fomenting liberty.

In October 1956 I received a two-week vacation package from the company. Sara and I had a delightfully relaxed ten days in the Mátra Mountains. It was here that we began to hear government warnings. All of us at the resort spoke about the possibility of unrest in Budapest. We were quite open with one another. We all had a sense that something was happening. With great difficulty we secured emergency transportation home.

On the way home we heard one of the vacationers say, "We have to get rid of Jewish leadership." My uneasy feelings increased tenfold, since this was from the mouth of a person with whom I had just played a friendly chess game. All of a sudden "Soviet leadership" or "foreign leadership" was becoming "Jewish leadership." I wondered about the safety of Agi. I wondered about the safety of all of us.

We arrived at the Eastern Railroad Station in the late evening. We noticed the AVO in great numbers. The streets, usually quiet around this time, were crowded with people. The whole city was in the streets.

The next day, October 23, 1956, I reported for work and tried to find out what was going on. Little groups talked in corners of the factory. No one was working. Everybody was whispering, gesturing, and going to other groups to exchange information. When the Communist Party secretary and company managers entered the factory, they looked at the workers and the workers looked back at them. No one spoke a word. Then the workers started to disappear from their workbenches.

News came that hundreds of thousands of people were on the street demonstrating against the government. I joined them. I had some mixed feelings about all this. I wanted the demands for more freedom met, but I felt uncomfortable marching with the same people who could easily march against me the following day. No one who saw the fascists march could ever look at mass gatherings again in the same way.

On the street people carried the outlawed Hungarian flag. The new Hungarian flags had been modified by removing the Soviet hammer and sickle. These flags with a hole in the middle were carried, waved, and displayed in the windows. Soldiers and police tried to keep order. Groups of uniformed police left their station and joined the marching, singing people.

- *13* -

I was again to be a participating witness to one of the great events of history. People—young and old, boys and girls, grandfathers and grandmothers—came out onto the streets in an open rebellion against the Soviet and Hungarian overlords. I marched with them in cautious joy.

I marched with the people of Budapest, shouting defiance against the dictators.

"We want free elections!"

"Don't stop halfway!"

"Away with Stalinism!"

"Down with Gerö!"

While loudly screaming these slogans, I feared another outcry which somehow I was subconsciously expecting and dared to hope would not come.

"Death to the Jews!"

I worried during the shouting about what the slogans portended. Would the next slogan, under the pretence of liberalization, demand opening the door to fascism and antisemitism? I was unqualifiedly against the Communist system. I was not against the Russian army. I was against Communism. I was also for the system where my life would not be endangered because I was a Jew. No one who has watched the marching, enthusiastic ranks of Nazis can ever be part of the group process of marching, shouting people for whatever good cause without an eerie feeling of warning.

I ran home to see what was happening in our area. The first person I met was my schoolteacher neighbor, Mrs. Oroszi, whose husband was a university professor. She was leaving the building carrying the forbidden old prewar Hungarian flag with the Hungarian crown in the middle.

"Where did you get the flag?"

"I kept it under my mattress for just this occasion."

This idealistic, mild-mannered, matronly teacher who had embraced Communism had kept the old national flag. Underneath all her ideology, she remained stoutly a nationalistic Hungarian. If she had hid the flag, I could only imagine the floodgate to patriotic feelings that had been opened and would not be stopped in the rest of the population.

Together with my family I joined the crowd marching on Andrássy Boulevard towards the Russian embassy.

"Russkies home" roared the crowd over and over.

Here I was again among slogans which were too simple for the complex set of feelings that I felt. The Russkies had saved my life when my own countrymen had treated me as less than human. The system that was erected thereafter was porous with inequalities and hypocrisy. If the Russkies left, which I wanted, who would be there to take their place? Hopefully not the fascist agitators who could turn patriotism around on its head. I hoped they would not equate Hungarian with Christian as they had in the past.

- *14* -

*R*umors and wild news began circulating among the enthusiastic crowd as we marched towards Heroes' Square. A small car at the intersection with a bullhorn kept stating that the AVO was shooting demonstrators at the radio station. The crowd changed direction. Part of our group surged towards the radio station. The other part of the group, which I had joined, continued towards the Stalin statue in the middle of Heroes'

Square.

A great crowd surrounded the Stalin monument. Ropes were wound around the statue. The statue did not budge. In the distance we heard the sound of gunfire. But the atmosphere here was more carnival-like. More and more people gathered around the square shouting encouragement to the people with the ropes. Finally, from a nearby factory, a truck brought welding torches and managed to melt the statue at the knees. When the body of the statue fell to the ground, the roar of the crowd reached a crescendo. Several demonstrators broke the statue into countless little pieces for souvenirs.

I had never seen more determination than in the faces of the people around me. The crowd began to grow more violent, its appetite whetted by its success with the statue. Hungarian army trucks appeared when the statue toppled, and some of the demonstrators fled. The soldiers, though, displayed the Hungarian national flag on their trucks.

"The army is with us. The army is with us."

From the army trucks rifles were distributed to the mob. Barricades were set up at intersections. A shiny car was stopped at the barricades, and it looked dangerous for its occupants. The armed people at the barricades relaxed when they realized that the car carried Western newspaper reporters. We began to hear rifle and machine-gun fire much closer. Sara and I turned towards home.

When we got to our block, an armed AVO soldier stopped us. His rifle was trained on us.

"Where are you going?"

We pointed at our home.

"Get home fast!"

Across the street from our building, sandbags were being made into barricades at the AVO interrogation-door entrance and the first-floor windows. We knocked at our apartment building's door, and the porter finally let us in. She didn't say anything. She had also scented the shifting political winds. Her position as an official of the government, which required her to report the comings and goings of the building's occupants, now placed her in jeopardy. Hungarians were experts in the shifting-winds department.

I woke up next morning to the sound of machine-gun fire. The heaviest fighting was taking place along the nearby main boulevards. From our third-floor apartment we had a view of the AVO building across the narrow street. All of its windows were open. All of its lights were out. From behind my bedroom curtains I noticed people moving around in the rooms. I heard their telephones constantly ringing. I could hear orders being issued.

"Get a detachment to the passport department."

"Close Eötvös Street. Let no one in. Let no one out."

"Captain, I need orders."

"Wait for instructions."

The telephone rang again.

"The passport office is under attack."

"Hold out. Reinforcements are on the way."

It was exciting watching this revolution develop from my safe vantage point. It was like watching a show from the tenth row of the orchestra. This revolution was certainly participatory theater, and I was part of it. From my window I watched prisoners being taken in, between the sandbags. The revolution was on, and the flame was spreading.

At dawn the radio had an important announcement,

"Attention! Attention! Imre Nagy has become the prime minister of Hungary."

Although Imre Nagy had spent more than twenty-five years in the Soviet Union and returned to Hungary in 1944, he had become a popular political power. His daughter had married a Protestant minister. He liked to sit in Budapest's cafes among the people. I was present several times at the Jokai Beer Hall when he walked in and began to engage in discussions on politics and the merits of different Hungarian soccer teams. Naturally he was arguing good naturedly for the Team Vasas, which made my friend Ferenc Nagy, who was a former star of the team, happy. Overall he was well respected by most of the people. His leadership would calm the rough seas of dissent.

The radio broadcast was repeated on the streets via loudspeakers. The usual *comrades* was omitted from the message.

"Workers, Hungarians! The government will announce new programs. Defend the factories which are your factories. Protect your machines. Order and calm. Return to work. Support your government."

But it was too little, and way, way too late. The revolt now had its own momentum. Nothing would calm the people. The revolt had outraced its own revolutionary leaders. The student and factory committees with bolder demands urged the people to a general strike. Workers showed up for their weekly salaries, but not for work.

The revolutionary committee of our company sent for me. Revolutionary demands had to be printed. With a skeleton crew and armed revolutionaries changing copies on the press, some work was being done. There were threats, fistfights, and political arguments. There was anger against anyone who had held power in the old regime, which meant anyone in a managerial or administrative position, and quite a bit of controversy over where the new zeal would lead.

The crew of typesetters, including me, did some of the preparation work for the presses and then decided as a unit to go home. We were in the yard when the personnel office doors were forcibly opened, and the files were thrown out. These were the private files on the workers. Béla M., as a former functionary, was forced into the yard and seriously threatened. I and the other typesetters calmed down a few wild demagogues, but not before Béla had received some punches in the face.

Then my turn for endangerment came. Someone pulled my file and began reading it. In my file there was a note that my wife had worked in the police department. I was accused of political duplicity. My accuser was beaten up by the other typesetters and thrown out of the yard. Rozoga was there, and no one said one word against him.

Again feelings flooded my heart. Were Béla M. and myself singled out because we were Jews? Was Rozoga, who was feared as an informer, spared because he was Christian? In spite of the few violent storms, it was remarkable that there were not more open fascist voices. At the same time there were lies and painful accusations.

At home I went to the doctor, my neighbor, and told him about my experiences in the shop. He listened cautiously and added that in Hungary revolutionary movements were always connected with outbreaks of antisemitism.

"It's part of our culture," He stated.

The few minor incidents of Jew-baiting in this uprising made the revolt almost pure in this respect. Two weeks after this discussion the decent doctor was in jail for counterrevolutionary activities.

Curfew began. Then it was extended. The government was undecided as to its position. Demands by the people were refused. More demands were made. An hour later the government accepted the demands. More extensive demands were made and refused. Then in minutes they were accepted. From the roofs surrounding Parliament Square, AVO soldiers opened fire on the gathering demonstrators. Bloodbath! Street-fights broke out all over. The Hungarian Revolution had its first victims.

- *15* -

The big question on everyone's mind now was what would the Hungarian army do when fighting broke out. I witnessed a column of tanks race towards a besieged government building. Confused citizens, milling in the streets and hiding in doorways, began to cheer the soldiers. The crews of the tanks began to cheer back, waving the national flag. Within hours it appeared that some troops were siding with the youthful revolutionaries and the rest were remaining neutral. The neutral ones handed over their weapons to the revolutionaries. The others actively joined the fighting.

Two to three days of heavy fighting occurred, with fifteen-year-olds carrying weapons openly on the street. Fourteen- and fifteen-year-olds were buried in the city square. Armed workers marched in the streets. The police tried to stay neutral. But the time for neutrality was over.

During momentary lulls in the shootings, people surged in great waves into the streets, hungry for any information. Strangers greeted one another like old friends in a village market. Everyone had witnessed something heroic. According to the news spread by its citizens, the city of Budapest was full of heroes. In fact, there seemed to be more heroes than the population of the city. Speakers, informed or not, made speeches from hastily made platforms. Everyone was an expert. Everyone had something to say. Platforms were constructed from chairs, boxes, or anything else. New demands were the most prevalent topic. Demands were to be made to the world. Demands were to made for retribution. There were no demands for calm.

At the clattering noise of approaching Soviet tanks, the street cleared and people ran for cover. We wondered if the tanks would shoot us, as we had heard that they had opened fire on another group of people who only were singing the national anthem and waving Hungarian flags. The tanks approached us and slowed. They turned off onto a side street. This time a bloodbath was avoided. People took to the streets again; some brave and foolish people followed the tanks at a distance.

From the farm belt, state farm workers sent food in a show of support for the people of Budapest. They shipped and distributed the food free of charge at the street corners. I was looking for a bakery, hoping to find some bread. The lines at the bakery and in front of food-distribution corners were too long. I started heading in another direction.

In front of an open apartment house I saw a crowd begin to form. Inside the yard there was a man with a machine gun raised above his head. There was a short burst from his weapon. He yelled and fired his weapon again. He was staring up at a window in the apartment, screaming, "It's time for me to walk up to your apartment and empty my gun there. Hey, I'm yelling to you! You stinking Communist. You and your fat wife in the third-floor apartment. You who have the three-room apartment. You bloodsucker! Show your face and come down and see my one-room unit for my family of four. No! Don't come. I'll walk up right now and throw you out of there."

From the second floor someone dumped water on the shouting man. The shouting man's wife then came into the courtyard and dragged her drunk husband back into the building. The crowd applauded. It was a happy ending. Bread and circuses for the revolution. Unfortunately, not enough bread and too much circus.

At the next corner was an unattended basket filled with money. These were donations for the revolution. Further down the street, on the sidewalk under the shade of a tree, lay a dead freedom fighter covered with the national flag. People who passed this fallen soul made the sign of the cross. Only his legs were left uncovered. The soles of his shoes displayed large holes. That pair of shoes sent a shiver throughout my body. A woman opened her window. She had flowers in her hand. I asked her for the flowers and lay them on the flag. An ambulance arrived and removed the dead man. His fight for freedom had ended here at Sziv Utca.

A stranger passed me and whispered, "Dangerous times."

He was gone before I could formulate a response. I wondered, "dangerous" for whom? For the AVO? For the Communists? It is always dangerous for anyone who runs into the wrong group at the wrong time, especially if he or she belongs to the wrong religion.

I realized as I continued my search for bread that the stranger who had whispered "dangerous times" to me must have witnessed the hanging of the unfortunate man whose body now swung from the lamppost. Who was he? What unfortunate group had he belonged to? Was he just at the wrong place at the wrong time?

Crossing the major boulevards was a dangerous undertaking. Four of us, after a lengthy evaluation of our chances, decided to try. We managed a few meters when machine-gun fire forced us back. A soldier in the middle of the street was crouched down firing his gun.

"If I had my pistol with me I would go on the rooftop behind that soldier and finish him off."

This was from an old fellow beside me. He was pale and shaky with fear, and yet spoke with conviction.

"Now every old fart claims heroic deeds," stated a young housewife angrily.

"We should sit down with the fellows on the other side and talk over our problems with them. We should all talk it over.

No decent Hungarian should try to kill another Hungarian. If we had wine in our hand, this could be settled. Would you try to kill someone who sits opposite you in a cantina?"

The latter question was addressed to me. Before I had a chance to answer, others started arguing about this possibility or the absurdity of it with great emotion. A fight broke out. We dispersed in different directions as embittered strangers. A few moments before we had been patriots trying to cross the street together.

I decided to go home without bread. As I threaded my way home, images came unheeded into my head. Images of young men standing naked in the rain while soldiers in Hungarian uniforms searched for hidden "treasures." Images of a cattle drive where the cowboys were dressed as Hungarian soldiers and the stampeding herd were other Hungarians wearing a yellow armband. Images of young men singing the most beautiful song as they reached their first Hungarian city after years in hell. Perhaps it was the argument with my fellow Hungarians, perhaps it was fear, perhaps it was the dead freedom fighter with holes in his shoes which rekindled these images.

On my arrival at the doorway of my apartment, the young doctor who was my neighbor hurried out. He was wearing a Red Cross armband. He told me that he had been on duty at the hospital the entire week. He had been treating the overflow of wounded. In the hospital one's political convictions were not important. All were being treated. Once a slightly wounded man had accused him of being a party member. The doctor replied,

"Do you want me to treat you or not?"The wounded man became quiet.

The doctor and I decided to return outside in search of bread. At the corner of Csengery and Szondy Streets a middle-aged man with a mustache under his red nose was loudly agitating a small crowd around him to take vengeance.

"Help me search the houses. I know where the AVO are hiding."

The doctor and I exchanged looks. This was a largely Jewish neighborhood. It smelled to us like another excuse to round up the Jews. We were ready to interfere if necessary. Someone in the crowd shouted,"Don't listen to him. He's an AVO jailer himself. He once interrogated me."

A fight broke out between the two men. The crowd swelled and watched the struggle without any visible emotion. I knew that one of the men would end up dead. It would depend on which man the crowd believed. This would be trial by passion.

The doctor and I walked on. Our search for bread continued. The doctor told me that he had just treated a badly battered member of the AVO.

"What did he do that he was so badly beaten?" I asked.

"He was the trumpeter of their marching band. He was lucky. He's alive."

When we arrived at the bakery I told the doctor to stand at the back of the long line. I then went to the front of the line and pretended to recognize the good doctor for the first time.

"There's the doctor who's been treating the freedom fighters for a week. Let him get bread first."

The line parted for him. He received his bread. We marched to the next bakery and repeated the theater there. Now we had bread for both families. This was not the most heroic of deeds, but our families now had bread. And remember, in the city of Budapest, the streets were filled with heroes.

- *16* -

From behind my curtained post in my bedroom, I watched as a motorcycle sped by with a sidecar. One shot was fired from the window across from mine. I heard the shot when the motorcycle was ten yards away from our windows and right past the AVO building. The motorcycle slowed down and began to reel from side to side. It turned over. I was hypnotized by the overturned motorcycle and the dead or comatose person next to it on the pavement. Who was he? What was he trying to do on this street filled with AVO buildings and soldiers?

At the next dawn, on the way to line up in front of a bakery, I saw the motorcycle on another sidestreet. A young, very dead youth was still in the sidecar. It appeared that later that night someone from the AVO had moved the motorcycle from its position near the AVO station and had taken the driver, who had been sprawled across the street, and put him back on the motorcycle.

I arrived shaken at the bakery. A huge crowd was waiting in line for bread. I was one of the lucky ones. I got a loaf. A loaf of bread and a dead man sitting ludicrously on his motorcycle!

That morning I tried to cross Heroes' Square to see my short friend Karcsi. I had not heard from him for almost three weeks. The beautiful and spacious square was empty. In the middle of the square, where Stalin had stood tall, only two bronze boots remained. Somehow, whenever I think of the

288

revolt, I think of those bronze boots. I could not cross to the far side of the square where Karcsi lived because tanks and armored cars were lined up in the People's Park. I turned back towards home.

At a streetcorner I found a basket half-full of paper money. The sign above it read, "Give to the Revolution." I put some money in the basket. Broken shop windows had signs which proclaimed, "Windows broken by government machine-gun fire. Do not touch items. Do not loot. Do not steal."

I walked to the main boulevard. There was a nude male body hung on a lamppost. A sign hung around his neck, "AVO traitor." Ugly scenes abounded. Ugly accusations proliferated. This scene was multiplied on every streetcorner.

"He's lying. I'm a barber, not an informer."

Someone started to beat the barber. Others tried to defend him. Members of the hated AVO were lynched. Others, thought to be the AVO, were lynched or beaten up.

The true face of the uprising was all of this. There was the gallantry and idealism of the students' revolutionary spirit on one corner of the street, and ugly, murderous happenings a few hundred yards down the same street. There were people who just wanted to think and speak freely, and there were people longing to blame everything on someone. I knew on whom the blame would ultimately fall.

Shootings were on again, off again the next two days. The shaky new revolutionary government urged the workers to return to their factories. About half the employees of our factory showed up and were busy evaluating the fate of the company's leadership.

Ugly whispered accusations surfaced, especially against my friend and the head administrator, Ferenc Nagy. To be a leader during these times was dangerous. He was present and sat stone-still, listening. He was pale and quiet. I couldn't stand it. He had offered me help twice. Once he had offered me advice when I was bloodied in a soccer match. He had also made sure I got a job in Budapest. I got up and in a clear voice stated that whispered allegations served no one. If someone had something to say, I urged them to have the courage to stand up and say it. I told the gathering that I owed Ferenc Nagy. The meeting abruptly ended.

As we walked out of the meeting towards the typesetters building, heavy shooting and fighting broke out right in front of us. A group of freedom fighters was attempting to cross the street from our side in order to enter one of the AVO buildings. Two young revolutionaries, rifles in hand, had run towards the AVO entrance. Shots rang out from the building. Both men were down, mortally wounded. One man tried to make his way back across the street. He failed, and both men died in the middle of the street. The man who had tried to crawl to safety died with his hand outstretched, still trying to make another half-inch.

This whole tragic episode lasted only for a few seconds. Six of us typesetters ran to the safe side of Aradi Street towards the typesetter's building. We banged on the door until the porter unlocked the closed gates. He let us in. We were safe for the moment. Among the six of us was an old machine operator, well respected by all of us. This old Social Democrat now turned very pale and in a tired, defeated voice said, "My son is an officer in that AVO building."

Not two minutes later, there was banging at the door. The porter had orders not to open the door to strangers. We convinced him to open up and let the strangers in against standing instructions, since this was such a dangerous time. Two armed and angry freedom fighters entered the yard. They looked closely at the porter. The porter was an old Jewish man with heavily accented Jewish features. The freedom fighters began cursing him, calling him "Jewish swine." Without thinking I kicked the leader in the stomach. My colleagues helped disarm the other man. Taking away their weapons, we pushed the two of them, now subdued, into the cellar.

What had I opened the door to in the name of freedom? What a confusing and unwanted situation this was. I was for more freedom, more expression, more open communication. I was for less oppression, but here I was face-to-face with what that legacy opened up in my countrymen—hate, prejudice, and blindness. Whose freedom were these fighters arming for—only their own? Not the old Jew's! Not mine—not in this fashion.

Among the six of us who had run for our lives and were present at this situation, two of us were Jewish. We discussed the situation openly and heatedly. The Gentiles said that this was a unique incident, and we were overreacting. The Jews knew differently. We let the two men out of the cellar. We returned their rifles. They left wordlessly.

- *17* -

On the fourth day of the revolt there were no signs of abatement. What began as a demonstration a few days earlier had turned into a full-scale war.

Underneath our windows Soviet tanks roared towards the sounds of artillery fire. All through this day furious battles raged. Hungarian army units one by one sided with the populace against the Soviet occupying forces. News arrived that in certain districts of Budapest, Soviet soldiers had been deserting to join with the revolutionaries.

I was assigned to stay on the roof that day as a fire-watcher. From the rooftop I had a clear view of the gathering revolutionaries surging towards our street and building. When I was relieved from my duty, I saw machine guns positioned and trained from the second and third floors of the AVO building towards the gathering people.

Young and old, men and women, boys and girls, intellectuals and workers, idealists and hooligans were all united due to hatred of the foreign system. They were marching unknowingly towards havoc and machine guns perched on rooftops.

One wall of our apartment building was only five feet away from the neighboring police station's back wall. Our bathroom window almost abutted their third-floor bathroom windows. Ventilation shafts formed the outside walls of the two buildings. The police officer who had given me papers when I had arrived in Budapest and had steered me to this apartment yelled to me from the police station via these adjoining bathroom windows. He asked me to keep the bathroom windows open this night. I did.

Through their bathroom window police pushed over planks to our bathroom window. Our buildings were now joined by a shaky bridge three floors high. Having discarded most of their uniforms and their weapons, one by one the officers crawled on their stomachs from their building to ours, from bathroom to bathroom spanning the ventilation shafts.

The officer told me that they had received orders from the AVO across the street to remain at their station and open fire on the gathering crowd. The people on the street would have been caught in a crossfire and massacred.

"We left our weapons behind," he whispered.

One by one they left our apartment unit and one by one entered a side street via our cellar.

Next morning the revolutionaries gathered in front of our building facing the open AVO windows in greater numbers.

Thousands were milling, waving Hungarian flags and singing the old national anthem. Delegations were sent and received by the AVO.

The demonstrators demanded the release of jailed prisoners. There was a denial that there were any prisoners. Slowly, over a long expanse of time, forty or fifty people were released one by one and entered the throng. The crowd roared and cheered and celebrated every freed prisoner.

From our vantage point high above the street, we could see Hungarian tank columns approaching. The turrets were aimed at the crowd and constantly scanning the crowd as if to point out that everyone would be in range of the shells. The celebratory roar now became a frightened, angry bellowing as the group recognized the trap they were caught in.

Somehow, somewhere in the middle of the crowd the red-white-and-green Hungarian national flag began to appear. The crowd separated as boys and girls, with shoulders touching and flags waving, marched toward the tanks. The tanks slowed and then halted. People began to climb onto the tanks. The Hungarian tank crews opened the hatches of their vehicles. The officers and soldiers joined the revolutionaries. Shots were not fired.

One by one more prisoners were released by the AVO Someone shouted, "My brother is still in."

"Let my friend out."

"Let them out. Let them out! LET THEM ALL OUT!!!"

As the releases went on, taking perhaps an hour, the AVO units were using an underground tunnel. They were abandoning the building.

The people on the street finally dispersed. The revolutionary guards were now stationed in front of the AVO building. By the next morning they too were gone.

The next morning a group of us entered the abandoned AVO building. In the top-floor rooms we found pile after pile of torn and partly burned documents. Pages and pages were filled with names and addresses. Next to most of the names was a remark "Transferred to . . ." and then the name of a prison or interrogation center. Here and there were the comment, "Discharged." This was a euphemism. The names were those of waiters, drivers, and writers. These were names of ordinary simple people who had files on them. Not just radicalized dissidents, but everyone had been watched. This is how order in the Communist state was kept. This is what had happened to those taken in the middle of the night.

In the basement were little damp cells with their iron doors now open. In each one there was a cot, one blanket, and a slop bucket. This was what was behind the curtained windows across my street. This was the sight and smell of repression, torture, detention, and maybe even death. In one storeroom we found potatoes. This was a great treasure to all of us. The revolution had been won. The Soviet army, we heard, had exited Budapest.

- *18* -

My neighbor, Mr. Oroszi, and I walked towards Terez Boulevard and witnessed the remnants of the Revolution. We found tanks and armored vehicles disabled and burnt out. We saw buildings in ruins. We saw dead Soviet soldiers near their skeleton tanks, encircled by crowds of people. The soldiers had jumped from their burning tanks and had been shot as they attempted to escape.

One of the soldiers was very young, not more than twenty. His eyes were blue and forever open towards the sky. Dust covered his face. As the dust continued to swirl, his face became even more pale and ghostlike. I stood next to his rigid body for a few minutes, watching the transformation of his face. Who was this young Russian soldier? What was his name? What was his city? Who were his people? Was he an enemy of the Hungarian people or a person caught in a momentum he had no control of? Maybe he was the brother or a friend of the Soviet soldier who had thrown my hat on the ground, bade me to discard my weapons, and liberated me.

I wondered about my brother. He was another dead soldier left on a road somewhere. I wondered if anyone had watched over his dead body. It would give me solace to believe so.

I was filled with mixed and ambivalent feelings. On one hand I had seen the strength of the popular movement for freedom. I was filled with pride in my country. On the other hand I was frightened by my fellow countrymen. I had seen their viciousness of spirit and cruelty of mind. Would I be part of their celebration or the brunt of it? I could only half-celebrate and half-pray.

From a nearby ruined and destroyed store I took a few sheets of paper. I returned to the soldier and covered his body, securing the paper under his rigid frame. As I covered him I said the first words of the Kaddish, the Jewish prayer for the dead. An enemy or my savior? I did not know and did not care. He was only someone's son, someone's brother to me. He deserved a prayer.

Soviet tanks and troops were evacuated from the war-battered city of Budapest. They left a wrecked city. The city took their dead from the city squares to the cemeteries.

With the departure of the Russian troops there was a sudden explosion of joy, hatred, and violence. The hatred pushed the fury of the crowd, so that suspected AVO and Communist functionaries, if found, were lynched. In Budapest the lynchings were relatively few, but in the provinces there were serious settlings of accounts. I am sure some of the murdered were innocent. Some were murdered in the city of Miskolc because they were party members, but mainly because they were Jewish.

Members of the Hungarian Olympic team were stranded at the railway station and didn't know what to do. Should they go to the Games and show the world the great Hungarian spirit or should they stay and fight for freedom? The sports committee finally decided to tear the old hammer-and-sickle emblems from their uniforms and go show the proud face of the new Hungary to the world.

- *19* -

Sunday, the fourth of November, I woke up suddenly. From our window I saw the horizon light up from the flames. The Soviet army had returned in great numbers and had just as quickly crushed the revolt. In front of our apartment building Soviet machine guns were set up. They would fire intermittently, making it impossible to cross the street or leave our building.

On the rooftops there still remained some freedom fighters who continued to fire down at the tanks. They would not believe that all was in vain. Now the crowds who had cheered these men and women on with cries for freedom changed their slogans. Now the freedom fighters endangered them. Now it was better to be neutral or on the Soviet side. There were cries of "Stop those men from firing! Get those people off my roof!"

There might even have been cries for bloodshed in order to save one's own skin. The wind shifts quite rapidly in Hungary.

On the same day that the Soviet army crushed the revolution, the Hungarian exodus to Austria began. Young people left, carrying their weapons to the border crossings. Rumors circulated that sections of the border were open.

Hungary's radio stations were now in the hands of Moscow. The revolution was called a "revival of fascism" by the Soviet reporters. There were descriptions of "Hitlerite" forces and the old "fascist army and their officers." People were arrested in Budapest. Friends were jailed in Kecskemét. Accusations about atrocities committed by the freedom fighters were made. Accusations were made about fascists joining the freedom fighters. We were informed of former Arrow Cross murderers, freed from jail, who dreamed of vengeance and felt that this was the time to reestablish a right-wing Nazi dictatorship.

We all listened to Radio Free Europe. It urged us to resist, to strike, or to escape. How dangerous would the escape crossing be? I now had a wife and child. It was not only myself who would be endangered. Daring people whose lives depended on it had made it. I decided that I had to get out with my family. It was now or never. I knew that this was our last chance to get out to the West and start a new life. The problem was how to do so without facing Russian machine guns.

Béla M. reappeared after a few days' disappearance. He had tried to cross the border, but was captured. He then had escaped from the Hungarian border guards. The former AVO units that usually guarded the border had been recalled to the city to try to restore law and order. The government promised that the AVO units would be disbanded. If this were true, then only the regular Hungarian army soldiers would be at the border. They actually aided the escapees some of the time.

Radio Free Europe constantly aired news from the thousands and thousands of people who had arrived safely in Austria. There would be broadcasted messages saying,

"This is Lazlo. I made it."

"This is Pali. I'm in Austria."

"This is your husband János. Follow me."

To get some facts about a possible escape plan, I went out to the Southern Railway Station to try to learn what I could from people arriving from the border areas adjacent to Austria. I found a colleague from the Globus doing the same. We pretended to be waiting for a relative.

At this time there were major food shortages in Budapest. Under the pretence of trying to buy foodstuffs from the arriving travelers, I managed to talk to a few people. My questions were unanswered. Fear regarding strangers had now become part of our life again. I didn't trust anyone. No one trusted me.

Pali Kerekes, my former group-leader at the five-per-two, and his wife Klara sought me out. They had received a message from relatives in Canada that an Austrian-Hungarian smuggler had been hired to get them out. The smuggler was now at their house and had told them to be ready for the next morning's train. He forbade them in the name of security to tell anyone. They asked me to make up my mind that instant. Would we join them in the escape attempt? They told us to meet them at the railroad station at a certain time, to pretend that we were strangers, and to follow them in their escape.

"Just get to the same compartment we are in and follow us," was their instruction to me.

We hugged each other and departed.

Alone in the apartment Sara and I began to talk. She began to cry, "My whole family is here."

"What is left of mine is also," I replied.

"What will happen to our possessions, our furniture, our apartment? How can we risk our daughter?"

We discussed whether we should stay or go. We stalemated. Then help came from an unexpected source, a right path so to speak. It was our ten-year-old daughter who led the way.

"Mother, trust us, we must leave! We cannot live here anymore."

The decision was made. We had to get ready.

We went to sleep immediately to ready ourselves for whatever lay ahead. I woke up many times to the sounds of my wife's crying. We tried to comfort one another.

"What should I pack?"

With this question the whole world of insecurity and impossibility opened up. How does one pack a life? How does one say goodbye to everything to begin again? What are the essentials? When it really matters, it is only people that count . . . but before that minute, "What do I pack?" And with that question I knew that we would go, and that together we would face whatever was ahead of us. The die was cast. We would pack and get ready.

- *20* -

We packed a light blanket for Agi, one change of underwear, and food for a day. We had a little argument about what to wear. Sara put on a light-green overcoat over her newest outfit and placed high-heeled lizard shoes on her feet. She would walk out of Hungary wearing the latest styles.

I walked out of our apartment in a heavy coat and wearing a fur hat. I took my best boots. I knew from my five-per-two days what was essential. We had to look as if we were going out for a stroll, not for an escape. One could not alert anyone—not the porter at the door, not a stranger on the street—that we were leaving. One of us looked like a fashion plate, the other looked like a survivor. We shut the door behind us. We marched towards the railroad station without looking back.

From the railroad station I telephoned Ferenc Nagy. I told him that we were going to try to cross the border. I asked him to cover for me at work for two days. Despite his strong Communist views, I knew he was a friend. I knew I could trust him. He wished us luck. We simultaneously put down the phone without either of us saying the final words of "goodbye."

We found my friend and his family waiting at the train station as promised. We ignored one another per instructions. We followed them to their compartment on the train. Sara and Klara looked at each other and started to cry as the train filled up. The train which was to carry us to the western border was packed. My guess was that at least half the passengers were going to try to cross the border.

The conductor entered the compartment and announced loudly, "This is the Austrian Express."

This calmed frayed nerves a bit. He knew that this train, which passed very close to the Austrian border, was a freedom train. Everyone knew it. That was reassuring, but if it were well known then it wasn't just escapees who would know it.

The train first stopped at Mosonmagyarovar. On the platform we noticed Soviet soldiers waiting for the slowing train to stop. Panic! We would be captured! We were doomed!

Our smuggler led the Kerekes family, with us following, forward from car to car towards the locomotive. In sudden panic everyone else surged toward the rear of the train. We were going against the scurrying crowd as we followed our friends and their leader. Some people were weeping, some screaming, some yelling senselessly. There were some who were already surrendering to the Soviets before they entered the train. There were others who were trying to leave the train and run somewhere for freedom. Our small group stopped at the first car and waited in the dark compartment. Everyone else was trying to hide or to give themselves up to the waiting soldiers.

From the opposite side of the platform, a flashlight was signaling. The smuggler opened the train door and rushed his group off the train. A few seconds later we followed. Pali and his family disappeared in the darkness. We were disoriented. We had lost our contact. A voice in the dark beckoned us, "Follow me."

We followed the invisible voice to a darkened house where fifteen strangers sat waiting.

Our new guide instructed us to rest for an hour. We were now completely separated from Pali and his family. We were far from our destination, and we had to trust ourselves and strangers. We were alone with our destiny.

At about ten at that night our unknown guide led us down an unknown road to an unknown destination with a group of strangers whose fate we would now share. We were committed to this unidentified path which would lead us to freedom or to damnation. Our fate was in his hands now and in the hands of the border patrol.

It was November. It was dark and cold, and the ground was muddy. Our guide told us that he had chosen a muddy, swampy area of the frontier where there were few guards. They didn't like to wade through the mud either. A doctor in the group gave medication to the two babies so that they would sleep and not cry out. Machine guns rattled in the distance. Each muddy step took enormous effort. Occasionally tracers fired from shotguns lit the area and the people's strained, fearful faces.

"Lie down, lie down," came the whispered command.

When the dark came again we were told to get up and walk. I saw Sara step out of her high-heeled shoes as the mud sucked them away from her. I remembered those five-per-two rainy, muddy days when our shoes were left in the mud. I knew the importance of shoes. I tried to retrieve them from the mud. It was dark, and we were lagging behind the group. Agi tried to help, but as soon as one shoe was retrieved and placed on her foot, the mud sucked the other away. I was angry and frustrated that shoes were forcing us behind the group. I was upset at Sara's unwillingness to let go of the vestiges of her old life. She had put on her newest shoes for this trip, and now she would have to walk barefooted in the thick cold mud. She so needed to cling on to the stable aspect of her known life that she had ignored my advice. It was ironic that at such a hazardous time Sara thought of shoes just as I had when in the labor battalion. Shoes had become some sort of connection to our old life.

We had fallen behind the group. The guide came back for us and gave Sara some schnapps to keep her warm and her mind off the fright and the cold.

Machine-gun fire erupted next to us.

"Be quiet! They're not shooting at us," the guide whispered.

"Stay down! Stay down!"

Sara's shoeless foot had started to bleed. Agi was holding on to her from one side. I was pushing Sara from the other side. The guide was putting more schnapps in her mouth. Shooting erupted to our right. Sara pleaded for it to be over and for someone to capture us.

"Let me go home. Let me be in my own bed."

I understood what it meant to yearn for one's own bed instead of the muddy, deafening, frightening world of war and survival. We three walked and walked all that night, clinging to one another.

Finally the guide told us to go ahead and climb across a six-yard-wide ditch. He said that the other side was Austria. It was dark. Here and there in the distance were moving lights. We guessed them to be the headlights of moving cars. Doubts entered our minds. Were we in no-man's land, or were we still in Hungary? Perhaps we had made it. Maybe the guide had tricked us. Maybe he had taken our Hungarian money and would leave us in the dark. Maybe we were still in Hungary. How did we know that Austria was really just across the ditch? The mud was the same deepness there. The night held the same cold on either side.

I went ahead to investigate. I found an electric pole. Very high on the pole was a sign. It was too high, and it was too dark to read. With great difficulty, with my muddy hands and shoes, I climbed up a yard or two. I couldn't read it in the dark, but it was in German. We were in Austria. We had crossed the border. We were now free in the land that years ago had taken my family to concentration camps and had killed them.

I walked back to the group in the mud. Everyone was half-asleep from exhaustion. When I told them the news, everyone began to walk towards the moving lights. We reached a paved road. A car was coming towards us and stopped. Everyone surged forward to try to talk to the driver. I walked to the passenger side, and opening the door, pointed to Sara, who was barefoot and bleeding, and to my ten-year-old daughter. The driver stepped out of the car and put my family into the back of the car. She took us and two other women to the refugee center. We were safe. We had made it!

- *21* -

A part of our life had ended. As the sun rose we all felt that a new life had begun. I was born and had lived my youth under a feudal system. My early adolescence was during a neo-baroque, grotesque, half-democratic government for the privileged Gentile society. I had managed to survive the Nazi dictatorship which sought my extermination. I had survived the Soviet dictatorship which sought my servitude. Now I would learn to readjust my life to a never-before-experienced democratic system.

We would learn somehow. I knew this as I sat in a strange German car, with a stranger in a new land. I knew that our future was bright. The country where we would ultimately end up would not ask my religion or my race. My new country would respect my ability and willingness to work and my adherence to its laws. I was thirty-five years old, my wife was twenty-seven, and my daughter was ten. We were ready!

Hot chocolate and warm food waited for us at the refugee camp. Hot chocolate! We were asleep within minutes. The following morning buses and convoys arrived. With them were oranges and chocolates. We had not seen oranges for years. For a moment I flashed on another time when I had watched the German soldiers having such a feast in the shadow of the synagogue. I washed that memory from my mind. The buses took us to a large camp in the city of Eisenstadt, not too far from the Hungarian border. We got room assignments. There were twelve to sixteen people per room. Blankets were issued. We were forbidden to leave the refugee center without written documents. I understood the need to register the refugees. Understanding and liking this new type of imprisonment were two different things.

We were in the yard of the refugee center among hundreds of wandering, restless people. Masses of humanity were moving, all anxious, all disoriented. I told Sara not to lose faith, but to wait for me here. It was easy to get out of the camp for an experienced camp escapee. I needed to take my future into my own hands. I didn't want to begin my new life by being part of a herd in a refugee center.

I walked into the city. I found the Red Cross station. They allowed me to select clothing for my family's needs. I found a good-looking winter coat for Agi. I found matching high-heeled shoes, not unlike the ones stuck in mud near the Austrian-Hungarian border, for Sara. I knew she would like the shoes, a symbol of dignity and femininity. I also got oranges, figs, and chocolates. I walked back to the camp.

I found Sara standing in the mud in the middle of a patch of water.

"Why are you standing in the water?" I asked her.

"You told me to have faith and wait for you here. I did."

She had the dazed look of compliance that I recognized all too well as a loss of spirit. The oranges and figs brought back a smile. For a moment we could forget our nonperson status.

The next day brand-new shiny buses began arriving.

"Italy, Italy. If you want to go to Italy enter Bus #1."

People looked at each other, and you could almost read their thoughts.

"Italy sounds good. It's sunny and warm in Italy."

The bus slowly filled and Bus #1 rolled out.

"Sweden, Sweden. All those wanting to go to Sweden enter Bus #2."

"Sweden is cold. The language is difficult."

The bus was only half-full when it rolled out of the camp.

"France. Paris, the city of love."

The bus filled in minutes and departed. I waited and waited. I remembered that a year ago there was a track meet at the stadium in Hungary. European, American, and Soviet athletes had competed. When I saw the athletes carrying the American flag, I knew something deeply and intuitively. I knew that America would be home. I knew, yet I can't explain why. I knew in my heart I would be an American. I would go to America.

No buses were going to take me to the United States. I went back into the refugee office. I asked a police officer there how to get to Vienna.

"It is forbidden! Vienna is filled with Hungarian refugees, and we have to register you here."

"I have friends waiting for me there," I lied.

When he asked their names and addresses, I feigned ignorance of his language, although I knew German. From Vienna I would find a way to get to America, but I had to get to Vienna first. I had made my choice of the path I needed to take. I had no money in my pockets. Sara had a gold chain with a charm. I took it to trade for Austrian schillings. When I again requested permission to go to Vienna and showed the officials my Austrian money, they acquiesced.

This was a difficult time for us all and not insignificantly for the officials who were trying to organize the thousands of new arrivals who were coming across the border. My hope was that Pali and his family had made it to Vienna and might help us. I had the will and the desire! Now all I needed was some luck and good fortune.

The noon bus took Sara, Agi, and myself from Eisenstadt to Vienna. It took nearly two hours. At the bus station a large sign in Hungarian greeted us: "Welcome to Austria." We walked a few blocks towards the center of the city when I noticed a large group of Hungarians waiting in line in front of a movie house playing *Gone with the Wind*. We lined up and went into the movie. It was the realization of my small dream of seeing this famous American film. Here we were, three refugees from Hungary, watching an American film in the center of Vienna.

Sitting in the theater watching this wonderful film, we forgot some of the immediacy of our problems. I felt a bit drunk with the headiness of the new experiences which lay ahead. I just enjoyed the moment. We would find a place to stay the night later, but later. Right now there were Rhett Butler and Scarlett.

It was early evening when the show ended. The sparkling Viennese city lights after the gloomy nights in Budapest made us feel as if we were in a different world. The bright display windows of the different stores were filled with long-forgotten, long-yearned-for merchandise. We were each holding one of Agi's hands. What if we were to lose her? We had no home, no address. This thought suddenly brought me down to earth.

We kept walking. We heard some people speaking Hungarian. They looked settled into the city life of Vienna. Walking down Kärtnerstrasse, I looked into an espresso cafe and recognized a former five-per-two comrade sitting there. I walked in, and we greeted each other joyfully and warmly. I told him my predicament. I told him I needed to find Pali Kerekes. He said goodbye to his friends and joined me and my very exhausted family. We walked a short distance to a side street. He showed me the hotel where Pali was.

They had made it! To meet again had enormous meaning for all of us. I asked them if we could sleep with them for a few mights. Pali, Klara, and their two children were staying in one small room. Sara and Agi would sleep there. Pali walked out with me. Together we explained my situation to the hotel maid. She gave me a blanket and showed me the bathroom which served the floor.

"Early out," she told me.

For the next few nights I slept in the bathtub. It was better than sleeping in the Carpathian Mountains during the rain. But not much!

In the morning I began to learn about the refugee situation in Vienna. Thousands and thousands of people were living in temporary shelters. Jewish, Catholic, and other organizations were trying to relocate, shelter, and feed the fleeing refugees. Lines of people stood overnight trying to gain an audience with someone who might help them.

The next morning I registered my family as newly arrived refugees at the police station. I received a document stating that we were officially recorded as a homeless refugee family. This paper entitled us to certain privileges, such as being able to use all public transportation free of charge. I told my wife that although we were temporarily homeless and refugees, we would not be so for long.

Near the police station I noticed a sign: *Druckerei* ("print shop"). I walked in and asked the address of the typesetters' union. Without too much difficulty I found it and showed them my Hungarian union card. I inquired about the possibility of getting a job. They said that they would give me a job, but there was bureaucratic red-tape surrounding the hiring of a non-Austrian. They told me to return in a couple of days.

I asked them politely for any help in securing living quarters. Although the interviewer looked compassionate, he could not help.

Another office employee, holding a newspaper, approached me and showed me an article in the paper about a beautiful and elegant young woman. The picture was of the Baroness Mauthner, who had volunteered for the Austrian Red Cross. Both men began talking at once, saying that according to the article the baroness was turning over her summer castle to Hungarian refugees. Both of them urged me to try to see her.

- 22 -

The interviewer at the print shop offered to write a letter of recommendation addressed to the baroness. I felt that those in charge of granting audiences with her might think it had some official merit.

I located the Red Cross office. Several hundred people were waiting in line for help. A policeman was trying to keep order. I showed him the letter addressed to the baroness and told him I had to deliver it to her personally.

"*Bitte*, follow me," he said wide-eyed.

He led me to the entrance and past a guard with a huge Red Cross insignia on his arm. He escorted me past twenty desks, each with a volunteer busy interviewing people. I was led into a private office and was asked to wait.

This was the most elegant setting I had ever seen in my life. The baroness herself, when she entered, evoked a style of wealth and gentleness which overshadowed even her elegant office. I introduced myself. In a few sentences I told her that I had read about her admirable intentions to help the Hungarian refugees, and I offered my help. She looked at me in great bewilderment. She asked my name again and asked about my family. I think I must have impressed her with my passion and some of my self-assuredness.

After some hesitation, she asked me where I lived. Without hesitation and with a burst of emotion I told her, "In a hotel bathtub." She told me to gather my family and wait for her at six-thirty that evening at the side entrance of the Red Cross center.

We were there waiting there with our meager belongings at six-thirty. A chauffeur-driven white Steier pulled up to the side entrance. Our mouths dropped open. Agi and Sara were put in the back seat. I was told to join the baroness in the front. The chauffeur was discharged, and the baroness took the wheel.

The trip that night through the Wienerwald was a special experience. It was dark, so there was no landscape to distract me from a ride filled with dreams. Nothing was impossible. The baroness asked a few questions. I answered her with slightly embroidered stories about the daring acts of the valiant Hungarian freedom fighters. She enjoyed the stories. I wanted the dark starry sky, the forest, and the drive to continue forever. I wanted to dream of possibilities forever.

A housekeeper was waiting at the door of the summer palace. The baroness left us at the castle and returned to the city. We were the first and only family in these castlelike buildings. Warm food for dinner was served by the cook. We were then escorted to a first-floor bedroom with a private bathroom. Sara and Agi took a warm bath in this aristocratic setting. I could not bear to step into a bathtub with my aching reminiscence.

The room that was ours had three beds. Real beds! We all shared one bed and put Agi in the middle. Agi turned toward us and said, "This is the way to begin!"

The Wienerwald, the Vienna Woods! I had heard and read about it. Now it was my address: "Odon Mandel, Mauthner Castle, Wienerwald, Vienna, Austria, formerly of the labor battalion." This certainly was the way to begin. This was the fairy tale beginning to our new life. It promised a rich future of joy.

Breakfast was served in a large dining room. Two rosy-faced, healthy women who were permanent employees of the baron and baroness served our every need. After breakfast they showed us the extent of the estate. We walked the surrounding forest. Coming back into the gardens we noticed a young girl, a few years older than Agi, watching us. I talked to her and found that she was the daughter of one of the caretakers. Her name was Maria, and she lived in a small building at the side of the castle. She approached Agi with a doll, and Agi started to cry. Maria led her away, talking to her all the while. This young girl reached out to another girl in such a sweet, loving manner. In her small body was a large, caring heart. How different she was from the children who had mocked Agi for her "foreignness" while she was hospitalized. This was a child raised with love and not hate. This little episode made me feel good about the human race.

A former governess of the Mauthner family was in charge of the summer palace and its refugee inhabitants. After lunch I asked her if I was free to go to the city.

"Of course you are free. You can go anytime," she said. "If you cannot come back the same evening, just let me know."

She told me that she would give me some money for transportation, phone calls, or any emergency which might arise. I was thinking about Pali and his family in that cramped hotel room and how hospitable they had been to us.

While she prepared my lunch and emergency money, I asked her if it would be possible to obtain help for Pali's family. She began questioning me. From her pointed query it was clear that she was trying to screen the refugees. The criteria were not clear to me, but I was certain that religion was not one of them. She told me that there was a two-room section of the castle that they could occupy. I dared not mention that Klara also had her elderly parents with her.

Pali's whole family was waiting for me in their cramped hotel room. I described our new home, the surroundings, and the food. I showed them an envelope with the address and my lunch and emergency money for the day. They were amazed. I told Pali and Klara that a two-room section of the castle was waiting for them. They were to leave with me in a couple of hours. I told them that we would get permission for Klara's parents to join us in a day or two.

I left them and returned to the union office to look for job opportunities. I regaled the two union men who had just interviewed me twenty-four hours before with my story of good fortune. They seemed graciously and genuinely happy for me. They also told me I had a job at the Circusgasse print shop. I immediately reported there.

The print shop was a large, modern establishment. It really had nothing to do with the circus except its location, which was on Circus Street. I was told to report for work the next morning. Not a bad start for a documented homeless refugee. I had a job. My family was on vacation in a castle, and on top of this I was able to help my friend and his family. I hurried back exuberantly to pick up Pali's family.

- *23* -

In their hotel room, the Kerekes were immobilized. No one had packed, and everyone looked frightened. My friend Pali was tall and dark-skinned with black hair and mustache. He was extremely dashing and good-looking. He looked like a casting director's dream of a handsome heroic figure. Under the swashbuckler's looks beat a kind but timid heart. At social functions he was always the center of attention. Yet he was a very cautious, anxious person. During our labor camp experiences he was tormented both from real and imaginary frights. Somehow these qualities had melded to make an excellent compassionate leader. Sometimes, like now, they were a deterrent.

"What happened?" I asked.

Pali told me that the part of the Wienerwald where the palace was located was much nearer to the Hungarian border than Vienna was.

"Perhaps it's part of an AVO trap. At night the AVO could sneak over and carry us all back to Hungary."

I was completely puzzled. Pali's fear was unbelievable and ridiculously foolish. Pali continued his explanation, telling me that someone had already been captured in front of the Hungarian embassy and been shipped back to Budapest. One never knew the truth or the exaggeration of such rumors.

"If it's true I have to protect my family."

He said this last sentence without looking at me. I had to leave without them.

Unexpectedly alone on the way home on the streetcar, I was upset and amused. I laughed at Pali's personality, which made him so fearful. I laughed at the perversity of life. I laughed at an almost perfect day, now less perfect. I went to see the Red Cross lady in her office and told her that my friend's parents had unexpectedly managed to cross the border, and the whole family was too exhausted to move. How pleasantly surprised I was at this delightful lady's answer. "I'll get them a room, too. Bring the whole family tomorrow." I would if Pali's fears could be assuaged.

After work the following day I all but ran back to the hotel with my good news. I could take Pali's entire family to their new superdeluxe temporary home. This time they were packed and outside within minutes.

In about a week eight other families settled into the castle. I felt proprietary since I had been the first one there. I was proud of the fact that I was able to make connections and follow through on intuition. I made things happen. This was the first proud achievement in my new life—to be able to make the future happen and not just wait for it to envelop me.

My earnings were tax free. I did not have to pay for rent or food. This felt very good for the first few days, but soon my self-respect demanded of me more than this easy life.

Before and after work I lined up with thousands of refugees in front of the various embassies. The holiday season was approaching, and the embassies were not prepared to handle the overwhelming rush of people looking for new countries to emigrate to. I was finally given a ticket with a number and a time to report for an interview. These numbered tickets had great value. People had begun to barter for them. The numbers to Australia and Canada had the greatest value. The majority of the refugees wanted to go overseas, to be as far away as possible from Europe and the Russian claw. The American embassy did not issue numbers.

I missed two days of work in the first week in an attempt to get a number. I managed to register for Canada, New Zealand, and Australia. The appeal of Canada and Australia were more self-evident than New Zealand. A factor in my youth had established the priority of New Zealand. When I was a student in Kecskemét, I had a teacher who described this country as the most wonderful place in the world. The irony was that this teacher had never traveled further from Kecskemét than to Budapest. Somehow his book-learned description remained with me. With my New Zealand number I got an interview and was told that New Zealand was accepting single people only. I inched nearer to the American dream.

Pali was relaxed, waiting for his Canadian immigration papers to come through. Since he had a lot of free time on his hands, he waited with me in the long, endless lines. Deep inside, I envied him and his sure knowledge of his future. I envied that he had someone waiting for him. I remembered wandering home after my escape from the labor camp and hoping that someone would be waiting for me. I was about to start again without the comfort of someone planning and waiting for my arrival. There were no relatives, no friends, no known addresses for us from anyone in the universe. We were on our own. Probably for this reason we clung together as a family as never before. Where would we end up? What language would we need to learn? What customs would be different? We hoped, though we had no reason to be hopeful, that we would be able to go to the United States of America.

I registered my family with the Jewish help organization, HIAS. I asked them to help me with the forms which would allow my family and myself to emigrate to the United States. The help they were able to extend gave me new strength and vigor.

At the Circus Printing Company my colleagues were polite, but remote and distant. I was a stranger to them and had benefits denied them, for my earnings were tax free. I heard rumors that there were unemployed Austrians, which may have explained any resentment of me.

These Austrians with their German language were also an ambivalent package for me to assimilate. Traveling to work each morning, I began to recognize familiar faces in the street-car. Someone sat in the same corner every morning. I convinced myself, without any evidence, that he was a former S.S. officer. I closed my eyes and could visualize him in uniform. The other one, the middle-aged tall fellow who always read his newspaper sitting across from me, probably lived in his Jewish neighbor's home. His Jewish neighbor had been detained and deported to a concentration camp, I fantasized. Shutting my eyes I could visualize the man who read the newspaper traveling to "his" home in the nicest part of Vienna. That tall, erect fellow with the green feathered hat had probably been at the river Prut when I had worked practically barefoot in the winter. Every day I had such thoughts even though Vienna was very kind to us. Vienna was kind, but could never be home.

My past history continually caught up with me despite the ever present hospitality and kindness of the Austrians to the Hungarian refugees. Nightmares occurred more frequently and haunted my sleep. I was among Germans again. I could never forget it. It was hard to reconcile these two feelings, especially since the negative ones were becoming more and more potent. It was the same strangeness of working for the Germans in the labor battalion and how professional they were compared to the Hungarians. But they were also very professional in their Jewish Solution. How could I ever forget? How could I ever forgive?

To get to the Wienerwald from work I had to take a streetcar and then transfer to a bus. At the bus stop was a small grocery store. I always spent my lunch money there on a small gift for Agi and her new friend Maria. Sometimes it was a small piece of candy, sometimes an apple. Whatever it was that I brought, I felt it made her happy. It made me happy to feel more like a father to her. I realized how frightened and alone she must feel in a new country where she didn't speak the language. There would be no more missed ice cream cones for her! That grocery store would keep alive a child's hopes and dreams, just as Aush's grocery store had kept my imagination and dreams alive during my childhood.

- *24* -

In late December 1956, I was standing in line in front of the American embassy when news spread that Vice President Nixon was in Austria to help solve the Hungarian refugee problem. This was followed by an announcement that he would speak to us from the balcony of the embassy. I remember only his translated first sentence. "Your waiting is over."

This promise from an American vice president kept our spirits high over the holiday season.

We spent New Year's Eve with Hans Boyer and his family in their small one-room apartment. I had met Hans at work, and we had become family friends. As I fell asleep together, I wondered about Hans. Where had he been fourteen years before? What had he thought when the Jews were taken from Vienna?

I realized acutely how uncomfortable I was in this Germanic land, even as I was surrounded by kind and giving people.

Even with these wonderful friends who showed us nothing but love and kindness, I felt a type of uneasiness. I understood what people had to do to survive, but I also needed to know the limits to which these people, my friends, had gone. I felt that I knew their hearts in the real way that friends did, but I also felt that until I knew what they had seen, and done, and felt during the war, I truly did not know. As close as I was with the Boyers, I wondered whether they had cooperated with the Nazis or resisted during the war.

The new year 1957 had a wonderful beginning for us. With American efficiency and speed we were registered for immigration. The very next day we had a physical exam. There were fifteen physicians in one huge room. One minute was allocated per person. One of the doctors was a Negro. Most of us gravitated towards him. Perhaps we felt that he would understand our plight and our status best. His being so different than the other Americans was a magnet to us. We liked the differences and our hope was fueled to be a part of that great American melting pot. Within days we were notified that we were to be at the railroad station on January 16 at eight in the morning. We were told that this was to be the second-largest Hungarian emigration from Austria to America. By special vote of Congress we would be able to receive American citizenship papers in five years.

We had saved almost three hundred dollars during our stay in Vienna. We went into the city and purchased presents for the people who had given so much of themselves to us. I returned to the union and thanked them for their help. After our spending spree, our family fortune amounted to one hundred and three dollars and twenty-four cents. It was not very much, but we were healthy, young, and together. We looked forward to spending our great wealth and the rest of our life in the United States of America. We exchanged our Austrian schillings for American dollars.

Saying goodbye to the Boyer family was very painful. We had too many wrenching goodbyes in our lives. With all my soul-searching, with all my unasked and unanswered questions, I embraced the Boyer family with true love and friendship. I finally felt the peace and ease which had eluded me.

The train took us to a refugee center in the city of Wiener-Neustadt, a huge former army barracks which was designated as a temporary assembly and housing area for those already processed and approved for entry into the United States.Our group of five hundred people was Jewish. They had been brought together by the Jewish help group. The non-Jewish groups were already at the army barracks. As we arrived we were greeted by stones and pebbles thrown at us by the non-Jews. A true Hungarian welcome!

The Austrian guards rushed to separate us from the non-Jewish Hungarians. We were placed in a far corner of the compound. There was a group of fascists who had been freed from Hungarian jails during the revolt and now must have felt that they should have ascendancy over "the stinking Jews." They were the formentors of bigotry. This small group of former fascists tried to ignite antisemitic feelings among other Hungarians.

Within hours Hungarian-speaking Americans arrived to investigate the near riots. The leaders of the fascist group were removed by the Austrian police. The whole episode made us feel validated in leaving Europe. It was a blessing in disguise. It was easier to leave. I was only concerned that this bunch would be following us to America.

During the trainride from Vienna to Wiener-Neustadt, I met a former Division I soccer player, Pista Fuzesi, and his family. Pista Fuzesi told me that he had met a former colleague of mine from the Globus, one of the M's, Sanyi M. He told me that Sanyi M. was in a very desperate situation. He was alone in Austria and unable to find livable housing. I knew that the Mauthner Castle had vacant rooms. Sanyi M. was a handsome fellow and fond of the girls, and they of him. A few weeks before the revolt he had told me that he was now a married man. I couldn't imagine him alone and homeless. I would try to find him and help him.

I asked permission for a day's leave of absence. Back in Vienna I went to search for Sanyi. I began my search walking the streets frequented by Hungarian refugees. I stopped at every espresso house looking for him. Finally I found Sanyi standing in a line in front of the Red Cross office. He was perfectly shaven and well groomed. Only after a very happy hug and greeting did I notice despair and tiredness on his face and the sagging spirits in his eyes.

I pulled him out of the line and began to question him.

"How did you get out? Why didn't you tell me you were going?"

Finally I asked him about his wife.

"Let's not talk about past history. She didn't want to come with me, " he said.

I didn't have the courage to ask him if he had even asked her to go with him.

We took the streetcar and the bus to Mauthner Castle, and I introduced Sanyi to the Red Cross woman. I asked her if she could help him settle. She told us that she was not allowed to take in new refugees. She explained that Baroness Mauthner was beginning to wind down her operation. Sanyi began to smile his winning sensual smile and apologized for his unannounced visit. She hesitated a minute and then offered us a glass of wine in her room. I left the castle alone after saying goodbye to my friend, who was now situated in a small room in the corner. As I said, Sanyi M. was a very good looking lady's man!

I returned to my family. We spent a few quiet and anxious days in Wiener-Neustadt waiting for our turn to set out. We were to go by train to Bremerhaven and from there by ship to the United States. Last letters were written to family and goodbyes said to those who for unknown reasons were not on the traveling list and, therefore, were left behind.

Our group was called. We went to the railway station. We boarded a Jewish refugee train. Religious organizations were in charge of organizing and financing the transport. Ours was organized by HIAS and was for Jews only. Other religious groups were on other trains or on other roads on their way to the same destination. Red Cross ladies waited for us at the railroad stations with food and gifts for the children. At the German border, German army bands waited for us and played the Hungarian national anthem. Because of the excitement, all of us became tired and slept most of the time. We all wanted to be alone with our thoughts.

Despite all of the pain and excitement at leaving again we tried to show our appreciation to the volunteers who passed out hot chocolate and cold milk at the train stations. I had a wild-looking tall fur hat. Many times people wanted to take my picture from the train window. Many times I was asked to disembark from the train for a photo session with the local volunteer ladies. I complied with all requests. We represented a typical Hungarian family, or so they thought. If only people remembered what they had done to such "typical" Hungarian families during the time of their Third Reich!

Once on German soil nuns and priests began to appear at every stop. We wondered if they had mixed our train schedule with that of the Catholics. Rosaries and crosses were given to all of us. More photographs were requested and given. Priests blessed the train with huge crucifixes. I remembered another cross which had taken me onward and forward in the labor camps. It would do fine here also. This cross would lead to the world of America.

At night, while I pretended to be asleep, fear became my traveling companion. Fear of the unknown stayed with me for a long time no matter how I tried to shake it. I asked myself why I had this feeling now, when I hadn't had it before. The answer was that now I was not alone. I had my family to take care of. I was not alone. I was responsible for them.

The other cause for my uneasy feelings and anxious thoughts was that we were a trainload of Jews on a German train on German soil. From the train windows I saw the railroad workers in their blue uniforms watching us. They watched with indifference. From my bruised eyes I felt that these same railroad people must have done their duty shipping thousands and thousands to their deaths, with their same blind, cold eyes filled with indifference.

Our train arrived finally at its destination. Nuns and priests gave out rosaries again. We took them. It could not hurt. Upon our arrival at the Bremerhaven station a waiting HIAS official explained to us that the efficient Germans had misscheduled the arriving trains. The Catholic train would not have nuns or priests or rosaries or crosses.

At the harbor a band was playing. We did not know whether it was playing for us or someone else. Seeing a busy harbor, its hundreds of longshoremen loading and unloading crates with huge cranes, was a new experience for most of us. We had lived our lives in landlocked Hungary. We had expected to see the blue waters of the North Sea. We were disappointed. The gray dirty waters of the harbor greeted us instead.

- *25* -

Our ship was the *General Altinge*, a World War II United States naval transport out of mothballs. Its last journey would be to take us to our new homeland. Males and females were separated and put in separate quarters. Children stayed with their mothers.

As the ship began to fill with other groups, we realized with great comfort that the Jews were housed in a huge separate compartment. We liked this arrangement. We were aware that antisemitic outbursts could happen. We did not want our voyage to America marred by all the hatreds of the past. The antisemitic scenes during the revolt and afterwards confirmed most Jews' dreams of forming a new life outside of Hungary.

I lay in my bunk alone as the compartment filled with other men. I would have loved to share my thoughts with Sara and Agi. This time I needed my family to talk away my uneasiness and misery. I felt again that I was utterly alone. People were talking and moving around. They appeared so self-confident and hopeful. I was not. I slid further into rumination and isolation. My neighbor, Pista, my soccer friend from Wiener-Neustadt, talked about aunts and uncles in America waiting for them. My other neighbor was constantly praying. As soon as he put away his tallis, he talked about his American brother who owned a taxi company. He would drive a taxi for his brother. What would I do? I thought and thought without a clue. What could I do? Everyone around me seemed so sure and determined. Almost instantly I lost my verve and optimism and was filled with strange thoughts and fears. I wondered if it had anything to do with the separation from my wife and child. It was as if my surety about myself were fed by my knowing that they were present and alive. With separation a small part of me died again.

I not only did not know what I would do once in America, but I did not know what part of the United States would be my home. A large map of the United States was pinned to the wall. The United States of America was so huge! There were so many unheard-of states and cities. I didn't speak one word of English. How far could I go with one hundred and three dollars and change? Everyone seemed to be going somewhere, to someone. The Mandels were just going. All of a sudden my goals became unclear. Why had I not gone with friends to Canada? Who did I think I was to take on this new adventure!

After a few hours of gloomy thoughts, listening and watching the comings and goings around me, a new vitality seized me. I knew Pali's family in Canada would have helped me, but I did not want their help. I wanted to do it alone. I wanted a brand-new start. My start! My way! My life! Too much of my life had been orchestrated my others. No more! My life was to be my own. Our small family would be the nucleus of a new beginning, a new legacy, a new tradition. I didn't know the future, but I did know that I could manage with my foot on the right path and my family at my side. This time would be easier than in 1945. I was not alone in the world. I had a family. We would care for one another.

The ship's bakery was looking for two volunteer bakers. Someone said that the volunteers would get a bonus of three dollars per day. Pista and I took the job the day of our departure. I was excited and anxious to work and earn my first American dollars. The head of the bakery spoke a few German words. Even with his help we had no idea what the bakers were trying to tell us.

One of the bakers, nicknamed Popeye, took me under his wing. He let me align the bread on the slicing machine. I had never seen anything like it before. A bread slicer, what an invention! I remembered my camp days and longing for bread. Now I was surrounded by loaves and loaves of bread, awaiting a machine which would neatly slice them.

"Teche desi, Teche desi," Popeye said.

I did not know what he was trying to communicate. I started to work faster, trying to please him. He came over and repeated those foreign words. I worked even faster. Later the translation came to me, "Take it easy. Take it easy."

As the ship began to move I went to the front. From that vantage I could see how beautiful it was to look straight ahead toward the unobstructed view of the North Sea. It was late January, and the weather was pleasant. The sun gave some last warmth, and there was almost no wind. On the upper deck, the refugees were crowded to take their last look at Europe.

On the dock, on a high platform, a band was playing the Hungarian national anthem. I started to feel emotional. The crowd joined the band in song. Within minutes I noticed that fistfights had broken out on the main deck. I stopped singing. It was not my song anymore. It was the song of a nation I was leaving. It was a song which represented the old, the homeland, the bigotry. It was not mine. I returned to the bakery.

The fistfights occurred because it was claimed that the Jews were not singing the Hungarian national anthem with enough emotion and enthusiasm. The captain issued orders to maintain law and order. Those found guilty of racism would stay in the ship's jail and would not be allowed on American soil. We liked our new country and its laws already. I returned to the bakery and its peace and quiet.

The ship picked up speed. In the bakery I looked for Pista. He was already seasick. We had been moving less than twenty minutes. We had not moved two hundred yards when his career as a baker ended. Seasick bakers were not allowed, and he was very seasick. I helped him back to his bunk, where he remained flat on his back for the whole duration of the voyage.

With great difficulty I found the women's quarters. Agi told me that her mother was very sick. Everyone seemed to be sick, at least three-quarters of the travelers. I found a Coca-Cola machine for the crew. I bought one Coke for my daughter, and I had a sip. Communist propaganda had claimed this poisonous Coke was a mind-altering drink. It tasted good to her and me. Everyday I bought her one, and she brought one in for her mother. I didn't mind being a mind-altered almost-American.

The bakery had lemons. I brought a few everyday for Pista and Sara to help ease their distress. Agi was happy, healthy, and ran around the ship. She and I were having an adventure, but most of the passengers were longing for solid ground.

In groups of tens and twenties we were called in for questioning. When I was called, the first question was,

"What is your name? Do you want to change it to a more American-sounding name?"

My first name in Hungarian was Odon. They could not find an American substitute.

Would I take Edmund instead of Odon?

"Gladly."

This ended my interrogation, and I became officially Edmund O. Mandel.

I enjoyed every moment of the voyage. I had a wonderful time in the bakery. I was busy and did not worry. I loved to go out with the bakers and look at the huge waves.

I rarely managed to see Sara. If I was forceful enough I could coax her out of her bunk with Agi's help to get some fresh air. She looked, like many of the others, terribly sick. The dining room was always half-empty. Besides being sick, no one enjoyed the taste of American food.

"No taste," they said.

Even the fruits did not taste the way they should, or the way we remembered the fruits in Hungary had tasted. We all admitted that American fruits were beautiful and healthy-looking, but lacked the taste of our remembrance. The cooked food was tasteless and uneatable. Food was placed on the table, and even if it remained untouched, it was thrown away. That was not understandable to people who depended on food for survival. We could not understand the waste. We had been starved too often to be able to understand this plenty and extravagance. I began to save some oranges and apples for leaner times.

My daughter's birthday came. Somehow I explained this to Popeye. The bakers baked a special birthday cake for her. Their kindness touched all of us. They responded in the most human ways to an eleven-year-old. Their emotions were not walled off. Their eyes were not distant and cold. These were people I could live with. These were people I could be proud to be among.

The last day in the bakery, Popeye presented me with a sailor's hat as a going-away present. Everyone tried to say a few words of encouragement as I said goodbye to my first American friends. Then, as always, I felt most comfortable with a vast breadth of friends. Just as I had Christian friends at school and through soccer which transcended what most of the Jewish boys had, I now had the American bakers as part of my expanded group. I hadn't just stuck to my Jewish bunkmates. I had to have a wider circle. This ability or trait to open my arms wide to new experiences helped me overcome difficulties in my life and always enriched me.

I still look back on my days as a ship's baker as days well spent. Perhaps these first days as an American emigre had something to do with my ultimate occupation. Waiting in my quarters I now had time to be alone and time to think. Sitting alone among hundreds, my old traveling partner, fear, returned.

- *26* -

On January 21, 1957, I sat on the upper deck noting the outline of New York harbor. I saw the silhouette of the city and the great lady who guarded its entrance. The most astonishing sight was that of huge trucks piggybacking fifteen automobiles at a time. What a country! We had arrived safely.

We were told that no food could be taken off the ship. I had a dozen oranges and apples. I could not help my survivalist nature. I thought ahead of food shortages or adverse situations. Before I took my first step on American soil, I broke the law and hid three oranges in my bag and walked off the ship, feeling guilty and nervous about it. I was asked my name by a waiting officer as we stepped off the ship.

"Edmund O. Mandel," I answered proudly.

My heart pumped faster when I said my new name.

The passengers from the ship were led to waiting friends and family and to the buses. People, shouting and crying as they recognized their newly arrived relatives, ran forward to embrace them. No one greeted us. Hungarian-speaking American soldiers were there to direct us. Everyone was polite and quiet. The three of us Mandels sat alone on a bus.

No one waited for us. We began to feel very sorry for ourselves. Years later those who were greeted so fondly and warmly told us that we were the lucky ones. Their relatives were not as rich, as well connected, or as generous towards them as they had anticipated. Being so alone made us adjust from the moment we disembarked the ship. We became even more experienced at readjustment.

The bus took us to Camp Kilmer, a former army base. The Hungarian-speaking soldiers remained with us. We were asked if anyone required kosher food. It sounded good to me, since I had not liked the American food on the refugee ship. I loved making my own choices. This was the United States of America. I chose kosher food as my first American choice. It was a big mistake! The selections were very limited. I noticed that the others had great breakfasts and dinners. I switched my choice, which was also an American prerogative. The food was wonderful!

The physical examination and interviews with the Jewish helping organizations filled our days. Wherever we had to go, a bus transported us. A huge Red Cross warehouse filled with used clothing was at our disposal. We selected a few necessary pieces of clothing made in the American style. The trouble was that we did not have any luggage to carry it.

My interviewer was a former famous Hungarian movie star who had moved to the United States before the war broke out. His name was Paul Javor. When I told him that I was a printer, he found a Hungarian printing shop in New York which needed a typesetter. I did not take his helpful offer. Somewhere Sara had seen a travel brochure about Florida. She had decided that was the place she wanted to live. I told the interviewer I wanted to go to Florida. He looked at me puzzled and questioned my logic.

"It's always warm there," I answered.

He tried to persuade me to change my mind. He told me about seasonal working conditions and low wages. I was stubborn. We had made up our minds to see the palm trees, warm sunshine, and coconuts. Within a few days we received permission from the Miami Jewish help organization. They would resettle us there.

The bulletin board at Camp Kilmer was filled with the names and addresses of refugees. Among all the names I found the name of a former labor camp comrade who had worked at Globus and his Los Angeles address. I wrote his name down and put it in my wallet. This unappraised action might have been an intuition about what would ultimately be our permanent home.

A van picked us up. The driver spoke only English. We did not know where he was taking us. He drove us through unknown sections of a great metropolis. We did not know whether we were in New York or New Jersey. We did not know if we were lost or found. Finally he deposited us in a motel near an airport. The driver showed us the airline tickets and with sign language communicated that he would pick us up at twelve noon the next day and deliver us to the airport.

Our motel room was beautiful. Our family had not been together for a long time, and we enjoyed every minute of it. In the room was a wooden box with controls on it and a window in front. I played with it, trying to figure out its purpose. It was a new experience to see a picture appear in the window. This was our first experience of television. We watched the whole night with great amazement. Wrestling matches were our favorite, since we didn't need the language to understand them.

When we woke up the next morning, my dear wife looked in the mirror and complained that she did not like how she looked. She wanted to appear her best when she arrived in Florida. We found a beauty shop. The charge for a new hairdo was ten dollars, which was ten percent of the family fortune. Sara seems to know intuitively what is right and what makes life beautiful. She pursues this regardless of rationale.

We were picked up as promised and delivered to the airport. It was the first airplane ride we had ever had in our whole life. Sara held onto her seat tightly. She was afraid she would get airsick. She had already suffered seasickness, and she was concerned about more of the same. In a few hours we landed at Miami airport.

A driver was waiting for us. In a half-hour we were again in a motel. The next morning, new interviews began. This time the questions were more practical: Did we have money? Were we healthy? Did we have relatives in the United States?

The lady who interviewed us issued us a rent-deposit check with two addresses in Miami. We had the choice of either one. We were also given coupons to buy necessary household items from a department store. The coupons were to purchase bedding, pots, pans, and other things to begin our new life.

Both apartments were located downtown. There were no palm trees, and we were far from the ocean. I'm not sure about the coconuts. I remember landing from the air and seeing Miami in a different, more becoming light than our living arrangements evidenced. We decided to look somewhere else.

I never seemed to follow instructions to the letter and always managed to go beyond the limitations imposed by them. We stopped at the first bus station heading towards Miami Beach. The bus slowed down a bit, but did not stop. Buses and buses passed us without ever stopping. We were unable to find an explanation and tried to solve this riddle by asking questions in Hungarian and in German. Finally a stranger noticed us and with great difficulty, in broken German, Yiddish, and English, told us that this bus stop was for *schwartzes* ("blacks") only. Ah, America! We learned quickly that race discrimination was still in effect in Florida. It seemed to me that it was not different than the *Nicht für Juden* ("Not for Jews") signs in Europe a decade earlier. He guided us to the next bus stop, which was "for whites only." I kept remembering that black American doctor with whom we had felt so comfortable as he seemed to embody what was American to us.

We enjoyed the sightseeing tour on the bus, and we looked longingly at the wonderful homes, boats, palm trees, and the blue ocean. We walked a bit. In front of a nice apartment at 6840 Abbott Avenue we heard an older man speak to his wife in Hungarian. We addressed the nice-looking older couple and told them that we were looking for a furnished apartment. He asked us a few question and told us that he was the landlord of this apartment. He told me the monthly rent. The rent was more than double the rent-deposit check in our hand. I told him I would go to work immediately and pay the difference. We moved in that day.

- 27 -

Our Hungarian-speaking landlord found Sara a job in a kosher restaurant. He made some calls on my behalf and sent me to see a Hungarian-speaking maître d', Mr. Katz, at the Fleetwood Hotel. Mr. Katz was a friendly man who looked elegant in his black formal wear. He questioned me and hired me as a busboy.

"Report for work as soon as you have a white shirt, black pants, and a work permit."

"What work permit? My wife did not need a permit to work."

He explained that in the hotel business in Florida everyone had to be fingerprinted at the police station. Photographs would be taken and work permits would be issued immediately. I did not know how to achieve all this technical bureaucratic process, and my fears must have shown.

Mr. Katz called over another busboy, Charlie, and spoke to him in English. Charlie spoke German. He told me that if I waited until his break, he would help me obtain the necessary documents.

The first thing I learned about Charlie was that he was broke. In almost flawless German he told me he was from Texas and had picked up German while in the military. He had a pleasant, carefree disposition and an open enthusiasm about the world. He was tall, good-looking, thirtyish, slender, and intelligent. As soon as we began to climb the steps to the police station, I noticed a conviviality which gave me a strange feeling. Several men, some uniformed and some civilian-clothed, stopped him.

"Hi, Charlie, how are you doing?"

They knew him too well. The detectives and policemen called him by his first name. Since Charlie was not the mayor of the town but only a busboy, the familiarity led me to the conclusion that Charlie must be a gangster.

I was fingerprinted, photographed, and immediately received my work permit. On the way back Charlie took me to the Goodwill Store, where I bought a pair of used black pants for one dollar. They were a bit large, but definitely wearable. Charlie also tried to persuade me to buy a used white shirt. I objected vehemently to his suggestion. I had too much pride to have used shirts or used underwear. At a nearby store shirts were displayed for ninety-nine cents. I bought a brand-new short-sleeved white nylon shirt. I washed it daily, shook it out, and within hours it was dry and brand-new again. The shirt was the first piece of my American wardrobe that I paid for with my own money. And it was brand-new!

We walked a bit towards the ocean.

"I have to check out something here," Charlie said.

He stopped in front of a very old and very dirty car.

"I have been watching this car for almost eight weeks," Charlie told me.

I was told by my new friend that if a car is found abandoned on a public street for two months, the finder of the car can take it after obtaining a police report confirming the date of abandonment. Charlie told me that within a few days this would be his car. I gathered then that Charlie's familiarity with the police was due to transactions such as these. Here was another person who seemed to know how to work the system.

I needed to enroll Agi in school. The school was very close to our apartment. Going back to school after five months absence and not knowing a word of English was a great concern to us all, especially Agi. With one of us on each side, holding one of her hands and sensing her painful uneasiness, we walked into the admittance office. Through a translator we answered the questions about her age and grades, and she began to whimper. Naturally her mother followed suit, feeling sorry for her and ourselves. The lady took Agi to class, introduced her to her teacher, and told her to be back next morning.

On the way home we regained our enthusiasm and optimism. We talked bravely about how much we had accomplished in such a short time. Both of us had a job, and our daughter was enrolled in school. We lived in a nice apartment in beautiful Miami Beach. We had warm weather, palm trees, and the blue ocean. We still didn't know about coconuts. We lived the life depicted in the travel brochure.

Our helpful landlord offered to take us grocery shopping for our very first time. He gave us a stainless-steel shopping cart and let us wander alone in this wonderland of foods, fruits, and dreams. We could not believe our eyes. All these strange beautiful fruits. The meats! The fully stocked shelves. Chocolates! Cookies! The various brands and types of milks and cheeses. It was like visiting Disneyland for the first time. We were surely in the land of milk and honey, and tried to memorize all the brands that would prove it to us.

How happy the family was when Sara brought home the bounty and began to cook in our new home. This was not an easy job for her.

"The stove—what is this 350 and 400 degrees?"

With the landlord's wife's help and explanation, Sara began to prepare our first American dinner. As she cooked, I watched her every movement. This whole setting of watching and waiting reminded me of the labor camp. There I was always very hungry, and I had watched the cook's every motion as he prepared our meals. Tonight the hunger was from a different origin. It was a hunger for the familiar. When dinner was ready, I told Agi that now we would have a wonderful meal just like the ones we had months ago in Hungary. Sara and Agi began to cry at the reminder of Hungary.

- *28* -

The Fleetwood Hotel was rundown and dilapidated. It was a pension-type hotel. Breakfast and dinner were included in the weekly rate. My salary was three dollars per day and tips. I worked seven days a week with no days off. My own breakfast and dinner were also included as part of my wages.

At work Mr. Katz told me to watch and catch on to what the other busboys were doing. "It's simple. Your waiter will help you if you run into any trouble."

My first job in the morning was to serve the juices as the guests arrived. Tomato or orange were the only choices, so that this task was easy. Only two new words to learn! My problems began with the glasses. There were none at my station. It appeared that the hotel did not have sufficient supplies when the dining room was busy. The dining room was huge, and I went from station to station picking up juice glasses. I got threatening looks for this territorial incursion. They had the same problem that I had with the shortage of glasses, and I was complicating their problem by pilfering from their stations.

Somehow I managed the first breakfast. I was now free from eleven until four. I enrolled in a daily English class during this interim time. It was held in a nearby library. I got a simple book with pictures and simple words.

This became my noon routine for quite some time. Charlie showed me a quiet beachside area where he spent his afternoons sunning. I sat under the palm trees in the grassy park studying my first English words: *goat, boat, coat.* Again and again I repeated these words. The scenery was beautiful, the weather mild and temperate; and I sat there with my elementary school book in my hand learning the vagaries of the *oa.* As I looked up repeating these words and word sounds from memory, I did not fail to notice the blue ocean, constantly in motion and the grace of the romantic-looking palm trees. I forgot the word sequence—back to *boat, goat, coat*!! I began to hate what these stupid English words were doing to this tranquil paradise.

I began to think. I'm thirty-four years old and cleaning tables with busboys who are sixteen and seventeen. My wife is working in someone else's kitchen. My daughter comes home from school everyday with a headache. I grew bitter, unhappy, and very tired. I did not feel that I was adequately taking care of my family. I forced myself back to my English book: *boat, coat, goat.*

The waiter from New York and I had eight tables to take care of. Usually thirty persons were accommodated by this seating. The expected tip per busboy was one dollar per person per week.

The people came in groups for a three- to four-week stay. I was counting the days.

"This table's tip for me is due this morning. That will be six dollars, or maybe a bit more."

One person did not show for breakfast.

"Where is he?"

"He checked out," the New York waiter told me.

"And my tip?"

He looked at me blankly. I did not understand how "rich" Americans, for that was what they were to me, could leave without giving me my well-earned dollar. I began to realize that this was also to be expected.

I learned the business fast. The hotel had quite a lot of older single women as guests. I gathered some white flowers and placed them in glasses of water on their tables. This little gesture brought me a few extra dollars per week. I realized that the little extras earned goodwill and tips. At the evening meal we were instructed not to offer juice. I began to visit the refrigerator in the kitchen to serve it anyhow. I thought that if I did a little bit extra these "rich" Americans might be more prone to remember me before checkout time.

At home I tried to urge my daughter to learn English with me from my supposedly easy-to-learn language book. I wondered if any of us would ever master the language. Yet, I knew it was essential that we do so. It was not more than two months after our arrival that I walked out to the yard looking for her. I found her playing and talking with children in the neighborhood in what seemed to me to be flawless perfect English. From that moment she became our translator whenever we needed one.

So Agi Americanized us by reading and explaining the news written for Americans. She explained movies to us. She explained what Rock Hudson, who played a gardener, was saying to the demure Jane Wyman. She tried to explain why Gary Cooper did not shoot this time but would wait for a showdown later.

In the meantime I had advanced from *boat, goat, coat* to the next few pages. No matter how hard I tried to learn during my noon break at the beach, I remained on nearly the same page. I arrived home from my busboy job at about the same time as Sara did from the kosher restaurant. Of the two of us, she had the toughest time. Not only did Sara endure the hard work, but she oversaw Agi's integration into America. It is most difficult to be an advisor to your child in a new country where you are almost a child yourself, learning with your child. Sara was working in a restaurant kitchen without the facility of language. She had no friends or family with her. She did not have the background of being a survivor which I had, and yet she was with me every inch of the way.

Back at the Fleetwood Hotel I ran into bad luck. The chef was an over-six-foot heavy-set American Indian. He kept warning me about the juice, and when that didn't succeed, he began threatening me. I did not listen to his constant warnings. The flowers for the ladies and juice increased my weekly earnings to fifty dollars. I began to feel like a provider, and that filled me with pride. No threats from the kitchen would stop my progress. One evening he caught me filling two glasses with tomato juice. Heresy! He wielded his largest kitchen knife high above his head and came after me. As a reflex I threw the red juice in his face and dashed from the kitchen into the dining room, running for my life. I didn't know if it was a threat or if he really would have stabbed me, but I wasn't about to stay around and debate him.

He came after me enraged. Now I was certain he would strike me. I had humiliated him in front of the kitchen staff, and now he found himself furious and out of control in front of an audience of hotel diners in the middle of the dining room. I kept running, and he chased after me. We went in and around the dining room tables. I was lighter and faster. I got away with my life, but not my job. I was fired immediately.

This happened during dinner when the dining room was busy. My waiter friend told me to wait outside. He went to Mr. Katz and tried to persuade him to let me keep my job. The guests must have enjoyed this little sideshow, and I was rehired as quickly as I was fired.

From then on the Indian chef never said a word to me. I stopped giving out extras. To me this was a compromise. But peace at the workplace and having a job were even more important.

My friendship with Charlie continued. The abandoned car, which was now his, allowed him to show me a little of Miami Beach. The trouble with his newly acquired car was that he had to stop every ten miles to fill the radiator with water and the motor with oil.

"Did you get a license?" I asked him.

"Not yet. I need money for that. Come with me to the dog races. I'll make a killing tonight and earn all the money I need."

I tried to persuade him not to go.

The next morning he greeted me with red bloodshot eyes. He asked me for a few dollars. Other times he requested me to give my blood at the Red Cross station, so he could have money. I did not. Even when he had money, he had it for hours only, and the next morning he was broke again. He was always on the verge of making money and making a big deal work, and yet never did.

The season was almost over. The weather became fiercely humid, and Charlie quit his job. After the breakfast shift he positioned himself in front of the hotel in an immaculate two-toned Pontiac convertible. He was wearing colorful shorts and shirt with white shoes. He waited there posing, hoping everyone would note his prosperity and fortune. No, it was not the dog races that accounted for his appearance of affluence. He had answered an ad to drive a car to New York for a fee.

"What about the outfit?"

"I picked it up at the goodwill store for almost nothing."

All of us felt the loss of a good friend at his leaving. He had charm to spare. He was, above all, a decent human being when it came to relationships with others. Three months after his departure from Miami, I received a letter from him. He urged me to move to Houston, where he promised to secure me a job in a print shop. My letter thanking him for his help and kindness in thinking about us was returned by the post office as "addressee unknown." In my memory I still see him posed in tropical splendor at the wheel of the flashy convertible.

As the winter season wound down, I realized that I should have listened to my Camp Kilmer advisors. Despite the seductive travel brochures, Miami was not the right place for a refugee family to begin a new life. Hotels and restaurants began to close shop. Mr. Katz, the maître d', offered me a job in the Catskills. He and my waiter both had summer jobs waiting for them. His offer was tempting, but I told him that this life was not for a family man. We needed a place to settle and live forever.

By this time we had met some other Hungarian Jewish waiters and busboys who worked at the new, elegant kosher Fountainbleu Hotel. Among them was Andy Roth. Andy had been taken to Auschwitz when he was twelve years old. His survival was a miracle. After that experience, the world, to him, was a playground. I found that to be true of many survivors. Those who were not broken were optimistic people who saw the world with a child's new eyes. No one who had seen the worst and endured, could look on the world with the same eyes. Andy remained a decent person despite his treatment—that was another miracle. His time there had left a few wrinkles on his face, but his heart was full and wonderful. He was unselfish, carefree, and always optimistic. Auschwitz was a period of his life which had taught him the meaning of life. Money and materialism had no significance to him. People and feelings did, but in a playful way. He did not worry about a job or what would happen tomorrow. He was a person who spent his life between Florida and the Catskills. This life suited him and his wandering, open-eyed nature. Four or five months here and four and five months somewhere else. He was happy then to get into his car and vacation somewhere else. Deeper, more intimate attachments were not his forte. Perhaps that, too, was a legacy of Auschwitz.

I talked to Andy about Mr. Katz's offer and my ambivalence. He advised me that California was the place to start a new life with a family. This reminded me of the address in my pocket, which I had copied at Camp Kilmer in an impulsive moment. Why I had done so is still a puzzle to me. Yes, Los Angeles, California, sounded promising and tempting.

I wrote a letter to my former five-per-two colleague who now resided in the Golden State. I hoped my letter would reach him. A few days before the Hotel Fleetwood closed its doors for the summer, my landlord told me that the FBI was looking for me and would return the next day. I was not sure what the FBI was or what the abbreviation meant. I am grateful for my ignorance, because the wait, otherwise, would have been terrifying and interminable.

The next day, instead of my usual *boat, goat, coat* routine, I came home to await their visit. A man came and questioned me. I answered him using my landlord as translator. My landlord looked deeply concerned. I thought that the FBI man was a government official whose job it was to check on my well-being and make sure that I was completely satisfied in having what I required in America. I did not think of him as checking on me in any negative way. I kept repeating that I was a printer and this is what I wanted to do. I told him I did not want to be a thirty-four-year-old busboy. He was a nice man and never lost his patience with me. He looked a bit bewildered at my answers, which never addressed his questions but only my concerns. It took me some time to find out the meaning of the abbreviation FBI. I learned also that it was routine for them to check on newly arrived people.

A few days later I received a letter from a local print shop to report for work. Perhaps I was correct about what these government people were able to do! Or perhaps this largess was due to my landlord. I never found out who had done me this favor. The shop was small. There were only two typesetters. They needed help in setting up the advertising pages in the calendar for 1958. What luck, I thought, calendars. I am an expert at calendars. In Hungary I remembered how I had maneuvered calendars into making bonuses two quarters in a row. This was an advertising calendar with special events listed in it. Two or three different ones per weeks—conventions, football games, theater, or public events listed in an organized format.

The trouble for me began when I noticed that my copy page ended in April and began again in October. I did not understand this and asked for help. I couldn't make myself understood. No one seemed to be concerned. No one seemed to understand what my concern was. No one seemed to understand my English. Months of *goat, coat,* and *boat* did not make it easier. Months of the copy was missing, and I couldn't get myself understood enough to explain the problem. I did not realize that this was an advertising calendar and only for tourists during the season. It was painful for me not to be fluent enough to explain myself or to understand their answers. Not realizing my foolishness at local customs made it more difficult for me. I felt so foreign here.

Just before my first paycheck as a printer, I received an answer from my Los Angeles friend. He was working. He was a typesetter with a salary of three dollars and seventy-five cents an hour. Jobs were available. The unpleasant surprise was my own Miami paycheck, which was one dollar and ten cents per hour. Just as my toothache made me jump for safety when I fled the labor camps, my one dollar and ten cent paycheck was too much misfortune for me to bear. If my friend in Los Angeles could earn over three dollars, then I could exceed him, since I was a better printer. Foolishly I didn't realize that his English was perfect and that I was still learning the phonetics of *goat, boat, coat*. We had a family meeting. I told Sara that I would leave them to try to relocate in California.

I asked for Andy's help. That same evening he called one of his friends in Los Angeles, and it was arranged that a friend of his would meet me at the airport.

- *29* -

As arranged, Andy's friend awaited me at the airport. I spent the first night in his apartment. The next morning he took me to a furnished single apartment at Crenshaw near Venice Boulevard.

I called my labor camp colleague. We spent a pleasant hour together. He briefed me about working conditions, wages, and unions. Before he left he gave me two addresses from the help-wanted section of the *Los Angeles Times*.

Two days after my arrival I began to work at one of the print shops. I was fired within hours. An eight-hour check was issued to me. I got thirty dollars. I was supposed to make changes and corrections in advertising copy. I could not read or understand. It was humiliating to fail so abysmally.

I tried the second address, which was also in the downtown area. I was hired for the afternoon shift, which was from three to eleven. Again I was fired within hours and given the day's pay as severance. Here I had two jobs in one day and was paid for two days when I had only worked part of one. I had lost two jobs as fast as I had found them. I had earned almost two weeks of my Miami salary. I tried to make that a solace for my embarrassment at not being fluent enough in English to hold a simple job.

It was dark when I got back to the apartment. My conscience bothered me. I had been safe and comfortable in Miami surrounded with family. What was I doing in California? Now my family was alone in Miami, and I was in California with the humiliation and problems of trying to support a family with dignity and respect. My thoughts tumbled.

"Why was I so impatient? Why couldn't I just be a busboy?

"I deserve to be alone in a rundown, dirty, smelly apartment.

"Why didn't I stay with my family?"

"Why did I pressure my wife to escape from Hungary? In Hungary everyone understood my words. I had friends there. In this huge American city I am alone. I know no one. Alone."

This gloomy feeling stayed with me for a few days.

I found a Printing Company Association whose function was to supply qualified workers to nonunion shops. The association sent me for job interviews. I was sent to the Industrial Stationery and Printing Company in Huntington Park. I had to take a bus downtown and from there a streetcar. People at work began to be curious about me. They asked me questions about the Hungarian revolt. I managed to be understood and overcame my shyness at my difficulty with the language. Since this was 1957, the Iron Curtain and the Cold War were the featured stories in all the newspapers. These good-natured colleagues saw me as a hero fighting the evil specter of

Communism. The image of a Hungarian freedom fighter helped me keep my job for those first few weeks.

- *30* -

When I received my first paycheck, I felt financially safe enough to write Sara to begin packing. I told her that Los Angeles was beautiful. It had an ocean and palm trees. I hadn't seen any coconuts, but it did have a year-around economy. I told her to come as quickly as possible. I still had several weeks to consolidate my new financial foundation before Sara and Agi would arrive.

It was the third Monday on my job when one of the typesetters entered with a deep suntan. When I complimented him on his color, he told me he had been in Palm Springs.

"It must be beautiful there."

"No," he said, "Too many . . ."

He finished the sentence by pointing at his nose. It was exactly the same gesture that the antisemitic freedom fighters had made at the Jewish porter during the Hungarian revolt. Not here! Not now! Not after all I've tried to leave! My body and mind stiffened, but I remained silent.

I walked away, keeping my painful awareness to myself. I wondered why I hadn't spoken out to him. Why hadn't I told him that I belonged to the big-nosed group? I had consciously decided to always defend my Jewishness. On the ship, sitting next to the seasick Pista, we had argued about our Jewishness and the stand we would take about it once in America. His contention was that we had been born in the wrong place on the wrong continent to the wrong parents, and had suffered enough for that.

"That was not of our own choosing," said Pista. "We choose to go to America. Let us choose the right names and the right religion so that we do not have a handicap anymore."

My argument was that in a free society like America I did not want to start with a lie. One of the main reasons I chose to leave everything behind was that I was tired of lying and pretending. Yes, being born in Hungary to Jewish parents was not my choosing. That is true. But that is who I am. That is unchangeable.

Pista chose his path. I, the Jewish boy who hid during the Sabbath in order to play soccer, chose mine. If this was so, and I was right in choosing my path, why did I keep quiet? For days I argued with myself, losing some self-respect over this episode. I had not stood up for myself. I did not stand up for the principles of the democratic government which had given me hope to build a better life for my family. I did not like my cowardice. The self-scrutiny served me. I learned my lesson that day.

Four weeks was a very long time for me to be alone in the big city of Los Angeles awaiting Sara and Agi. Sunday morning, the day of their arrival, I awoke early in a larger and nicer-furnished apartment on Arlington Avenue near Olympic Boulevard where I had moved anticipating their arrival. I washed the walls. I cleaned the kitchen. I finished my breakfast, but it was still only seven in the morning.

I took a bus to a parklike area overlooking the Pacific Ocean. I was overwhelmed. We would be together soon as a family. I knew we would be happy here. Somehow, right then, I was positive I would succeed. Somehow, having a small base to build on, I knew that I would be the head of my family again. I was sure that my wife would not have to work in somebody else's kitchen. I felt that I would be able to provide a better education for Agi than I had received and better than I could have provided her in the old country. I was happy about the way our lives were beginning to take shape. I also knew that I had not been born to work for someone else.

As I walked, I thought. What could I do? In what kind of business could I be my own boss? I did not know, but I would keep my eyes open. I would keep these secret ambitions to myself. We needed to save a thousand dollars for an emergency. Then I would begin a business of some kind. A business of my own. I promised this to myself and to the Pacific Ocean.

I got a bit tired of walking and sat down on a bench. I closed my eyes and somehow the waves lulled me. The waves sounded to me like the cheering crowds in the Budapest stadium during one of my soccer games. I had a hard time convincing myself that it was just a fantasy. It felt good to think about soccer again. I opened my eyes and thought that this was a good omen. Someone was cheering for me in Los Angeles. I still had many hours to wait until the afternoon plane. I decided to walk back to our apartment, where one of my friends would take me to the airport to bring Agi and Sara.

On the way home a car stopped next to me and a fast-talking salesman picked out windbreakers from the back of his car, trying to make a sale. The merchandise looked nice to me, and it cost two dollars and ninety cents. I could not resist. Back home I tried it on. It looked so good on me. This is the way I would meet my family—with my American windbreaker on.

I arrived at the airport in my new sporty jacket, feeling very Californian. At the airport Sara looked at us curiously. From her look I realized that I had been taken. The vendor had picked me out as an easy mark. I looked gullible and not the typical American that I had thought I was being taken for. The fast-talking salesman had been right about me. No matter. I wanted to show my family that I was a full-blooded Angelino. I knew I was not there yet, but soon.

We were finally home. We knew that this would be our last separation.

- *31* -

I felt secure in my job. I began working normal hours. I began to feel more like a full-blooded American until some incidents brought me back to reality. These made me realize that I was still a student and had a lot more to learn.

One Saturday evening Sara and I were sightseeing on Wilshire Boulevard in Beverly Hills. I found a little red metal box on a pole on the sidewalk. I couldn't figure out what it was. It was too small for the mail. I tried to solve the riddle of the box by pulling at the handle. The fire alarm blasted. We were scared. What had I done? It seemed to me that within seconds sirens were approaching from the east and from the west. We did the only thing we could. We vanished from sight.

"What will happen when they take fingerprints?" I thought.

I walked around for several weeks awaiting the Black Maria to pick me up for questioning. One of my early lessons was that a mistake in America was not a crime.

We learned slowly, step by step. My company organized a Sunday picnic for the workers and their families. The men began to play baseball. I had never seen this game before. I had never touched a baseball. I was put in the far corner of the playing field. I tried to ascertain what the point of the game was and tried to put my hand into a funny-looking glove.

Someone hit a long hard ball which came towards me. This was my chance. I looked up to the sky, watching the ball arc towards me. A perfect ball to head back to the center of the field. I positioned myself perfectly, soccer-style, for a header. For some reason, at the last second, I reached up and caught the ball in my gloveless hand. It hurt like hell. Everyone ran to me to check me out. I could barely admit to myself what a header would have done! It would not have improved my language ability.

This was a relaxing and prosperous six months of my life. My English began to improve. I obtained a driver's license. I was so proud to pass the test on my first try. I bought a two-tone Pontiac just like the one Charlie had posed in. It was a good omen.

Having a car gave us great freedom to explore. We traveled all over California. We had a tent which allowed us to enjoy the bounty of the land. We loved this place. It was paradise. Sand, desert, orange trees, palm trees, oceans, and mountains. All were here. All but the coconuts! The weather was always perfect.

We found a public swimming pool in Burbank, the Pickwick. It reminded us of the public swimming parks in Hungary. There was a dance floor in the park with loud good music. Agi liked to go and watch the boys and girls. One day she strayed from us, and I went to look for her. I found her dancing! She moved like all the other youngsters. Where did she learn? How did she become so American? How did she become so grown-up? She was not a little girl any more.

It was also time to move from our small, cramped furnished apartment. We leased a one-bedroom apartment in a duplex at Curson near Olympic. We furnished it. It was simple, but new and ours. We paid cash for the car and for the furnishings. All this from six months' earnings!

I tried to be an American. I tried to look like an American. I tried to think like an American. My success was meager. I knew how a Hungarian worker thinks. I knew how a Hungarian intellectual thinks. I had learned the same nursery tales that they did. I had played the same games as a child. I knew the way to raise a glass of wine in a restaurant. I knew how to greet guests when they came to visit. In America everything was different—history, thinking, recreation. On Sundays in Hungary we used to put on a necktie. In America we put on T-shirts. I was used to kicking and heading a large ball. In America they threw a small very hard ball, and you never would put your head near it. Essentially it was the heritage, the personal and joint history, which separated us. In the beginning I felt it absolutely unacceptable that we did not have American friends. I slowly realized that it would take a long time.

Once or twice we invited my shop foreman, Dwight, for dinner. These were strange and exhausting evenings for all of us. Agi was constantly being asked to express our thoughts in a more precise way than we could. We searched for ways to communicate a commonality. We wished to rush the process where we could know each other's hearts. When we invited Dwight and his wife for the third time, they noticed a Seder plate on our kitchen wall. Dwight asked us about it. We told them we were Jewish and used the plate on the religious holidays. They did not understand this.

"Aren't you Hungarians?"

"Yes, we are Jewish Hungarians."

They pondered this. This was the last time we got together socially. To be a freedom fighter was one thing, to be Jewish quite another.

For all of us newcomers, the language problem and our heavy accents placed a great burden on our children. At home most conversed in their mother language. The children spoke perfect English without an accent. We watched our children become noticeably ashamed at our being foreigners and so different from their friends' parents. One of our friends had been a chief engineer and had been a professor in a world-famous university in Hungary which had been established in 1695. I overheard his two boys talking to my daughter. They were saying that their father was so ignorant. I guess all of our children thought us ignorant.

- *32* -

Everybody talked about Disneyland. Even friends and family from Hungary would ask about it in their letters to us. We decided that it was time to visit Disneyland. We wandered in the crowd enjoying the day. Of all the thousands of people there, we ran into Pista, who had been a wonderful soccer player before becoming a seasick baker. We were so happy to see one another. Two hundred million people live in this country. Eight million live in Los Angeles, and two Hungarian refugees ran into one another in Disneyland. It was amazing!

Pista said that he was here to relocate his family from New York. His first job in Los Angeles was to coach a semiprofessional soccer team of Hungarians. He was thirty-eight years old and still played. He was a bit slow and a bit overweight, but his technical skill was that of a Division I professional player. I immediately began to think about soccer again. A close friendship developed between our two families. His career and mine were very different, but developed side by side. I rooted for his success, and he rooted for mine.

BOOK THREE

- *1* -

On Saturday and Sunday mornings I used to wake up early and leave my sleeping family. I called this time my discovery time. I wanted to be the first one to discover a new tree, a new flower, or a new street. I loved seeing the green grass of the yards, the exotic flowers, and the strange-looking trees. I watched with great admiration the way the newspaper boy delivered the morning papers from his bike. I wondered about his being so poor that he needed to deliver papers. I wondered at his father's shame at his son's needing to work at such a young age. Then I recognized him to be the son of one of wealthiest families in the neighborhood.

During these walks I kept up an interior dialogue with my little friend Karcsi, who was eight thousand miles away. In my mind I described to him the neighborhood of my new country. He had always been there to support my new endeavors, even when parents could not. I would keep him at my side now.

This was the first time in my life that I felt the luxury of peace. I did not fear persecution. I had none of the fear or terror which had so accompanied me in the past. For the first time I could heed Roosevelt's words which I had first read in pamphlets dropped from airplanes—"The only thing you have to fear is fear itself." It is only when one feels reasonably safe and secure that one can forgo fear. For me it only came now.

My occasional bad dreams now were of being back in Hungary. I would dream that I had lost my passport which would make me unable to come home. I realized that home was here. Home was the United States of America.

Slowly I gained the strength and courage to express my thoughts out loud. I could talk about Republicans and Democrats without uneasiness as to the consequences. I could talk openly about Eisenhower and Nixon. I could be for or against Adlai Stevenson and the Kennedys. It might be a passionate discussion. There may be angry words. But there would not be terror or death.

I had my own opinion about unions forged from my experience during the Communist regime in Hungary. I had hard thoughts about unemployment offices where people drove up in brand-new cars. They knew how to work the system, something which a whole country had learned under Communism, but I didn't understand their need to do so in this land of opportunity. I expressed strong opinions about the nonexistent free medical care in America. I did not hesitate to express my opinions about Elvis or the musical value of rock and roll. I had my own opinion about the incomprehensibility of baseball.

I witnessed my first freely held elections and was overcome by the simple beauty of the process. I followed every word of Walter Cronkite. For weeks I had a ringside seat in front of my television, watching the political fights as the GOP fought to decide who would be their nominee for the presidency. The show was every bit as good when I watched the Democrats doing the same. To be able to listen to others promote their causes via radio, television, and newspaper was amazing. It was all so exciting to me. To be able to listen, to discard, to accept. To make one's own choice—that is democracy. It was vastly different from the elections in Hungary, where the citizens in "open" election voted the Communists to power in 1949 by a 99.9 percent margin. In America there would never be that kind of consensus.

I was eager to read everything that had formerly been forbidden to me. I read *Dr. Zhivago* by Boris Pasternak boldly. I was so glad to read Leon Uris. After years of living among rumors and confiscated news, I could now formulate my opinions and views with first-hand knowledge. I could go to the library or bookstore and read anything without being accused of being subversive. I could read any book and any writer without thinking about any consequence other than the broadening of my own mind.

I was free to drink Coca-Cola until my teeth rotted, if I so chose. I could watch my favorite television programs and especially liked *Gunsmoke* and *Have Gun, Will Travel*. My favorite motion picture was *Marjorie Morningstar*.

I now began to learn American history. I began to count down the years and finally the months until I could earn the prize I had been waiting for—the prize of American citizenship. I was free to err and make mistakes. I was free to fail or to succeed. It was largely up to me, and I had no question but that the future would be bright.

- 2 -

*T*hen the unexpected happened. Sara and I lost our jobs on almost the same day. There was a general business slowdown, and we were among its casualties. I was frightened at the economic insecurity, but learned a valuable lesson. This wonderful country was also a tough country. It did not take care of its citizens like certain socialist countries. You could rise to a higher level than you ever imagined, but you could also come crashing down. There was almost no limit as to what you could do or how low you could sink. You could not count on things lasting forever. You must continuously and unceasingly work for your success.

I made the decision that as I looked for a new job I would simultaneously make inquiries about business opportunities where I could be my own boss. I remembered making such a promise to myself while walking on a bluff overlooking the Pacific Ocean waiting for the plane which would bring my family to me. This might be the time to take such a plunge.

I began my search for a job in earnest, driving as far as San Bernardino to answer help-wanted ads. I also was reading the "Business Opportunity" parts of the classified ads hoping to find a small retail or service business which would require only a small down payment to purchase. I also needed a business which would require an experience that was not peculiarly American. I soon realized, as I answered these ads, that I did not have the right experience or the proper capitalization to venture into the market yet.

I answered an ad for an advertising agency which was looking for a typesetter. As soon as I walked into this small firm, I felt that the job was custom-made for me. There was no modern typesetting equipment. There was a small, old hand-operated typesetting machine and cases of type which needed to be hand set. There was only one person running the typesetting shop. A second person was needed.

I filled out my resume. It was put on the bottom of many others who had also answered the ad. I judged there to be twenty-five applications before mine. I wondered what I could say to the owner and how I could impress him that I was perfect for the job. I then thought of an idea.

I went to see hopeful, optimistic Andy Roth. He was my friend who had survived the concentration camps with aplomb and vitality. At my urging he had relocated in Los Angeles. His carpet-cleaning business was now successful and growing. I asked Andy to apply for the job as a typesetter. When he responded that he had no idea what typesetters did, I responded that that was the point. I told him to tell the owner that this old-fashioned typesetting was not in his field of expertise because he was used to modern equipment. I told him to convince the owner that he knew of only one person who was expert with this kind of equipment. The name of the expert would be that of a Hungarian refugee, Ed Mandel. That same day I got a telephone call telling me that I had the job.

A short time later, I received a call from my old employer in Huntington Park. He wanted to rehire me. I took on a part-timenight shift. So I was working two jobs while my daughter began her high school years at Fairfax High School.

- *3* -

*T*he long-awaited five-year residency requirement for United States citizenship was over. Sara and I enrolled at a night school for our upcoming citizenship test. We learned about the Declaration of Independence, the Constitution, the legislative, executive, and judicial branches. In school we passed the trial test with flying colors. We were ready for the big day.

I was called in first. A judge asked me a few questions which I answered correctly. I could not answer the question about the number of articles in the Constitution. I passed the exam and told Sara, who was still waiting to be tested. She was beside herself in anxiety awaiting her test.

"I don't remember anything. My mind's a blank."

She was called to be examined looking distraught and returned ten minutes later with a triumphant grin on her tear-stained face. She had passed also.

"It was a breeze," She said.

We received our citizenship certificates after a moving swearing-in ceremony at Los Angeles City Hall five and one-half years after the *General Altinge* had deposited us in New York harbor. The date of receiving the top prize any person can receive, that of becoming a citizen of the United states, was August 17, 1962.

How can I explain how it felt to stand in the curtained booth checking my choices off at voting time? Choices, I finally had real choices. I could help choose the direction of this country. I could choose to tax myself. I could choose not to. The world of freedom opened up to me that voting day as I stood inside that small booth. The claustrophobic booth encompassed the world's most expanded idea, that of individual freedom of choice. I saved my ballot stub.

Things were going so well that I had to check my complacency and remind myself to push further. This is the toughness of America. There is always the need to push further and further. To stand still is to fall behind. I remembered my wish to have my own business. I had to make an opportunity to find my way into the business world. I had to find the path and take the correct fork. I had to push myself forward.

This was easier to say than to do. It took me years to find my way into American life. There was the ever present problem of language. There was the problem of the fast-paced American lifestyle which could leave me in its wake if I slowed down or faltered. As gratified as I was for the opportunities America showered on me, I had a silent complaint. I knew how much easier it would have been in Hungary had times been different. Returning from the war in 1945 as a twenty-two-year-old, inexperienced young man, I was able to enter the business world without difficulty. The language, customs, life pace, and lifestyle were no mystery to me in Hungary. Here I could barely be understood. I was working against the current here. I was still swimming, still afloat, but exhausted at the extra exertion. I had emerged from the darkest, most backward Communist regime to fall into the middle of the most highly advanced country in the world. It was hard work to learn and keep striving.

During the first five years in the United States, I wondered at all the striving for technical achievement which marked the American way of life. There was not an equal striving for cultural ascendancy, which seems to be a very European style. All the joys of theater, opera, and symphony were barely enjoyed in the country which had the money and the time to promote such activities. This was difficult for me to understand. These regal, fast-moving Americans rushed in cars to get to new places. They rushed to homes, movies, and restaurants. Life in America was one big rush. It was hard for me not to long for the very luxury America could afford but rarely seemed to offer. I longed for the luxury to expand my soul.

Contrary to the Old World craftsman who was proud of his handmade artistry, Americans loved the new, the stylish, and the quick. Mass production was the American way, and it catered to tastes which changed yearly. It was amazing to watch advertising dictate changes in fashion, music, and entertainment. Old World stability gave way to New World change and excitement. This constant search for the new and different was also the secret of American success. It was just hard to get used to.

Americans did not seem to know the pleasure of a simple, leisurely walk, of an animated conversation among peers, or the comfort of quiet family life. Even those who walked did not do so out of pleasure, but for exercise. In time the pace of America and the pace of the Mandels seemed to fall more into step. We both needed time to adjust to one another.

Understanding this country and loving it were two very different feelings. We loved America unabashedly the first time we stepped onto her soil. The resources and beauty of the country were easily loved. We loved the people here. They were such vital people. I argued with Republicans, and I loved them. I argued with Democrats, and I loved them. As time passed I learned that these racing, busy people were much more humane and helpful than my former neighbors around the Danube between the Dniester and the river Prut. They had a new history and, therefore, had far less to feel guilty for.

During this time I both yearned for the Old World order and culture, and at the same time was ashamed at my regressive thinking. I also yearned to be more forward-thinking and Americanized. There were times we looked back nostalgically to the Old Country instead of looking forward to the new. As time passed, this looking back through the rearview mirror grew less frequent. The seduction of America became more complete.

It took years to get used to the local customs and to behave accordingly. It took very little time to fall in love with these friendly, loud people who drank Coca-Cola continuously, chewed gum constantly, and had an insatiable appetite for mass-produced food. Americans were loud, honest, and without guile.

I could not understand why Americans said "Thank you" when you complimented them on their tie or appearance. It was not something Europeans did. A compliment is the truth, and one does not thank another for the truth. One thanks a person for a gift, but that is different than the truth. Nor did I understand why someone would fall silent if I asked them the price of something they owned. It would not be considered bad taste in Hungary. It was felt that curiosity and interest in the person extended to the price of things. When I got paid at work, the check would always be given to me face down on the workbench. I would always turn it over to see the amount. My employer would turn it over again. Money was more taboo than sex. In Europe the napkin is placed to the left side of the plate during a meal, never on one's lap. To place a napkin on one's lap would be a breach of etiquette. One's clean and folded napkin was a testimonial to one's good manners. I remember countless exasperated waiters handing me my napkin when I left it folded at the side of my plate. As soon as they gave it to me, it was placed to the left of the plate where it belonged.

I began to love football games, basketball games, and ice hockey teams. Baseball still eluded me. I found myself mystified and unable to understand this great American pastime. I kept hoping that in a few years soccer would gain the popularity it had in the rest of the world. I believed then, as I do now, that no sport can compare to my favorite one.

Time after time I would wonder how these fine American people would react to a racist situation like that in Europe. How would Americans react to the rounding up of minorities and to their extermination? I wondered whether their sense of decency and tolerance would prevail, or whether something more primitive would take its place. I wondered if Americans felt safe enough to tolerate differences. It terrified me to see on television Americans give the fascist salute. I became concerned one day after I was given a pamphlet on a street corner that contained racist remarks. It was very easy to say that there would be no pogroms or concentration camps in America. I knew differently, since I had felt the same before in my birth country. I knew differently because of the segregation in America. It was no easy question to answer. I prayed for America to truly live up to its tolerance and its democratic principles.

- *4* -

Among the thousands and thousands of Hungarians who left Hungary in 1956 were many world-class athletes, including members of the 1956 Olympic team.

Puskas, the greatest soccer star in the world at that time, did not return to Hungary after the competition. He was not alone. He came to America with the Real Madrid team from Spain. World-class runners and coaches also stayed. Among them was Igloi, who was considered the best long- and middle-distance track coach in the world. He settled in California and started to coach American athletes as well as his seasoned runners. A few meets were held in the Los Angeles Memorial Coliseum, where his runners competed. Pista and I went to every meet and rooted for the Hungarian runners. The Real Madrid soccer team played in the Coliseum against a Los Angeles all-star team which Pista coached; I co-coached.

Driving south on Jefferson Boulevard towards the Coliseum on the way to these meets, we used to stop at a hamburger drive-through. It was at the corner of Thirty-Sixth and Jefferson. I was amazed at this most American of concepts. As we entered the parking lot we used a standing telephone which routed our call to the hamburger stand in the middle of the parking lot to place our order. By the time we drove to the window and paid, our food was ready. It was a remarkably efficient, purely American, small business which was part of a small fast-food chain. Big Daddy was its name.

One day while going to practice, Pista and I made our usual detour to the hamburger stand. It was closed. There was a "for lease" sign on it. I was disappointed in that I had looked forward to my hamburger. At the same time I was elated, for I knew that this was it! This would give me my start in the business world. The right path was in front of me. I just had to take it. Pista dreamed of soccer balls that day, and I dreamed of hamburgers.

- *5* -

I learned that Big Daddy had gone bankrupt. The landlord
was willing to lease the place to me without the equipment, as
that belonged to the creditors. I didn't have the money for new
equipment, nor did I have the experience to go to the bank for
a loan. In order to capitalize I formed a partnership with a Polish refugee. With a new sign and new fixtures we opened.

We gave it a new, very American name, Daddy O. My partner
and Sara ran the daytime shift. Two girls and a short-order
cook ran the second shift with me. With this arrangement I
was able to hold onto my regular job as a typesetter.

No one involved in the venture had any experience in this
kind of business. We were eager to learn. My first customer
was a young black boy who walked to the window and ordered
a root beer float. I searched the menu behind me for inspiration, and with relief did not find the item even listed.

"Sorry," I told my first customer. "We don't have floats."

The boy looked disappointed, visibly deflated, and ordered a
plain root beer instead.

"You have that, don't you?"

"Yes," I answered.

"Put a scoop of softened ice cream in it. You have that don't
you?"

"Yes."

"Thank you for my root beer float!" He said in a self-congrat-ulatory way, looking back at me.

"Right!"

I learned fast.

This small business was a lot of work. The amount of money it added to our salaries was not sufficient for two families. It was a wonderful way to learn about running a business and the trials and rewards of this kind of work. I knew it was what I wanted to do. My partner and I began to look for another business. We thought that the two of us could own jointly two businesses.

We learned shortly that the Carousel Ice Cream Store in Brentwood was for sale.

As we entered the Carousel there was a case with chocolates from around the world followed by a case of cakes, and lastly, display upon display of different kinds of ice cream. It had all the charm of a Viennese pastry shop.

It was summer and the place was packed. Sandwiches and beautiful ice cream extravaganzas were being served. The people being served were young people from the neighborhood, and it reminded me of youth, ice cream, and hopefulness. We noticed the elderly managers who were working hard, con-stantly serving the people and keeping up with the orders.

My partner did not want to go forward with a discussion to buy the place. I did. I felt that it would be a big step for me. The neighborhood and the business itself were full of class and atmosphere. My partner paid me back my investment in the hamburger place and we separated.

The owner of the store was Mickey Cohen, the famous gang-ster. His sister and her husband were the managers we had watched that afternoon. I really did not know about their con-nections with crime, and I guess I really wouldn't have cared. I wanted to buy this business, and eventually I did. With a small down payment it became mine.

Well, again I had to learn a lot—on my feet, and quickly. Our customers were from the neighborhood of Brentwood and students from the nearby UCLA campus. Actors and actresses frequented the place, sometimes for a sandwich and sometimes for a simple ice cream cone. Among them I remember Angela Lansbury, Robert Young, Vincent Price, Eva Marie Saint, Steve McQueen, and Mort Sahl. Quite a few young television actors came. When Ricky Nelson came in, he caused quite a stir among the young waitresses in the shop. Walter Winchell, the gossip columnist, was a frequent customer. He had just begun to lose his clout at this time. Not at the Carousel. Everyone in my store was treated with great care and respect.

- *6* -

Business was good. Summertime was even more special, with all the comings and goings of so many bronzed and ebullient people. Sara waited on the tables, serving ice cream dishes. On weekends Agi was a waitress also. Our specialty was pink whipped cream on top of the ice cream dishes. When youngsters asked why the whipped cream was pink, we always told them about our pink cow in back of the store. Another often-asked question was whether I was Mickey Cohen. That question was always followed by the next, "Do you at least have a gun?"

When Agi graduated Fairfax High School, we had amassed enough money to make a down payment on our first home in the Westgate area in Brentwood. It was conveniently close to the store. This was a time of great happiness in our lives. I was a small businessman who now owned a small home in the United States of America. All this would have been beyond my wildest dreams years ago among the freezing laborers housed in subhuman living conditions. This was also a time of constant work. Sara was never at home when I was, and vice versa. We had no time off for months at a time. But the proudest moment of this time was Agi's graduation. I listened to "Pomp and Circumstance" as my daughter was handed her diploma from an American high school.

The business was wonderful for the family, but the long hours were taking a toll on me. Even though the Carousel had the reputation of being the largest single-owned ice cream store in Los Angeles, certain concerns began to enter my mind. The sandwich part of the business had always been borderline, but when Hamburger Hamlet moved in a few hundred yards away, the food part of the business disappeared.

One of our lunchtime regulars, an attorney, brought two strangers into the store one noontime. One of the men was David Shein, the owner of the Ambassador Hotel. They asked me to sit down with them and offered me the management of a coffee shop in a new hotel just east of the Ambassador. I said I would do it. Years later I learned about Mr. Shein. He was a member of the notorious threesome of McCarthy, Cohen, and Shein.

For a year or two I ran the two businesses. Slowly a voice became louder and louder. I realized that this business, while lucrative, was not really to my liking. It was a good start, but I did not feel that I was using my capabilities fully. It did not satisfy my ego to stand behind the cash register or to serve ice cream cones. I did not have a nature that allowed me to look happy for customers when I was not. I wanted to do something more creative. I hired a business broker, almost without thinking about it, to sell both places. This was accomplished in a month. I wanted out, and I underpriced both businesses for a quick sale.

The broker who sold my two places offered me a job in his brokerage firm if I could pass my license. He told me I was a born salesman. He encouraged me a great deal, suggesting a great future and lucrative financial rewards. I liked both his comments and the idea.

In great need for a vacation to recharge my slowly evaporating energies, we decided to revisit our homeland. I packed up real-estate and business-brokerage textbooks to study during the vacation. We planned to spend two weeks in Hungary and a week or so just driving around Europe. We asked for and received a thirty-day visa to revisit Hungary.

Our hearts were pounding as we entered the checkpoint at the Austrian-Hungarian border. The gates and men with machine guns reminded us of our escape.

"We are back in hell," Sara said.

We knew that this visit would be painful, as we would see the full extent of what we had left, both the most beautiful and the most ugly. At the same time our feelings were full to see family and friends and Kecskemét again.

Standing and looking down into the Danube from the beautiful Margaret Bridge on the visit, I realized that I had never seen it as angry blue as it was that day. I imagined seeing blood flowing down river with the current. The blood of my brothers and sisters!

"What am I doing here? Why did I come back?"

The memories of my murdered family and friends haunted me and made it quite impossible to feel relaxed and enjoy the undeniably beautiful city of Budapest. Sara came to my rescue.

"We will leave Hungary tomorrow," she said.

Walking back towards Budapest to say our farewells, I studied the faces of my fellow Hungarians. I was not sure what I

was looking for. An unbidden thought came—"My winter coat."
I was looking for my winter coat. In the midst of this summer's
day, I was searching Hungarian's faces for my stolen youth. I
still wanted what was due me—the freedom to grow up unen-
slaved and unendangered.

Walking back to my sister's apartment, I remembered all the
dead ones. The fathers, mothers, sons, and daughters who
were lost forever. During this hour I relived the years of my
youth in this city. The dreams and disappointments of trying
to be a superstar soccer player cut short. The years of strength
and defiance and the years of humiliation and persecution all
played themselves before my eyes. We left the next day.

Saying goodbye was very painful, especially the goodbye to
my beloved friend and mentor, Karcsi. I remember each aspect
of time and place of this farewell and how the tears ran down
our faces. It would be our last goodbye.

We were certain of one thing. It was good to be out of there.
The rest of the vacation after the Hungarian prelude was fine,
and I found time to study for my business-brokerage license.

Back in Los Angeles I passed the license examination and
began to work in a new and completely different environment
as a salesman.

I had a private furnished office and a part-time secretary. I
sat behind my desk in a white shirt and tie. I hoped that I
would be able to meet the challenges in this new field. Sitting
behind a desk made me realize that I had to get out and find
sellers in order to carve out a living for myself.

I sent out form letters on elegantly printed letterhead offering
my services. When I received a reply, I got up from my desk
and started to work. I loved meeting with business people. I
liked the talking, discussing, and arbitrating that went on. I
felt that this type of business suited me more. Every new meeting was a new opportunity for learning. I felt that it would only
be a matter of time before things would click for me.

I learned a lot during this time. I had a chance to meet with
presidents and chief executive officers of large companies.

With time I overcame my fear and shyness and presented my proposals with great conviction. I, Edmund Odon Mandel, former member of the five-per-two slave-labor company, a Hungarian refugee, now an American citizen, could manage even with my thick accent. Even though I did not make a penny during these months, I learned that I could arbitrate and present myself and my case with a new self-confidence.

To supplement my income, I took on a night shift in typesetting work. Although the hours were long, I liked my life this way. I felt that I was part of the real American business world. Every change was a new opportunity for learning and going forward.

Finally, after a lot of false starts, I got my first real break. A Long Beach–based automobile parts company, Chief Auto Parts, answered my form letter soliciting businesses for sale. The two owners of this small chain had disagreements with each other. They trusted me to find a buyer for their lucrative enterprise. Their business was good. To find a buyer was easy. My part of the commission was over forty thousand dollars. In time Chief Auto Parts became the second-largest chain of auto repair shops in California. Whenever I saw its advertisements on television it made me feel good, since I was the one who had brought the buyer and seller together.

I stayed a year and a half in the business-brokerage business, working nights as a typesetter. The learning was some compensation for the fact that except for the auto parts business venture, I hardly made any money.

- 7 -

It was part of my daily routine to read the "Business Opportunity" section of the *Los Angeles Times*. One ad caught my
immediate and utmost attention: "Old established salad company for sale." I read it again and again.

During the years when I had Carousel, our cole slaw and
potato salad supplier was a small company called Risvolds. I
knew immediately that this ad had to be referring to Risvolds. I
knew this opportunity was for me. Everything about Risvolds
was something that rang true for me. They were a responsible,
reliable company with a fine reputation that was well
deserved. They delivered a perfect product without advertising
or sales support. This was a real fit for my needs and my
desires. I was ready for it.

I went to visit the owners. The company was located in Santa
Monica. My first impression was one of disappointment at how
small a company it was. I think my hopefulness had fueled my
imagination into overdrive. I looked around at the smallness. I
noticed the lack of technology or machinery. It was a kitchen
operation. It was "homemade," as their label contended. Everything was done by hand. I was soothed by the idea of what a
fine product they produced. I was also soothed by the fact that
this way of doing things was something I had grown up with.
This was the craftsman, or European, way. Within a few days

373

and without any hesitation I bought the small food-processing plant.

The former owners, in their late sixties, stayed with me for three weeks teaching me the business. Sara was with me from opening to closing. The workforce consisted of two old ladies, Betty and Metty. These ladies peeled the cooked hot potatoes by hand. Betty was around seventy. Metty was the same age, and half-drunk most of the time. There was also a driver who made the deliveries in a small truck. The trunk was twenty years old, and the man three times that.

In those three weeks I realized that the small building was restricting my dreams. If we were to grow, I would have to move to a larger and more modern plant. I began my search for a small plant suitable for food production. I found a landlord on Jefferson Boulevard who trusted me and the future of the business. He converted a vacant warehouse to conform to the health department regulations partly at his expense. I signed a ten-year lease on six thousand square feet and six months later moved in.

The day we began in the new plant, the size was so overwhelming that I wondered if I hadn't gone too fast and overextended myself. I asked myself the same questions I had asked myself each time I made a leap forward: "Why am I doing this? Who do I think I am? What risk am I putting myself and my family in because of my ambition?"

But I had always been a leaper, from the first time I biked alone into Budapest to see my favorite team play soccer. I could do more than merely exist or survive. I could overcome. I could create. I could help make my own future rather than take what was given me.

- *8* -

Slowly we began to mechanize. Slowly we needed more workers. Slowly the volume increased with the demand for our product. At first the two old ladies peeled potatoes in fifty-pound batches. Now four women hand-peeled the potatoes. One was young and beautiful. It was Sara.

Business was good, but I was running out of money. I needed help to grow. Through friends I met Morton Kahn, a third-generation American my age, and we remained partners until we sold out twenty-five years later. Within five years we had outgrown this location and found a new one in Gardena. It was from this plant that the business really took off.

Our most popular item was potato salad. When I took over the Santa Monica plant, we were producing nine hundred pounds of potato salad per day. In our mechanized, modern Gardena plant we produced eighty thousand pounds of potato salad per day. I remembered how I had bartered used clothing for potatoes while starving in the Carpathian Mountains. Somehow I had parlayed the starvation of my youth into a creative venture that was feeding the west coast of my new country!

- *9* -

During this time I realized that I had no time in which to bask in the warmth of my achievements. The work inspired only one thing—more work. There was always the necessity to grow and to produce more. This, I think, is a uniquely American experience. The growth and expansion made possible by this work ethic is also responsible for the lack of the fulfillment and happiness that a more relaxed lifestyle would allow. I had to continue to create more items and newer items. It was a never-ending dilemma. No longer satisfied with what was, I always had to better it. In doing so, I was left with less and less time for reflection and enjoyment. This was the gift and curse of the capitalist system.

Many times, with family and friends, I would express my desire to be content with the level of achievement already gained. To do so, though, would be fatal for business. All my life I had wanted there to be no barriers to whatever potential I had. Now I wanted to stop creating, growing, and expanding. I wanted to be able to just be.

Sometimes I would envision what it might have been like to have had Risvolds in my hometown before the Communists took over. I envisioned waking up late in a small house, playing chess, having a two-hour lunch at the famous Beretvas Coffee House, and visiting the plant for a couple of hours. But this was not Hungary. Reality dictated that security for my family was the first priority. Security meant expansion, long hours, and continual growth. There would be no two-hour lunches.

Sara's job during this time was the emotional one of keeping the family together. As I look back, I realize that I did not participate in this sphere as essentially as I would have wished. I was part of every discussion, but there was an observing stance to my family participation. My main center of focus and concentration was the workplace. I was distant to the joys and pains of my daughter falling in love, her graduation from college, her marriage, the birth of our granddaughter and grandson, and eventually her divorce and remarriage. I was part of all of this and yet was not involved in the noisy, tumultuous emotional arena in which Sara lived easily, and sometimes not so easily. My eye was on the future, when I would finally be able to relax and play catch-up. The irony was that one never can make up for what has already transpired. My catch-up would wait for another time and another arena. It was with regret that I realized that my childhood had been interfered with by the war and that I hadn't enjoyed Agi's young adult life because I was trying to make her life better than mine.

It took me quite a long time to be able to stop being ashamed of my accent. It took me quite a long time to be proud of my achievements. It took me quite a long time to be able just to relax and be happy to be me. I still had too much to prove to myself. It took me quite a long time to allow myself the dignity and self-satisfaction of a man who works hard and dreams large.

$$- \; 10 \; -$$

*T*he sixties was such a remarkable time for me to watch. I watched true democracy work in the most painful of ways. I saw the dilemma of freedom of speech and expression. I saw the flame of idealism shot down at Kent State. I saw the loss of purpose in the war due to fear of public opinion. I saw a president covering the truth, and I saw the people's belief in their government falter. I saw the victims both in the faces of children at My Lai and in the faces of our soldiers, who were not greeted with wine and lace tablecloths in the centers of our cities, but with insults and name-calling. I watched with astonishment as the flower children put flowers in the muzzles of the guns of soldiers who were guarding the army depot at Federal Avenue. I was confused as young men openly burned their draft card. To do this when American boys were dying was unbelievable to Hungarian-Americans. It caused hurt and pain among my friends because it reminded us of when fellow Hungarians had turned their backs as we were taken to the labor battalions.

I shivered at the optimism and hope of Kennedy's inaugural speech and also at the horrifying image of the riderless horse carrying his casket.

I watched the youth stand up for their ideals during Johnson's presidency. I watched the euphoria of their shared energy eventually swallowed by the excesses of drugs and alienation. I watched the flower children demonstrate against their government and be hardened into nihilistic hopelessness. This was all about democracy also.

I watched the turmoil of the civil rights movement, when white and black America joined hands. I cannot express how a naturalized citizen like myself felt when first hearing the hymn "We Shall Overcome." I watched with grief as leaders were stricken down for breaking the barriers. I applauded the civil rights advancement and hated civil disobedience. I could not believe that anyone could defy the rules and laws of the United States. After escaping so many times from tyranny and death to finally reach a country of law, I could not abide any disobedience.

During this decade of divided America, I watched shifts in alignment. No longer was it Republican versus Democrat. It became pro- and anti-war which marked distinct camps. I watched, and I was both impressed and repelled by democracy. It worked. It worked in the orderly passing of power after an assassination. It worked. It worked in the passive resistance of Martin Luther King. It worked in the public struggle against the Vietnam War. It worked sometimes in the most chaotic and painful ways. I watched as the leaders of both parties swayed in purpose and lied instead of explaining the war to the country's citizens. As a new citizen I had trust in the government. I watched deception instead of full disclosure. I saw a government which did not believe in itself.

I believed in an America that most Americans no longer believed in. I believed that in this democracy, when an elected official said that a war must be fought, that it must. I believed in an America where everything could be worked out. I believed in an America that only a new American could believe in. But throughout all of this, the democratic process survived; it was torn with bulletholes and stained with tears—but viable.

I watched the sexual revolution take over America in this decade. The sexual freedom which was spawned on the college campuses soon ignited in every form of American life. Sex became the alternative to the alienation which was afoot, and it served the same role it had in Hungary. With more and more disillusionment there was more and more sexual activity to counteract the depression. It all had the quality of *déjà vu* for me.

In this decade the first men landed on the moon and raised the American flag. I was one of the people who watched the landing via a television set. I was so proud to be an American and alive on that special day.

The sixties taught me that the more things seemed to change, the more they stayed the same. There could not be a more turbulent period, yet with all the upheavals and upsets, life went on. Political changes were just swings to the right and to the left, but the steadfast middle remained. America could withstand some momentous changes without resorting to concentration camps, human tattooing, and gas chambers. There were terrible errors and human victims, but not wholesale murder and enslavement. This country, my country, which lay between the Atlantic and the Pacific, could be buffeted by political waves which were turbulent and potentially destructive; but the basic country was so stable that it could withstand these climatic changes. Soon the waves would be integrated into normal conditions. We would hopefully learn from Vietnam, from presidential assassinations, and from civil right advocates and agitators. Even if we failed to learn and progress, the republic would continue in a democratic manner.

- *11* -

In the late sixties and early seventies national soccer championships and professional soccer teams were organized. My friends from the Old Country and I had high hopes that soccer would flourish in time in America as it does all over the world. At the beginning of the championship season Pista and I saw almost all the games. In the stadium we spoke to each other in Hungarian. Other people also spoke in foreign tongues. English was rarely the language spoken. This discouraged us.

Through Pista's recommendation I was offered the job of coaching the California Suns, which was a new professional team. I had to fight my deepest inclination to take this coaching position, but my business required my full attention. I had to reluctantly decline. The team folded after one or two seasons. It was discouraging to see team after team dissolve because of poor attendance. It was discouraging to see only Europeans, South Americans, and Mexicans at soccer games. I wanted my country and my sport to come together.

When I took my grandchildren to the park, I brought a soft rubber ball. Soccer was something I could show them. I would be able to impress them. We started to chase the ball. Other children started to watch. I organized a small game of four on four, boys versus girls. How surprised I was when I noticed the good-natured arguments and how much fun the game was to these young children. I also noticed the proud smiles of the mothers who cheered the teams on. No one had a better time than I did. My feelings soared.

A year or so after this, my grandkids started to play organized youth soccer in the San Fernando Valley area. I helped a little, but after one season I felt that I had to move elsewhere. My secret desire was to make my grandson Michael the superstar I felt I could have been, had not history cheated me. My daughter and I both realized that this was too heavy a burden to bring to the soccer field. I felt cheated at not being able to coach my grandson in the game which was so precious to me. Perhaps because it was so precious, it put too much pressure on Michael and the game. It would be better adaptation to use my desires, longings, and talents in a less familial setting.

I went to the neighborhood American Youth Soccer Organization near my home to offer my talents as a volunteer coach. I finally received a call from Region 76 of the AYSO, telling me that if I was still interested in coaching, to be at LaCienega Park on the coming Friday at 5:00 p.m. When I arrived, there were fifteen boys and twice that number of anxious parents waiting. The boys were six years old. The next day was the beginning of their season and marked their first game. Their coach had become seriously ill. I was concerned about the AYSO rules. I was concerned about not knowing the boys' names. I was concerned about whether the boys would understand my fractured English. I signed up immediately.

My AYSO coaching career began on that day in the fall of 1977. I noticed immediately that when I began to talk, the boys would look at one another in puzzlement. I knew that my accent was causing a problem for them. I slowly and painstakingly told them a story about the small village in Hungary where I was born. I told them how old I was and how it came that I had learned the game of soccer. I told them how happy I was to able to teach them how to kick the ball and how to enjoy this wonderful sport. By the time I had finished my story I knew that I had reached them and that they had gone past my accent into understanding. I felt I had gained their trust because I had told them something about myself.

Soon I began to know the names of "my boys," their individual personalities, their mothers and their fathers. I began to love this team and all it represented. We were given the name Hawks by the AYSO committee, but I could not pronounce the word easily. In talking to one of the fathers about this, he suggested the word Rangers because he had served in the special forces in Vietnam. I did not know or understand the connotation, only the easy pronunciation. From that time onward all my teams would be called Rangers. Every day that we had practice I would tell them a little story that would punctuate a point I needed them to learn. The stories came from my youth and were about qualities of spirit which I had learned. Just as I had sat under a shady tree and listened to "Aush stories," I hoped "Coach Ed stories" would also expand and instruct.

One day, after a practice, a mother informed me that her ex-husband would pick up their son from practice. I watched father and son as they left the park. Steven's father had taken his hand, and Steven was trying to extricate himself from the grasp. Steven finally succeeded, and he kept several paces behind his father as they walked towards their car. My whole lifetime was that moment: the sadness of the missed relationship, the son's need for his own path, the father's desire for a relationship, and the unbridgeable gap between the two of them. So much pathos, so much passion, so much feeling. Something happened to me that day. I wordlessly knew that I must reach these boys. I would understand them. I would touch their hearts. I would, in small measure, make up for all the missed opportunities in my life. I would heal my own heart. I would find my "winter coat."

Steven became one of my favorites among favorites, and I began to look after him. I loved all my boys, but certain ones of them became special to me, and I to them. The special ones were the very young, usually the small in stature. They were strong and stubborn, and I sensed in them an inner strength and also a special vulnerability and conflict. All were good athletes, but not great. They had, though, a quality of heart and determination that attracted me to them, and vice versa. They also seemed to have very supportive parents who were with them for their successes and their defeats.

One day I was giving my usual exhortation to the parents about the need for their avid participation. I used an example that I had used before. I told them that my parents had never come to see me play soccer, and that I had left home as soon as possible. I told the parents that this time with their sons was invaluable and irreplaceable.

I coached soccer with vigor and added emotionality. It was not the emotionality of "get that goal" or "tackle that man," but the emotionality of valuing each and every boy on the team. At the end of the season, I was richer for the five months I had volunteered. I had given, but had received the greatest gift of all in return—the respect of the boys. The enthusiastic faces of the boys after a win and the moist eyes at a loss followed me months after our last game. I asked Steven's mother if she would be the team mother, thereby allowing Steven to be on my team again. She happily agreed. I was allowed also to choose an "adopted grandson" for the team, as every father was allowed to have his own son on the team. That honor was given to Brad, the smallest boy on the team.

- *12* -

During business hours I spent more and more time planning the new soccer season and thinking about the upcoming team, my fourteen new sons. My partner and production manager knew about my new involvement with soccer. Sometimes, when there was a problem or tension about production in the factory, they began to ask questions about the last practice, the team, or a particular boy. They knew from experience that after such questions and the subsequent discussion the tension in me would be less and the solution of the problem would seen self-evident.

My Hungarian-American friends seemed to humor me and began good-naturedly to wonder at my mental soundness, given the deep involvement I had with my boys. They pretended interest in my short or not-so-short descriptions of the games or about the boys. Down deep, though, I knew they were bored and did not understand the profound meaning that this had for me.

In the meantime my business was steadily growing. I felt fortunate and happy in the way my life had developed. Sara and I began to travel during off-seasons. Almost every year, no matter where our destination was, we routed ourselves through Hungary for a few days. No matter what else had happened, I was born there, my youth was there, part of my family is still there, and part is buried there. No matter what happened in

Hungary or how much pain, it is for me, now and always, my homeland.

In time I felt happy and content sitting with old teammates and old friends in Hungarian coffee shops, having espresso and talking about things on which I had completely different views than theirs. I felt that there was hope in the new generation of Hungarians and that they would not tolerate the crimes of their elders. I would remember back to December of 1944, when I returned to find my home defiled and ransacked. I hoped that my friends in Hungary were truly my friends and felt the way I did about that terrible part of our shared heritage.

I felt that a complete healing would be possible for me until an incident occurred during an outing to a Hungarian soccer game. I had gone to the soccer match with some Gentile former teammates. During the game I heard behind us a few antisemitic remarks. I stood up to leave and was stopped by Ferenc Nagy, who said loudly, "Human stupidity always waits in the dark for an opportunity to surface."

My teammates assured me that this was a rare and aberrant occurrence. I sat down and pretended to believe what they had told me, but I did not.

On the way home from the game, I started to tell my former teammates about "my boys." I realize now that I was trying to recover from the blow of knowing that Hungary would never change fast enough for me. I was bragging about my team when one of my friends said, "If they are so good, why don't you bring them over to play here in Hungary for a few games. You can show them this country. We can show them soccer."

This sowed a seed. I began to think about it. The American boys who made up my present team were too young to travel, but maybe one day I could bring my boys, my American boys, to my homeland to really repair and renew something. I could also give the boys a touch of the old and the beautiful. I could show them the soccer game well played in the classic style of Europe. The style of quiet and graceful finesse, not the long kicks into space, but the perfect craftsmanship of a well-placed ball sent to a teammate.

- *13* -

Years quickly passed. I had kept my two boys, Brad and Steven, and using them as a nucleus made my team year after year of new recruits. My five- and six-year-olds were now twelve and thirteen. Of course, they were still Rangers. We were a bit of a legend now in that we always were division champions.

I must admit to a special talent I had in reaching these boys. Winning and scoring was not my message. Having courage and heart was. I was teaching them skills in survival that I believed in, but in the atmosphere of a game.

It really felt like a family. After eight years coaching, I knew many of the boys on almost every team. "Hi, Coach" greeted me everywhere. During times of Bar Mitzvah, I was sometimes included. I was one of the few asked to come to the Torah. During Confirmation, I also was sometimes invited. I proudly attended. This seemed like the time, and this seemed to be the team I wanted to take to Hungary to play. I began to talk about it. To my great surprise a parents' committee was formed almost immediately, and an organization was put into place so that this could occur. Somehow my dream had coincided with the dreams of others.

- *14* -

So this is how it happened that in 1985 fifteen boys and their coach traveled to Hungary. We were now the USA Rangers and were decked out in red-white-and blue uniforms. I had talked to the boys about what being American had meant to me, and I hoped that they would be proud and walk tall. They were, and they did. We won a few games and lost many, but always felt good about ourselves.

We left Budapest and traveled to the Lake Balaton country. Then we detoured to visit Kecskemét. I had not intended to tell them why the bus had stopped, and why I was carrying flowers. This was their trip, and I wanted them to see the good side of Hungary. The ten-minute stop at the mausoleum in Kecskemét honoring the Auschwitz dead was my separate pilgrimage. It was something I had to do and always did on each visit to Hungary. Because I am so emotional and had tears in my eyes, the boys knew something was afoot. I told them in three sentences about what had happened here in World War II.

That was how it came about that fifteen American boys, black and brown, Jewish, Catholic, Russian Orthodox, and Protestant, and their coach came to stand in a mausoleum with yarmulkes on our heads. I tried to read to them the columns of names that represented my family—my mother, father, sister, brother, nieces, nephews, cousins, aunts and uncles—but the columns were too long. I tried to tell them a little bit about the names of some of my friends, teammates, and school chums, but the list was too long. I did not know if I had done something wrong in sharing this moment with them. Everyone was silent.

We walked back to the bus and sat down. The bus started up. Steven walked to me and sat down on my lap. Brad leaned over me ostensibly to ask me a question about chess. One by one, in that real, authentic way that defies plan, each boy during the bus ride engaged me in words, hugs, and gestures. This moment was forged in rightness. It was the right path.

The End